50-50 Parenting

Other Books by Gayle Kimball

The 50-50 Marriage

Harriet Beecher Stowe's Gospel of Womanhood

Women's Culture: The Women's Renaissance of the Seventies

50-50 Parenting

Sharing Family Rewards and Responsibilities

by

GAYLE KIMBALL, Ph.D.

Lexington Books

D.C. Heath and Company • Lexington, Massachusetts • Toronto

Library of Congress Cataloging-in-Publication Data

Kimball, Gayle.
50-50 parenting.

Bibliography: p.
Includes index.
1. Parenting—United States. 2. Sex role—United States. 3. Dual-career families—United States.
I. Title. II. Title: Fifty-fifty parenting.
HQ755.8.K56 1988 649'.1 86-46027
ISBN-0-669-14866-0 (alk. paper)

Published simultaneously in Canada
Printed in the United States of America
Casebound International Standard Book Number: 0-669-14866-0
Library of Congress Catalog Card Number: 86-46027

The paper used in this publication meets the minimum requirements of American National Standard for Information Sciences—Permanence of Paper for Printed Library Materials, ANSI Z39.48-1984.

ISBN 0-669-14866-0

89 90 91 92 8 7 6 5 4

I have a quarter input into family decisions. It's all very democratic. Other parents think kids are totally illogical and stupid. No one is as happy as we are.

— *A Texas girl, age eighteen*

Being a father is more rich and complex and emotionally involving than the care and feeding of a good dog or a sports car. Priorities are so screwed up.

— *A Maine father*

Being a parent is stressful. There's no way I could parent alone; I would do a poor job because I would be so harried. It's a lot easier to have half of the job of parenting.

— *A California mother of a toddler*

To Jed
who teaches me unconditional love
and who likes to see his name
in his mom's books.

To Barbara and Tom Kimball,
caring parents.

Contents

Introduction

MOST couples find parenting to be the most difficult facet of marriage. Marital happiness declines with the arrival of children and rises with their departure, according to a multitude of scholarly studies. Shared parenting helps make a couple's activities more similar and equitable, which heightens intimacy. A male professor explained that in role-differentiated families like his first marriage, "When the two parents are leading such different lives, it is very hard for them to find a common ground. You don't have a lot in common so it is very destructive of the relationship between the parents and not very good for the kids." I found that coparenting produces children who are more confident and see a wider range of options than children of more traditional parents. Coparented boys we interviewed, in particular, do better academically and on tests of self-esteem than boys with more traditional parents.

To find out how couples share their most complex and perhaps most influential role, I interviewed hundreds of parents, children, key family experts, and progressive employers. The purpose of this book is to provide examples for parents and policymakers moving toward equality in various family styles.

A major problem contemporary parents face is the expectation that mothers will do most of the child rearing, even if they are employed. The majority of mothers of young children are employed and also do 70 percent of the family work, which is clearly a strain. Mothers of preschool children are especially burdened and have little time for themselves. Working mothers often struggle with guilt about not being able to give enough time to children, husbands, and work. These stresses harm our families.

Shared parenting eases the burden for working mothers, enables fathers to be close to their children, and fosters democracy in the home. Although most Americans value equality, few practice it in their most intimate relations. The parents described in this book show us how to start putting our goals into practice. They are creating a new parenting style that must become the norm as we catch up with the reality that the majority of parents are employed and that children need equal time with their fathers.

Sadness over lack of closeness with our fathers is too common. Another generation of adults should not have to call home and hear their fathers say, "Hi, I'll put your mother on the phone." We need to expand the definition of the father as the good provider to include the good nurturer. Men I interviewed like being an active part of their children's lives and open up emotionally by caring for them. The consequences of fathers' involvement with their children can be far-reaching, extending to care of our polluted and war-torn planet threatened by nuclear disaster and poverty. Our future will be a better one if our children learn to practice shared responsibility at home. As we approach the year 2000, our employers, schools, and governments with their antiquated organizations need to catch up with current changes in family life.

To find progressive models of coparents I interviewed diverse types of families around the United States. I talked with divorced and stepfamilies as well as dual-earner couples in first marriages to reflect the fact that less than 11 percent of U.S. families now fit the stereotype of a full-time homemaker, an employed father, and school-age children. I looked at how parents share parenting, why some are more equal than others, what work place and other changes can help families, and future directions that family life might take. We interviewed and compared children in egalitarian and traditional families, a unique contribution to family research. (Appendixes 1 and 2 provide information about the children and parents interviewed.)

A major finding from the interviews is that good intentions between progressive and loving parents are not enough. Careful planning and structure are required to coparent. Priorities must be consciously established and followed. My surveys of coparents reveal that their roles get more equal as children get older and that parents with professional jobs are more likely to be equal than parents in jobs requiring less education or having less flexibility. Couples in first marriages are a little less likely to be equal than couples in second marriages; divorced fathers reported doing more hours of child care than divorced mothers. Individuals who score masculine/instrumental on a sex-role survey are much more likely to be egalitarian than individuals who score feminine/nurturant. Couples are more equal in their division of housework than of child care. For example, even though they consider themselves egalitarian, men in first marriages spend a mean of twenty-nine hours a week doing child care while their wives report spending forty-one hours.

What effect does role sharing have on marriages? Role-sharing parents are as happily married as other couples specifically recommended to me as happily married. The role-sharing men are a little more happily married than the other men, an encouraging result. Marital satisfaction in both groups is linked with an androgynous or masculine personality type, perhaps because high masculinity scores and high self-esteem are linked. Children with egalitarian parents report satisfaction with their families, appreciating responsibility and talking with their parents about family matters.

Coparenting is clearly the goal towards which parents and their employers should strive—children benefit from two involved parents, fathers delight in nurturing their children, and working mothers work too hard. Coparented children and child development experts arrive at the same conclusion, believing that families function best with authoritative rather than authoritarian or permissive parenting. This is precisely the type of parenting found among coparents, who rely on democracy as well as clear limits and structure. Coparenting now is rare and difficult, requiring tight planning and careful organization because social institutions such as the work place ignore families' needs. Also, male success is too rigidly defined by work outside the home and the family is seen as a feminine realm in which inequality in family work seems "natural." To give children and families the equality of attention they deserve requires rethinking traditional gender roles and how work is organized. The outcome will be to improve the quality of family life. To struggle against what feels "natural" for the sake of children's well-being is not easy, but it is an exciting challenge.

I have talked with progressive parents and their children for the six years during which I have worked on this book. To continue the dialogue, I invite readers to write to me about your experiences with role sharing and combining work and family. How working parents cope is the topic of my next book; I would like to include your comments. Please write to: Dr. Gayle Kimball, EWS-420, California State University, Chico, CA 95929

Self-Test for 50-50 Parenting: How Equal Are You?

To find out how your family rates on equal parenting, each parent should check the column on the right to indicate which partner usually does the following chores. This list can also be used to divide family work fairly. Your children can also supply their perspectives on the children's report, which follows this test.

	Mother	*Father*	*Both*
1. Who changed most of the baby's diapers?	_____	_____	_____
2. Who took time off from work to care for a young child?	_____	_____	_____
3. Who usually gets out of bed at night when a child wakes up?	_____	_____	_____
4. Which parent is contacted first when a child becomes sick at school or day care?	_____	_____	_____
5. Who usually stays home from work with a sick child?	_____	_____	_____
6. Who usually goes to parent/teacher conferences?	_____	_____	_____
7. Who checks to make sure that homework is completed and paperwork from school returned?	_____	_____	_____

	Mother	*Father*	*Both*
8. Who makes dental and medical appointments for your child and takes your child to them?	______	______	______
9. Who plans birthday parties for your child?	______	______	______
10. Who buys gifts for your child?	______	______	______
11. Who shops with your child for clothes and other items?	______	______	______
12. Who mends your child's clothes, washes them, and puts them away?	______	______	______
13. Who prepares your child's lunch?	______	______	______
14. Who usually cooks breakfast?	______	______	______
15. Who usually cooks dinner?	______	______	______
16. Who shops for the family's food?	______	______	______
17. Who pays the child's allowance and makes sure the chores are completed?	______	______	______
18. Who takes care of the bedtime routine?	______	______	______
19. Who gets children to clean up their messes?	______	______	______
20. Who usually cleans up around the house?	______	______	______
21. With whom does your child spend the most time?	______	______	______
22. To which parent does your child feel most free to make a request or			

	Mother	*Father*	*Both*
an inquiry, as about using the family car or staying out later than usual?	____	____	____
23. Which parent worries about not spending enough quality time with your child?	____	____	____
24. Who is your child more likely to talk with about a problem such as a conflict with a friend or worries such as those about nuclear war?	____	____	____
25. Who plans most of the family social and fun activities?	____	____	____
26. Who spends the most time in sports and other game-playing activities with your child?	____	____	____
27. Who pays the bills?	____	____	____
28. Who is responsible for investing family savings?	____	____	____
29. Who does your child see do most of the outside yard work and home maintenance?	____	____	____
30. Who does most of the car servicing and mechanical repairs?	____	____	____
31. Which parent is more likely to arrange for home maintenance or auto repair services?	____	____	____
32. Which parent is more likely to repair or assemble your child's toys and bicycle?	____	____	____

	Mother	*Father*	*Both*
33. Which parent is more likely to instruct your child about how to use tools and encourage the child to assist in home maintenance and repair work?	______	______	______
34. Who does your child see drive when both parents are in the car?	______	______	______
35. Which parent is more likely to decide on a disciplinary action, such as a time out or being grounded?	______	______	______
36. Which parent is more likely to have the last word in a family dispute?	______	______	______
37. Which parent will or has taught your child to drive a car?	______	______	______
38. Who does your child think is the boss of the family?	______	______	______
39. Which parent does your child see with more leisure time?	______	______	______
40. Which parent is more likely to plan family vacations and outings?	______	______	______
41. Which parent is more likely to talk with your child about the parent's own childhood and current activities?	______	______	______
42. Whose workplace has your child visited?	______	______	______
43. Which parent sets and enforces time curfews and establishes where the young person can and cannot go and with whom?	______	______	______

	Mother	*Father*	*Both*
44. Which parent has taken or will take your child to visit possible career and college sites?	_____	_____	_____
45. Who discusses stereotyping as portrayed in the media?	_____	_____	_____
46. Which parent has or will talk to your child about the dangers of drugs, drunk driving, and sexually transmitted diseases? Also, the use of birth control if sexually active?	_____	_____	_____
47. Who encourages your child to aspire to develop his or her abilities?	_____	_____	_____
48. Overall, who would you say does most of the parenting activities in your family?	_____	_____	_____

49. What do you most like about your child-rearing practices? _________

____

____

50. What would you most like to change and why? _________________

____

____

Scoring

While no test can provide a precise measure of equal parenting, your answers will indicate basic styles of parenting. If you checked "Mother" most often in questions 1–25 (which relate to the typical mother's role) then that is a strong indication that the mother is carrying the heaviest—and stereotypical—part of the family work. If you checked "Father" most often for questions 26–38, then that indicates that the father's role closely follows the stereotypical one. The last set of questions would most likely be split between the two, and are there to remind you of some of the important issues in equal parenting, such as combating stereotyped images in the media. If you checked "Both" most often throughout the test, and particularly in questions 1–38, then you are on your way to an equitable sharing of the work—and rewards—of parenting your children.

Please send your quiz results to Dr. Kimball to be included in the next edition of this book. Include a description of your family.

Dr. Gayle Kimball
EWS-420
California State University
Chico, CA 95929

Children's Report

Have your children answer the following questions, and then compare their views with yours and those of the children described in chapter 5 and appendix 2.

1. Who is the boss in your family? Explain. ______________________

   ____

2. Name two chores that your mom almost always does.

   ____

   ____

3. Name two chores that your dad almost always does.

   ____

   ____

4. What are two family rules important to your father?

   ____

   ____

5. What does your father do if these rules are broken? ______________

   ____

6. What are two family rules important to your mother?

____

____

7. What does your mother do if these rules are broken? ____________________

____

8. How do you get your parents to buy you something you really want or give you permission to do something that you really want to do?

____

____

9. What do you do with your family for fun? ____________________

____

10. What activity do you like to do best with your mom? ____________________

____

11. What activity do you like to do best with your dad? ____________________

____

12. In what three ways are you like your father?

____

____

____

13. In what three ways are you like your mother?

____

____

____

14. Do you spend the most time with your mom, your dad, or both of your parents? ____________________

15. Does your mom, dad, or both of your parents spend the most time helping you with school work? ____________________

16. What is one thing most likely to cause a disagreement in your family?

____

17. How does your family resolve the kind of conflict you just described?

____

____

18. If you are a parent someday, what things will you do differently from your parents, and why? ______________________________

____

____

19. What things will you do the same as your parents, and why? ______

____

____

20. What do you think about both parents working outside the home? __

____

____

21. What advice would you give to a newly married couple who are thinking about having a child? ______________________________

____

22. Who is your favorite television character, and why? ______________________________

____

23. If you could only have one child, would you choose a girl or a boy? Why? ______________________________

____

24. If you plan to get married, describe your ideal partner. ______________________________

____

25. What three things could you say to describe yourself to someone who wants to get to know you? ______________________________

____

____

____

26. What three things do you most like about yourself?

____

____

____

27. What one thing bothers you the most now, a problem that you are working on solving? ______________________________

____

28. What is your favorite subject in school? ____________________

29. What subject are you best in? ____________________

30. What is it like to be the oldest or only/middle/youngest child in your family? ____________________

____

31. What do you like about being in your family? ____________________

____

____

32. Are there any suggestions you have for your family? ____________________

____

____

Please send this report along with the self-test to Dr. Kimball for the next edition of her book.

1

Advantages of Equal Parenting

Right from the birth on, because I was so involved, we became closer as a family and as partners.

— *Jim, father of one*

Shared parenting, despite the inevitable problems, is the only way to go—both from the viewpoint of lessening the burden of any one parent and, more importantly, that children know they have *two* people who care. Nonsexist child rearing remains very difficult, as our society, though it may pay lip service to sex equity, is still supportive of traditional sex roles.

— *Annie, mother of two*

A MAJOR social change in the twentieth century is the large-scale entry of mothers into the paid work force. Over half of our children now have employed parents. The family of the 1950s, with one breadwinner and one bread baker and children under eighteen, represents less than 11 percent of American families.[1] The resulting social expectation is that men will play a more active role in family life. Learning to blend what we have stereotyped as men's and women's work is stressful, because our organization of work and family life is patterned on a nineteenth-century model that rigidly divided the worlds of women and men. Now that the majority of women work outside the home, most men do not have wives who greet them at the door with their slippers, dinner in the oven, and children's homework completed. Yet husbands of working wives do not do much more family work than husbands of homemakers.[2] Women have changed, but men and social institutions have not, as Arlie Hochschild observed after studying dual-earner families.[3]

Our hierarchical family form still reflects the power structure of nineteenth-century industrial society, whose pyramids of authority are also retained in corporations, in the military, and in government. In families, an example of men's greater power is that only one of the seventy-two fathers in a recent study of new parents changed work or educational goals after his baby's birth, while all of the mothers did.[4] Another example is that dual-career couples are much more likely to move for the man's career than the woman's.[5] Even the married coauthors of a book for dual-career couples struggled with inequality. Francine Hall explained after her divorce, "Our marriage was fine as long as I went along with him, made [job] compromises or sacrifices and didn't talk about them."[6] The implication of all this is that what men do is considered more important than what women do. Hopefully we can give our children a message better suited for those who will be coparenting in the 2000s.

Partly as a consequence of mothers' employment, popular interest in fathers is growing. A major theme in current writing about men is sorrow over men's lack of closeness to their fathers. For example, in *Finding Our Fathers: The Unfinished Business of Manhood*, Samuel Osherson observes, "The psychological or physical absence of fathers from their families is one of the great underestimated tragedies of our times."[7] In interviews with men around the country, Anthony Astrachan confirmed that most men regretted that their fathers were either silent or absent.[8] Ninety-five percent of the men in seminars led by psychologist Ken Druck report "psychological or physical absenteeism in their fathers. . . . The human side of Dad often was not available. Many of us are still operating on the format that at some basic level the woman is emotionally responsible for the family."[9]

Some men numb their sense of loss by abusing alcohol or drugs, or exorcise their frustration through violence. Others are redefining masculinity and learning to nurture each other and their own children. Men who actively nurture can have far-reaching beneficial influences on children—and on our environment.

The recent expansion in the number of working mothers with young children indicates how rapidly women's roles are changing.

Currently, over half of mothers with preschool children are employed, compared with only 12 percent in 1950. Two-thirds of mothers of school-age children are employed. Almost two-thirds of divorced mothers work full time, compared with a third of married mothers.[10] Yet changing traditional attitudes to actually practice equity is difficult, especially when many young adults believe that the women's movement of the 1960s and 1970s succeeded in securing equality for women at work and at home. In fact, fathers with working wives average only 30 percent of family work, spending fifteen to twenty-five minutes a day in direct child care activities.[11]

In 1985 and 1986 I surveyed 84 egalitarian coparents (interviewed for this book and for *The 50-50 Marriage*) and 299 randomly selected dual-earner couples to learn what percent of child care and housework they do each week.[12] Egalitarian couples are those that try to divide family work 50-50; randomly selected couples may not make this effort. (A description of these couples and how they were chosen can be found in appendix 1.) A little over a third of men in dual-career couples say they do half or more of the child care each week, compared to almost two-thirds of the role-sharing men. Forty-four percent of dual-career men and 71 percent of role-sharing men say they do half or more of the housework. Wives generally agree with their husbands' assessment of child care, while only 55 percent of egalitarian wives agree that their husbands share housework equally or do more. Around a third of the couples who think of themselves as egalitarian in fact adhere to more traditional patterns of family work.

Economics explains some of the unequal division of domestic labor. Women earn 64 percent of what men earn. Only 16 percent of white women had four years or more of college in 1984, compared to 24 percent of white men (and 10 percent of black women and men), although this is changing since women are currently half the college undergraduates. Joseph Pleck examined why husbands of working wives do 30 percent rather than 50 percent of family work, despite the fact that the "majority of men are more psychologically involved in their families than their jobs."[13] Pleck's conclusions are that men have long and inflexible work hours and earn more, and if they spend more time with the families, they produce less at work. They follow the example set by their fathers. Social attitudes and the media reinforce inequity, men lack some domestic skills, and men may not receive support for change from their wives or friends. Pleck notes that only around half of wives want more help from their husbands. Michael Lamb added that "people who have positions of power don't want to lower themselves to positions of low status and low power," which characterizes our attitudes towards child rearing.[14] Evidence is the low pay given to child care workers.

Many women still consider the home to be their realm, and thus couples regard unequal distribution of family work as fair. However, women still have less power than men in major family decision making and do most of the unpleasant and uninteresting work like changing diapers. Their time seems less valuable, partly because they earn less and partly because they have less confidence that their time is important. Fathers lack examples of how to share equally in family life and often feel confused about men's changing roles.[15] An example of a mixed message is an automobile commercial in which an involved father tells his young son, "I'm not going to trade in my [driving] gloves for dishpan hands." The media often portrays men at home as bumbling and incompetent, as unrealistically calm and always in charge, or as removed—reading the newspaper. Even the involved father played by Bill Cosby had to sneak in spaghetti sauce from the store when his efforts to cook it failed.

Most Americans retain the nineteenth-century belief that raising children, especially young children, is the mother's main responsibility, while the father's job is to earn money. Congresswoman Patricia Schroeder observed, "Our problem is that the people of my generation still think the best of all worlds is children staying at home with Mommy while Daddy is out slaying dragons. That is not the real world."[16] Americans believe that mothers of young children should be at home,[17] and only a minority (from 10 percent to 35 percent depending on the study) believe that men should do more family work than they do currently.[18] Contradictorily, most Americans, especially middle-class people under forty, say they value egalitarian division of child care, housework, and decision making.[19] Around 15 percent probably actually share family work equally.[20]

Roots of Inequality in the Family

Parenting inequity is actually a relatively recent phenomenon; before the 1800s both parents worked on their farms and supervised their children. Protestant fathers were responsible for the religious education of their girls and boys. For example, Samuel Sewall's seventeenth-century diary recorded, "It falls to my Daughter Elisabeth's Share to read the 24. of Isaiah which she doth with many Tears not being very well, and the Contents of the Chapter, and Sympathy with her draw Tears from me, also."[21] Sewall was concerned enough about his daughter's spiritual well-being to write about it in his diary and to cry with her.

With industrialization men left their homes to work in factories and offices, where expression of emotion was discouraged. Women's historical work of finishing raw materials—such as turning wool into clothes—was taken over by machines. Abundant cheap immigrant labor made middle-class women's paid labor unneeded. To keep women at home, nineteenth-century culture created an image of "the lady" who did no physical work. She was put on a pedestal and told she was too angelic to function in the outside world without tarnishing her purity. The sexes were polarized. Middle-class women's major work came to be nurturing children in single-family houses, in an exclusiveness and isolation unique to industrialized nations in the last two centuries. Even in the Victorian era, wealthy mothers usually put daily care of their children in the hands of a governess or nanny.

The impact of industrialization on parenting practices indicates the extent to which economics shapes family life. During World War II women were encouraged to leave their homes to work in defense factories, and their employers or the government provided child care facilities. The film *Rosie the Riveter* showed that women liked working outside the home. When soldiers returned from the war, Freudian psychology was popularized to tell women that they belonged back at home. Career-oriented women were described as suffering from a masculinity complex, as castrating, in competition with their husbands, in search of a penis, frigid, neurotic, and unfeminine. A husband who "let" his wife work outside the home was either a poor provider or unmanly.

The function of the truly feminine woman was the birthing and caring for her children, although this woman was defined by Freudians as naturally narcissistic, passive, and masochistic—traits that do not make for effective parenting. In fact, the fifties homemaker was often labeled a "smother mother" who produced overly dependent children.

The psychoanalytic view defined the father's role, especially in early childhood, as secondary. In his 1981 book *Sons and Mothers*, the psychiatrist Paul Olsen asserted that the mother is always "the most powerfully influential force" in a son's life.[22] Social scientists believed that infants bonded mainly with the mother. Books about parent/child interactions were really about mothers, in particular mothers' interactions with infants. Information pertaining to fathers was usually provided by their wives. Therapists told their clients that the mother had to devote herself to her children to avoid maladjusted offspring. A study of Ohio mothers in the 1950s described mothers who believed that it was important to meet their own needs as "hostile."[23] Researchers were surprised to find in a follow-up study that the daughters of "hostile" mothers grew up to be high achievers.

As Betty Freidan explained in *The Feminine Mystique* (1963), the fifties image of the happy housewife was used by social scientists and popular media to keep women at home. Ideology changes, but from St. Augustine to Freud the prevailing ideas have defined women's nature as subordinate. Friedan's book struck a responsive chord in many homemakers who were not fulfilled by white wash and shiny floors. *The Feminine Mystique* was a major force behind the feminism of the 1960s; middle-class housewives read the book and decided that it was not unfeminine or neurotic to want adult interaction and an opportunity to use their skills doing paid work that stays done, without incessant interruptions.

Research in the 1960s began looking at the effect of maternal employment on children, but ignored the effect of paternal employment. The major finding of this research was that children do best when their mothers are satisfied, whether they are at home or employed.[24] In the last decade studies have finally looked at how fathering is different from or similar to mothering and the effect of involved fathers on children and wives. (Some of these studies are described in appendix 3.) The Fatherhood Project at the Bank Street College of Education in New York City represented an increasing realization that the father's role is significant and needs study and support. The project, begun in 1981 by Jim Levine, produced the book *Fatherhood U.S.A.* (1984) and other written guides, developed "Fatherhood Forums" around the country, and established an ongoing clearinghouse of information for fathers. Popular magazines are beginning to include articles about how to involve fathers, although the parenting magazines still are written for mothers.[25] Advertisements for *Parents Magazine* still offer articles on how to be a better mother, ignoring fathers. *Parenting*, a magazine begun in 1987, does include fathers in their articles and advice.

The 1980s image of motherhood is a supermom who wears a three-piece suit to her high-powered job, cooks gourmet dinners, is a scout mother, has extraordinary energy to satisfy her family's needs, and looks ravishing. Women feel guilty when they are tired and do not match the output and glamour of supermom. In 1986 *Newsweek* reported that "the myth of the Supermom is fading fast—doomed by anger, guilt and exhaustion."[26]

In fact, women in high-level management frequently have had to choose between career and family, unlike their male counterparts. A *Wall Street Journal* survey of top women executives showed that only around a third of those under forty had children. One explanation is that only 5 percent of executives' husbands assumed sole responsibility for any child-rearing tasks.[27] Other studies confirm that achieving women are much less likely than their male counterparts to be spouses and parents.[28] Women still feel that they have to make a choice between career success and family obligations. Combining marriage, parenthood, and career poses no role conflict for men, since women give them support services.

In the future parenting will be shared so that women will not be so exhausted and will have more options and children can have close bonds with their fathers. To make this trend possible, men are beginning to shape new definitions of masculinity. Shepherd Bliss, a professor of men's studies at John F. Kennedy University, explains, "We don't have a word yet to refer to the kind of man we want to be, but he's visible."[29]

Other major changes are taking place in the American family. More individuals (27 percent) are living alone. Some are young adults, other are widows and divorced people. Families make up 72 percent of the households, down from 81 percent in 1970. As the divorce rate skyrocketed in the 1970s single-parent families became the most rapidly increasing family form; around half of the children born in the 1980s will live at some time in a single-parent family. A surprising 20 percent of births are to single mothers, and almost half of single-mother families live below the poverty line. A fifth of our families are headed by women. Almost half of all marriages are remarriages. Single-parent families and stepfamilies are becoming the most numerous family forms.

Families and their children are in trouble and our society is giving them very little assistance, as indicated by the millions of latchkey children. The adolescent suicide rate is increasing rapidly. A million teenagers get pregnant each year and as many run away from home. One in five children lives in poverty. Many children are abused by their parents, many use drugs, and one in nine will appear in court before age nineteen.

Despite the rapid changes in families, young adults' attitudes have not caught up with reality. In 1985 and 1986 I asked 755 college students to predict how they will organize their future careers and family lives. Most of the students plan to have careers and to marry and have two or three children—current families average one. Many expect that women will stay home for years with their young children, an expectation also found in other surveys.[30] Students plan to sandwich traditional parenting between contemporary two-career marriages. Some recognize that they will probably not be able to afford to leave work for an extended period of time, but almost half the women plan to stay home more than a year with their first child. Few men plan to stay home for an extended period. The minority predicted equal sharing of child care (women, 29 percent; men, 31 percent), housework (women, 42 percent; men, 46 percent), and earnings (women, 30 percent; men, 14 percent), typical of other surveys of college students.[31] Their predictions are very close to the unequal division of labor described by dual-career couples earlier in this chapter.

Young adults expect to divide care of young children and wage earning along fairly traditional lines; however, currently most mothers with preschool children are employed. Employed mothers average three months' maternity leave. Most college students will not be able to afford their goal of a long maternity leave. Working mothers often feel guilty and monopolize their babies; a study comparing working mothers and full-time mothers of twelve-month-old infants found no difference in the babies' attachments to their mothers, but a weaker bond between fathers and babies of working mothers.[32] Both men's and women's attitudes must change to make equal parenting possible.

Institutional change must occur too. Progress is beginning on a small scale, with some employers now offering flexible work hours, job sharing, permanent part-time jobs, parental leaves, and child care benefits for employees. More states are encouraging no-fault divorces and joint custody of children. The Pregnancy Disability Act of 1978, a federal law, prohibits employer discrimination on the basis of pregnancy. In 1987 the Supreme Court upheld a California law that provides four months of unpaid maternity leave.

The media are beginning to reflect family changes, producing popular films such as *Kramer vs. Kramer* (1979) and *Mr. Mom* (1983) about involved fathers who overcame their original ineptness and fears after being thrust into child care. Many current films revolve around fathers and their children: Molly Haskell suggests that children are providing the adoration of males once provided by their wives in films such as *Author! Author!*, *Ordinary People*, *Table for Five*, and *Tender Mercies*.[33] However, policies enabling widespread coparenting are still rare and newsworthy; involved fathers are unusual enough to make an interesting film.

Advantages for Children

Despite the pervasive belief that young children should be reared almost exclusively by their mothers, children who are coparented have many advantages. They have more options and care; they learn less rigid sex-role limitations, as reflected in their career choices;[34] and they tend to progress better both academically and socially than children raised mainly by their mothers.[35] A coparented eight-year-old, Califia, explained that when one of her parents is busy, the other is "nice enough to do something with me so I'm not bored. I feel happy with my parents." In one survey children with dual-career parents said they liked the positive role models, the financial security, and the opportunity to develop independence.[36] Two-thirds intend to follow their parents' example. Daughters were especially proud of their mothers. The problems reported by the children were the parents' time pressures and fatigue. But two parents can divide up housework and child care. When U.C. Berkeley women students were surveyed about their childhood reactions to their mothers' working, only 7 percent replied that they were often resentful.[37] Children I interviewed agreed that it is not fair to insist that one parent stay at home full time.

Children who have close contact with their fathers excel: One study found twenty-month-old children with involved fathers to be more self-directed and persistent in completing a task.[38] Other children with highly involved fathers had higher verbal intelligence and exhibited a sense of control over their lives.[39] Boys especially flourish from the contact. One study found that preschool boys with involved fathers had better social adjustment than other boys.[40] According to Warren Farrell, when a father is often away at work or tuned out reading the paper at home, a boy learns unrealistic ideas about masculinity from superheroes, sports figures, and TV entertainers.[41] In fact, boys spend ten times as many hours watching television males than their own fathers. These models of masculinity set up a standard of performance, toughness, and success that is unobtainable. For example, an egalitarian father I interviewed expected to be like batman when he was married, able to solve all problems. Boys need contact with real men, not fantasy figures.

Studies consistently show no significant differences between the development of children with employed mothers and nonemployed mothers. A government-sponsored panel concluded after an exhaustive review of existing studies that mothers' employment has no "pervasive effect—positive or negative—on the education, family or career paths of their sons or daughters."[42] The panel found that the more critical factors in shaping children's growth were the mother's educational level and personal satisfaction, the father's job status, family income level, race, and geographic location. Preliminary results of a recent five-year study of 130 children, begun when they were one year old, again found no difference in the development of children whose mothers are homemakers or employed.[43] What did matter was stimulus and attention such as parents reading aloud to children.

Elementary school children who scored lowest on an "adequacy of mothering index" in one study were mothered by homemakers who felt that it was their duty to be at home.[44] Working mothers and homemakers spend about the same amount of active time with their children, like going over homework.[45] Working mothers give up their leisure time from activities such as watching television, although they still feel guilty. Time spent in quality day-care centers does not disrupt children's development unless the care lacks continuity. Day-care centers often provide parent education that supports close bonding with children. Although the findings are not definitive for infants under six months, when Michael Lamb compared more and less securely attached babies, their mothers' employment status was not an issue. What mattered was women's attitudes toward being mothers.[46]

Dorothy Dinnerstein, Nancy Chodorow, and Lillian Rubin all believe that having the mother as the primary parent leads to deeply rooted inequities in society in general.[47] Children resent their mother's power and their dependence on her. We generalize from our mothers to women in general, and both genders join in desiring limitations on female power—all because the woman is the main parent. I would add that as mothers serve their children they are also expected to serve adult men as secretaries and wives. For men to nurture children on a daily basis breaks the expectation that only females serve and nurture. If men share parenting, the barriers between the two sexes will be less firmly drawn, the resentment of women less widespread, and male and female attitudes toward intimacy and nurturance more similar.

Dinnerstein and Chodorow argue that girls maintain their ties with their mother, while to develop their masculinity boys must destroy the bond with their nurturer, lessening their capacity for intimacy. The *McGill Report on Male Intimacy* concluded after surveying 737 men that "the average man is barely familiar with his family, let alone intimate with its members."[48] The author explains that one reason men are not more loving is that they fear loss of control and power. If men had intimate relationships with their fathers, they might have less fear of being controlled by a woman. This is a provocative theory; we will not know if it is valid until we find more people raised equally by both parents or by a father. After talking with men around the United States, Anthony Astrachan agrees with the theory. He found that about 10 percent of men really support equality with women; the others do not want to share power with women because of "the fear of mother that is part of every child's psychological development and every culture's mythology."[49] He concludes that the most agreeable path to gender equality is active fathering.

Common sense tells us that children benefit from the nurturance of both parents. Boys need time with their fathers to learn how to be men. Girls need time with their fathers to learn how to develop close relationships with men and to encourage girls' career achievement. Also, fathers involved in tending their infants are less likely to abuse them later. This is contrary to what experts have declared about the primacy of the mother-child bond, the father's inability to nurture, and the relative insignificance of the father's relationship with his young children. A divorced father explained, "Sharing parenting has been good for my sense of self: It has made my son and I able to live very happily together."

Advantages for Fathers

Fathers who share the care of their children feel close to them and are deeply touched by these bonds, as studies reveal.[50] A father said,

> *You can't describe to non-parents the feeling of being needed and unconditionally loved. I don't care who the people are, if they're adults and they love one another, there are conditions. With a child, it's total dedication. You can't describe the feeling when you walk into a room and the child sees you and grabs onto your leg, and you're their rock!*

A father of two young children added that coparenting encourages marital involvement; he is learning to negotiate and give and take with his wife over family issues. Parenting teaches him to be more forgiving, gentle, flexible, and patient and to enjoy the present. These qualities are exactly those needed to save our planet from destruction. Another father explained, "Society cheats men by not giving them an opportunity to share some of the amazingly neat experiences, like seeing your child stand up for the first time."

Herb Goldberg, a writer, psychologist, and father of a daughter, observed that traditional fathers often lack a close relationship with their children.[51] Goldberg believes that the traditional man's response to being a father is to intensify his role as the good provider, making a home where his wife can mother their children. A study of new parents confirmed that "virtually all of the men believed that being a good father meant first and foremost being a good provider."[52] They valued their relationship with their children but were not responsible for them on a daily basis. However, many men want to be more involved with their children than their wives permit.[53]

A man who consciously and passionately decides to be a father will feel bonded to his baby, Goldberg says. He will do the things that mothers traditionally do. Fathers are as sensitive as mothers to infant cues, are affectionate with their babies, and play in a way that babies love.[54] Parenting probably comes easier to the mother, Goldberg observes, because men have been trained to relate better to objects than to people. He notes that men are working to expand their roles and that they are much prouder to be active parents than were previous generations. In Goldberg's view, fathering humanizes men so they are less inclined to give everything to the pursuit of money making. He reports of his own fathering:

> *Some of my deepest moments of pleasure are with my two-year-old, probably my most pure conflict-free moments. She brings out the best in me. She's incredibly entertaining. I feel more connected, in touch with the needs of someone else, deeper highs than ever before.*

Advantages for Mothers

For mothers, an advantage of equal parenting is emotional well-being. Depression is a pervasive problem for full-time mothers of young children.[55] "When I was home alone with my baby, I was getting very, very depressed. It was hard for me to stay home alone and not to work," said a female attorney. A full-time father reported that he also began to "feel isolated, to be withdrawn and get depressed." As with any life centered around one activity, if something goes wrong for a homemaker, there is no alternate source of satisfaction. A never-ending job with the same people can be wearing and irritating.

Child care is especially difficult because of the constant interruptions and demands coupled with little acknowledgment. A parent rarely feels a sense of accomplishment for work completed. One father described how he developed from a high school fullback to an architect, receiving ample praise at each stage. As a parent, though, praise came hard. One evening his wife came home from work to a house smelling of warm urine from dirty plastic diapers he had put in the dryer, mistakenly thinking they were washed. The baby was whining and teething and the dog decided to join the action by wetting the floor. The father had had no regular lunch or coffee breaks, no pay raises, and no sick leave; he could not quit, and was getting very little praise for hard work.

Children have a mind-boggling ability to create chaos, so it is easy for a parent to feel like a fire fighter continually encircled by new brush fires. The job of parenting is made more difficult by the romanticization of children as sweet, lovable beings who automatically turn out well if they have good parents, guided by a mythical maternal instinct. But children have not evolved beyond selfishness, as any parent knows who tries to concentrate on a task or a telephone call. Their rapid mood fluctuations require centeredness, patience, and compassion. The authors of *Lifeprints* suggest that the major reason that women have less "well-being" than men is mothers' primary responsibility for child care.[56] Parenting is too demanding, important, and ultimately rewarding to be delegated to one person.

In confirmation of this, three-fourths of working mothers, including those with children under five, say they would not choose to stay home even if they could afford it.[57] Many studies show that working wives have more self-esteem and better physical and emotional health than homemakers.[58] College-educated women are usually more satisfied when employed.[59] Women with responsible jobs seem to flourish, although the benefits of a subservient job are doubtful. Most homemakers plan to enter the paid force despite the fact that husbands of working wives spend only 10 percent more time in family work than the husbands of homemakers, and working mothers sleep, read, and watch television less than any other adults.[60]

The overwhelming majority of employed mothers are "exhausted and emotionally drained," according to a survey of 255 Los Angeles women, as well as plagued by guilt.[61] In survey after survey, including some I have conducted, employed mothers' main complaint is their lack of personal time. A mother of a toddler explained, "Being a parent is stressful. There's no way I could parent alone. I would do a poor job because I would be so harried. It's a lot easier to have half of the job of parenting because that allows you to get on with what you're involved with."

Coparenting is necessary to alleviate the strains felt by employed mothers. Despite the advantages of multiple roles, some women are so burdened that they leave careers that do not recognize their needs as working parents. A business school professor observed, "Women have given up the goal of being superwomen because it is impossible."[62] Recent books such as *Staying Home Instead* tell mothers "How to quit the working-mom rat race and survive financially."[63] No such books are written for fathers. This lopsided condition will change only when parenting is shared and our society recognizes its responsibility to ease the strain of working parents.

Advantages for the Couple

Equal parenting enhances the couple's marriage despite the fact that many men complain about doing housework.[64] Jim explained, "Right from the birth on, because I was so involved, we became closer as a family and as partners." In most families, marital happiness drops with the birth of a child, especially during the preschool years, and rises when the child leaves home. Mothers of young children most often consider divorce.[65] The happiest couples are those with no children: Happiness declines with each additional child, although parents do report great satisfaction from parenting.[66] The only study I found showing marital happiness as remaining high with the arrival of children surveyed parents who divided the care of their children fairly equally, at least 60-40.[67] Laurel observed after coparenting, "Getting married does not necessarily lead to the shift of maturity from an 'I' to a 'we' orientation. Having kids does, and the marriage can reap the rewards of that shift."

The eighty-four role sharers I surveyed had marital satisfaction scores equal to those of couples recommended to me as happily married for over twenty years. In fact, the egalitarian husbands scored a little higher than the other husbands. A Washington couple, June and Steve, reported that after their first child's birth "our worlds were slowly growing apart. After the second child, we decided to do shared parenting and providing. We have recaptured that feeling of mutual respect we shared when first married and are closer . . . companions." Sharing important activities leads to closeness and deeper understanding.

Divorced couples have much to gain by sharing parenting. The burdens on single mothers are enormous (only about 10 percent of single-parent families are headed by men). Single-mother families are likely to have low incomes. When custody is not shared, fathers frequently reduce financial support and contact with their children. In fact, most fathers do not pay full child support and many pay none. These divorced fathers feel cut off from their children, the mothers are burdened with all the responsibility, and children feel abandoned by their fathers and suffer from a low standard of living. When divorced fathers are encouraged to share equal responsibility for their children through joint custody and coparenting, some of the harmful effects of divorce are alleviated.

The United States lags behind the other industrialized nations in its support for families. The number of women in the work force has increased, but families have had very little help from schools, employers, or government. Every decade for the past sixty years the White House Conference on Children and Youth has proposed maternity leave, sick leave for parents, more day care, visiting housekeepers, after-school programs, job programs for youth, and maternal and child health care, as exist in most other industrialized nations.[68] But little action has occurred.

Sweden is perhaps the best model of a rational, humane, and egalitarian society. Swedish mothers and fathers have the right to divide a year's paid parental leave from work and to work a six-hour week with reduced pay until the child is eight. National and municipal governments subsidize child care at sliding-scale rates. Home care is available for sick children. Nurses visit babies and new parents in their homes. When I made a study visit to Sweden in 1980 I was astonished and delighted to observe that large department stores provide child care for shoppers and that numerous city parks have safe play areas for children.

Our parents did not raise us to do equal parenting. Most of our neighbors and friends do not do equal parenting. Margaret Mead explained that no society that wants men to work outside the home allows men to become involved in parenting; "if they did the fathers would become so 'hooked' they would never go out and do their thing properly."[69] Our institutions mistakenly assume that a housewife is maintaining the family; the twenty-first century is rapidly approaching without social recognition of current family needs.

Coparents struggle to forge better child-rearing practices. Their numbers will increase as we learn from their example, recognizing the benefits of fathers' involvement, and pressuring the institutions that surround the family to modernize. Children are our future and develop best with the care of both parents.

2

How to Coparent

> We have both consciously determined that our family is our priority and career is of lesser importance.
>
> — *Susan, mother of two*

> Gear up to take responsibility, like it's not somebody else's job, it's your job.
>
> — *Steve, father of two*

THE 291 coparents I interviewed feel strongly that sharing child rearing benefits both parents and children. Gail, raised in Indiana by a doting mother, grew up very dependent. Her mother rarely left Gail and her sister alone. Gail did not want this kind of life for her own children.

> *I hated school because when I was apart from my mother, I wasn't happy. My mother was always there with us; I can think of a couple of times that she went away, leaving me panic stricken that she would be killed. I didn't want my kids to have those fears that I did. I had no relationship with my father, although he was there, which I didn't think was good.*

When Gail returned to work her husband, Dan, assumed equal responsibility for their children. The fact that he periodically gets laid off from his factory work and is then home full time gives him time to cement his bond with his children.

Establishing the family as a priority is crucial for coparents. To have time with his two young children Steve decided to work part time, as did his wife, June. He explained:

> *When I was working full time, I loved the kids, sure, but they weren't a part of my daily experience. I didn't have nearly as much emotional involvement in their lives as I did when I was home more. There's been a lot of talk that the father doesn't really bond like the mother does, but I didn't feel any lack of intimacy or bonding between me and the kids. That is wonderful, so powerful and positive, it softened me up quite a bit. It helped me to be a more loving and better person.*

If politicians had this softening experience, peace might not be so elusive.

Obstacles to Coparenting

Married parents I interviewed have a difficult time putting their beliefs into practice. The intact married couples who returned written surveys reported that most spend equal hours (12) on housework, while women spend 41 mean hours weekly on child care to men's 29. These hours are similar to those that a randomly selected group of parents of elementary school children in Boston spent interacting with their family, a broader definition.[1] In stepfamilies where children are generally older, women's mean hours are 24 and men's are 13. However, men spend more time than women on child care in the divorced and househusband families that I interviewed.

One reason coparenting is rare is that child care is difficult. Margaret and Bill, who share a job in Washington, D.C., report that staying home with children is harder than working with adults. Dealing with all the "little nitty gritty care of young kids" is very demanding, Margaret relates. Since Bill is at home half the day, he knows what it is like to be the primary care giver to their four young children: "seeing it from both ends, we know which end is the more difficult." Bill observes that most parents do not share the *responsibility* for child care; the burden falls on the mother. The father may take the children to the babysitter, but if the children or the sitter are sick it is the mother's problem. Bill finds this pattern an "unequal and unacceptable" arrangement. A benefit of equal parenting for Margaret is that Bill no longer thinks he could manage the children better than she does; he has experienced firsthand the frustrations of being the sole adult with the children.

Most mothers carry an extra load of responsibility for the administration of the family. Karen, a social worker, reported that she and her husband, Daniel, took years to negotiate their partnership. He is a teacher who gets home two hours before she does and has the summers off to care for their three children. "It's still difficult," Karen says. "I still feel I'm responsible to see that family birthdays, holidays, etc. are successful. *Mother* is still an emotional role—not easily defined." Women often are the ones who are aware of household needs. Even a full-time father told me, "Paula will declare that this or that needs to be done and then I'll get with it and mop and stuff."

The work of initiating and maintaining role sharing often falls upon women too. A Michigan woman says it drives her crazy when men's family work is equated with women's. It is not the same, Mary Kay observes, because women have the ultimate responsibility for maintaining the home. A New York woman in an egalitarian relationship with a divorced father of two girls was surprised at how unequal their parenting was when the girls came to live with them:

> *It was not just that he expected me to do it—I expected me to do it! He wasn't patient enough or didn't respond quickly enough—just didn't seem to be a good enough parent and I would just do it myself. He did do a lot of concrete stuff—much more than many fathers.*

The next summer when the girls were with them she arranged specific duties for him, like transporting the children. She was away an evening a week so that he had some time doing total child care, but again she did the arranging.

Men are more likely to receive recognition for the contributions they make to child care than women, whose work is usually taken for granted. Bill, a reporter, thrives on the attention he gets from his children's friends, who think it is marvelous that he is at home during the day and participates in the neighborhood babysitting cooperative.

Men do not *assume*, as women do, that their time belongs to their children. Even a father who is closer to his daughter than her mother is and does most of the child care in the evening and every other weekend, when his wife is at work as a pharmacist, said:

> *My wife still has responsibility for most of the big decisions in her life, especially health care (due to her profession, at least in part). Lee probably is her Daddy's girl, however, if there's a choice to be made. Parenting is hard work and we're glad we have only one child. As she gets older I realize how much work she was when she was younger. As a parenting male I've been involved in more of the drudgery than traditional males, and* sometimes I can resent that loss of time. [*emphasis added*]

I doubt that many mothers think of their time expenditure with their children except to feel guilty that it is not enough. Child care is assumed to be the women's duty. The authors of *Beyond Sugar and Spice* state, "unlike women, men don't fear that someone will stop loving them if they make a demand."[2] Linda, a mother of two sons, explained,

> *Early on, it was extremely hard for me to insist that he do things, like get the baby for me to nurse. There was some kind of program in my head that said I wasn't doing a good job as a mother if I needed help. I would get angry with him for not realizing I needed help, but I never articulated that. By the time I was to the point where I would say, "I really need help," or "I need to get out of here," then I was angry because he didn't figure that out. This was a real Catch-22 for him.*

Most younger couples begin role sharing during the pregnancy by going together for prenatal checkups, birthing together, and sharing the nighttime feeding of the infant. The father gets up with baby to change and burp it after the mother nurses it. Steve, a civil engineer, advises fathers: "If they're serious about it, they will start it from day one. Gear up to take responsibility, like it's not somebody else's job, it's your job." His wife, Laurel, said it was almost incidental that she bore the baby and produced its milk, since they shared in every other way.

A few couples felt that breast-feeding separated roles too much. Since the father could not breast-feed, he would not get up in the middle of the night and change diapers. Breast-feeding "starts to change the dynamics," observed a Massachusetts day-care worker who bottle-fed his baby. Some fathers give bottles of expressed breast milk or formula in addition to the wife's breast-feeding. While the baby was still waking up at night, Adrian would get up and get his wife, Lisa, something to eat, and they would commiserate and talk about the baby together. Nursing is counted as family work: A New York lawyer does most of the driving his boys around because his wife is breast-feeding their youngest son.

Coparenting Techniques

The main coparenting principle that couples use is to alternate tasks in a structured manner. For example, one parent dresses the children in the morning while the other prepares breakfast. They may alternate tasks, one parent sleeping later one day and then getting breakfast ready the next day. They may take turns driving the children to day care, school, lessons, or sports activities. They may alternate cooking dinner and attending to children at the difficult transition time after getting home from work. One person gives baths, reads a bedtime story, and tucks the children in bed, while the other partner does the dishes. In one family, Dan cooks dinner on Monday, Tuesday, and Wednesday, and Karen does it the rest of the week. Dan cooks breakfast on Sunday and Karen does it on Saturday. Dan does the laundry on Tuesday and Karen does it on Friday. She does twelve to fifteen loads a week! Some couples take turns cooking dinner, and both put the children to bed each night. If a child is sick, parents take turns staying at home or taking the child to their office.

Parents may give each other time off from family responsibilities, one parent taking the children on a Saturday afternoon, or each taking them on specific nights during the week. A California couple each has two nights to themselves every week: The off-duty parent can choose to stay at home and read while the other parent goes out with their children, or the off-duty parent can go out. An Iowa couple gives each other three times a week to pursue outside interests in sports. They found that without scheduling time, it slips away too easily. This technique sounds artificial to some, but it is necessary to change old habits. Also, children thrive with routine and structure.[3] Elise, the mother of two children, relates:

Sometimes we fall into the counting trap! I put them to bed three times this week; it's your turn. I've picked them up every day this week. I gave them a bath two times so far. We count our fingers and compare notes in shouts and screams and then collapse laughing. It all evens out. Twenty years from now who cares that Philippe picked them up every day the week of November 19th. Or that Elise put them to bed four times the week of September 12th.

During some periods one parent may assume much more of the family work because the other has special time demands. Sometimes parents each concentrate on one child: A Wisconsin mother says that she supervises her younger son's homework because she can "best handle his uncooperative moods," while her husband works with their oldest son. As children get older, they do not require the same supervision. A teacher says that his children, ages thirteen and eleven, are able to stay by themselves until he gets home. His wife leaves them a note, a snack, and calls them from work when possible (illustrating women's assumption of administrative tasks). "Other than driving them to soccer practices or scout meetings, etc., etc., etc. I do not consciously organize their time," he says. David, a West Virginia father, reports that his daughters, ages sixteen and thirteen, now take care of themselves, except to get transported to a doctor or dentist appointment. His wife, Judy, agrees that child care is not a question. Now the issue is getting them to do their homework and chores, and "enriching their environment, leading them to stimulating activities, playing and working with them."

Employment has a lot to do with how parents share at home. Some couples were able to work three-quarter or half time each. One couple managed to find jobs where he worked Tuesday, Thursday, and Saturday, while she worked Monday, Wednesday, and Friday. Some arrange it so that one goes to work early and the other comes home in the afternoon. Matt, a New Hampshire attorney, takes off Monday and Thursday mornings from work to be with his two children. His wife, Susan, a health care administrator, picks up the children from day care at 3:45 P.M. Matt does the most to get the children ready in the morning and Susan does the most at dinner time. The schedule sounds smooth, but Susan reports that they had to work hard to arrive at it. They charted out the tasks and timing of them, since it takes a great deal of coordination to get two little children and themselves out of the house on time for work. Matt arrives home at 5:30 so they can all eat together. Both parents have to be very firm with their employers about not wanting to work full time while their children are young. "What it boils down to," says Susan, is "with us, there is no chore I do with the kids or Matt does with the kids that the other one doesn't do; there's nothing that is mommy's or daddy's specifically to do. There's nothing that I know about them that Matt doesn't know or vice versa." In spite of this flexibility, Susan finds she is still more responsible for the daily running of the household than Matt.

Ken, a health care consultant who traveled frequently in his work with hospitals, found that his daughter's birth was a salvation for him. She caused him to step back and evaluate what he was doing. When he realized he did not like much of his work, Ken cut back to half time. His decision was a struggle because as a man he was used to defining himself by his work accomplishments. His acquaintances were taken aback by his reduced focus on paid work.

Living close to work helps in coparenting too. A newspaper editor in Colorado thinks he is more involved with his children than any of the other fathers he knows, partly because his children can come to his office and he can also work at home. Bob, a sports reporter, does many of his interviews with coaches and players on the telephone or in the park where he can bring his two children. Two New York attorneys who are partners in a practice with a home office share taking care of their son with their secretaries. Their older son plays in his room two afternoons and goes to day care the other three weekdays. As a short-term solution, one professor took his infant to his office for half days, using a desk drawer as a crib; his wife, also a professor, did the same in the afternoon.

Working parents usually share the care of their children with paid child care workers. A Wisconsin mother feels that the sitter they had for their daughter from the time she was two years old until she was five was a "fantastic" substitute mother. "The sitter had the patience to do all the 'motherly' things I didn't do," she said. A day-care provider in New Hampshire is "so loving, competent, creative and involved that it allows me to work and know that the kids are really happy," reports Susan.

Not all reports are glowing. A critical view of day care was given by the Washington, D.C., father, Bill, who shares a job with his wife so they do not have to use day care. He believes that day-care workers are underpaid and that the care is often substandard. At the end of nine hours, when the parent comes to pick up the child, "they might well be received with the negative reaction that is the child's way of showing that they truly miss their parent."

Nine or ten hours is a long time for a child to be away from home; parents of young children need access to flexible work schedules and part-time jobs. However, studies do not show any major differences in children raised at home and those who attend good consistent day care.[4] Many of the parents I interviewed reported that their children got bored staying at home with one parent all day and liked contact with the other children and adults in day care. Twin boys in Iowa love their day-care center; they are learning and having a good time in a nonsexist environment, reports Larry, their father.

The Swedish plan of a six-hour work day for parents of preschool children is one to emulate. But since most of us do not have this option, some parents have a babysitter who comes to their home, some hire a college student for after-school care, and some share the cost of a babysitter with a neighbor. One divorced father hired a live-in babysitter who receives her room, food, and $200 a month. Another couple who had an eighteen-year-old live-in to help with child care sometimes felt they were taking on another child, however. Parents who hired live-in adults of different ethnic or cultural backgrounds were pleased with the new vistas opened to their children.

Some parents share child care with neighbors and friends. A couple with one child sometimes swaps weekends with a couple with three children: One couple goes off on a trip by themselves while the other devotes themselves to activities with the children. The couple with only one child gets two weekends off for every weekend on with the other couple's three children. In a New England town, five or six cooperative families living on the same street provide backup for a teenage sitter or for older children whose parents go out for the evening. The women share tending vegetable gardens and the men split wood together. For fun they make maple syrup, go on bike rides, and have neighborhood cookouts.

Children's grandparents are another source of help for coparents. Some who live near enough care for children daily or for an occasional weekend, but most just take the children while their parents go on a vacation. A Midwest father reports that grandparents "are terrific for sending the kids to for a visit, but terrible for discussing child rearing with. The most support we get is from talking to other parents with kids who are our kids' ages." A New York teacher says his wife's mother, who lives with them, is a big help in getting their daughter off to school and in being home with her after school. He reports frequent conflicts, however, in their child-rearing philosophies and practices: "Generally Beth understands that her grandmother is old and doesn't mean to oppose or differ with us, it is just her age and past."

Other sources of support for child rearing that parents mentioned were older children, church and women's groups, a small town where people know each other, a helpful pediatrician who helps parents "to see the bigger picture" of the developmental process, and newsletters such as *Growing Child*, which sends monthly updates geared to your child's age. An Ohio mother of three concludes:

> *Actually, I don't think we have a lot of support as parents to our three children—our parents are out of town. So many of our friends and co-workers have no kids, are divorced, or only have one child—which is a totally different ball game. We get support from extended family—cousins, etc. Several times a year we have huge family reunions and admire each other's kids. It helps! The few neighbors with kids are supportive.*

Children in shared parenting households are often involved in making decisions about their own care and other family matters, including the purchase of a car suitable for them, their vacation plans, what to do on the Sunday family outing, meal choices, buying clothes, and choice of camps or other summer activities. A Michigan family reports that they ask their two children for their opinions on just about everything. The family watches the news together and talks about current events and the truth of commercials. "Do you think that's right?" and "What would you do?" are frequent discussion questions. Some families have weekly meetings, often on Sunday evening, where family decisions are made. Annie, a Wisconsin mother, reports, "I make a point of giving my sons practice in decision making. They weigh the pros and cons and look at consequences in situations such as how to spend their free time, how to spend their allowances, and choosing clothes." By contrast, in a traditional family I surveyed, the mother said of her eleven-year-old twins, "At their age, we basically tell them what to do." Now, at age fifteen, one of the twins is doing very poorly in school because he has not learned to assume responsibility. Sharing in decision making may be one significant reason that children in egalitarian families have higher self-esteem than the children in the traditional families we surveyed.

Housework

Managing two jobs and a family is a juggling act. The mother of a five-year-old reports that when her daughter walks in the house everything falls apart, like the story of the wolf who blew down the little pigs' houses. A California father will think he has gotten everything shipshape and then a day later it falls apart—his living room had laundry all over it, for example, when I spoke with him. When a house with three teenagers and their friends gets cleaned up, it gets messed up right away, says one mother. She plans on hiring a crew with shovels to clean up when the kids leave home. But Susan believes that in a "co-parented household, housework can be less of a burden and more of a mutual carrying for family life." It helps her to think of a Zen Buddhist saying, "Before enlightenment, chop wood, carry water. After enlightenment, chop wood, carry water." Attitude is the difference.

Since infants sleep frequently, one might think that they could not create housekeeping problems, but the parents' lack of sleep and the baby's frequent interruptions make completion of simple tasks such as doing the dishes a major accomplishment. Laurel and Steve both stayed home from work for eight weeks after their daughter was born. They were surprised that they could not manage to get out to buy dishwashing soap for five days after the birth, although they were very much in need of it. "We were exhausted at the end of the day and we wouldn't know why. We were amazed: How could getting nothing done take all day?" It took them about a year and a half to get over the shock that a newborn causes. The infant of a Massachusetts mother never wanted to be put down; the mother rose at six, but at noon she would find herself still not dressed and the beds not made. Being awakened every two or three hours around the clock turns parents into zombies. Taking a nap—not doing housework—is the priority when the baby sleeps. MaryKay, a Michigan mother, said her first years as a mother were "in a fog. I hardly remember them." Completing a task is difficult with an infant around, like trying to complete a task when the phone rings every ten minutes.

One way parents cope is to lower their standards. An Illinois family frequently eats baked potatoes and easy-to-prepare Mexican and Chinese food, using their microwave oven. Some families buy frozen prepared dinners. "My corners are probably dusty," says a Colorado mother of three. "If I were as paranoid as some of my friends are about their houses I'm sure it would be a lot bigger deal." A Utah family said it looks like a bomb has hit their house. Karen, a Massachusetts mother, said that the general level of cleanliness in their house has plummeted since their baby was born. Toys are spread out in every room, beds do not seem to get made, and clothes pile up on the dressers, a constant source of irritation. A Mississippi couple cleans their house and within an hour their son has everything out again, but they have learned to live with this. Some coparenting couples who can afford it hire someone to come in once a week or every two weeks to do heavy cleaning, figuring that they are sharing their income and creating a job. However, 80 percent of the dual-career couples I surveyed do not hire household help. For some people, having a nonfamily member do housework violates their sense of what it is to be a good spouse. When they realize that time is so precious that it is better spent on family members than toilet bowls, they can override their childhood beliefs.

Even couples who decide to share housework equally face problems. One couple, Charles and Kathleen, thought that since they were both feminists and agreed to share 50-50, their problems were solved. But they still fought about family work because each person thought that he or she was doing more than the other. Charles had to "overcome internal messages that when I was doing housework I wasn't doing anything important." Their solution was to make lists of all household chores including dishes, cleaning, giving baths, and school-related responsibilities. They even counted how many diapers each of them washed. Then they divided up the tasks. The lists made it clear that one person was not doing more than a fair share. For another couple who both felt like they were doing more than 50 percent, keeping track of how much time each spent on chores helped them realize that there was much more work to running a family than they had realized.

Just as Charles struggled with his internal messages that doing housework is a waste of time for a man, Betty, an Iowa coparent, realized that she had her own female programming. She resisted her second husband's sharing the cooking. "I really don't like him taking over the kitchen, taking control of that," she confessed. He gets home before she does so it makes sense for him to start cooking, and she got tired in her first marriage of taking care of everyone. Her husband's socialization reinforces hers. He observed: "It is true that I rely on her. I would much rather ask her what she wants to have for dinner in the morning than make the decision."

Carol and Dave find that they have reverted to a fairly conventional division of male/female tasks, although equal in terms of the time they spend. They wanted to learn various skills but fell back on what they already knew due to "exhaustion. It's just a matter of who can do what the easiest, which has to do with what you're brought up doing," Carol explains. She does more of the cooking and organizes house cleaning, while Dave does more of the dishes and takes charge of the cars. Often who does what job is determined by what matters most to each person. A North Dakota couple noted that the husband does more work around the house because cleanliness is more important to him. In contrast, a California professor remarked to his mate, "There is stuff that I see should be done and stuff that you think should be done and the stuff you think should be done is a lot more. I do half of what I think should be done." He noted that over their four years of living together, she has lowered her expectations and he has raised his. Unfortunately, this is not enough to please either of them.

Recognizing that men and women are socialized differently helps put these almost inevitable struggles into context. The best solution seems to be itemizing all the tasks that need to be done for the family to function, noting the time that the tasks take and then dividing them up on the basis of preference or availability. Jobs that no one wants to do can be rotated or hired out. Sharing housework and child care is fair, conducive to family closeness, and a useful example for children who will form role-sharing families in the future.

Involving Children

Another way of dealing with housework is to include the children. "It's everybody's house so everybody should be involved in taking care of it," concludes a Colorado father. The divorced mother of two boys tells them if they do not do their share, then she has to do three shares, and since they are really nice, her boys do their part. Some parents use this appeal to fairness; we all live here, we are a team. Other parents motivate their children to do housework by providing or docking their allowances. Using money for control, "takes away the need to yell and scream and nag," said a Minnesota mother. A child psychologist, Janet Rausch, provided the following suggestions for getting young children to do their chores.[5] Define a time limit for finishing the chore and set a timer. If it goes off before the job is completed, an additional job is required or the parent picks up the toys and puts them out of use for several days. Give a reward, such as a sticker on a chart, for completion. List chores so that the child will not feel they are never ending. These techniques minimize nagging, which children do not listen to, by providing clear consequences.

Coparents want their children to develop into self-sufficient adults who can do their own mending, cooking, and laundry. They tell sons that they do not want them to marry to have someone to take care of them. One mother taught her son to cook as soon as he was tall enough to reach the stove. Children also need to learn the consequences of their actions by being responsible for the results; creating a mess means cleaning it up. Being responsible leads to self-confidence and independence. Useful suggestions for involving children in housework and other organizational tips are described in other books on the topic.[6]

Family meetings can be a time to define and assign tasks. One family has a Saturday morning ritual over tea of listing the jobs and activities for the weekend, including the time required. They also go over their calendar for the week. Their combined "votes" then prioritize chores from their list. Their five-year-old daughter, Whitney, adds her suggestions to the list and participates in the voting. A Minnesota family of five goes out to dinner every two weeks. While they are waiting for their meal they plan weekly dinner menus and make shopping lists on index cards. Each child will shop, card in hand, for the menu they select.

Some families have permanent lists of assigned jobs, while others post a weekly or monthly rotation on the refrigerator. A Washington family rotates their daily tasks, which include doing laundry, washing breakfast dishes, setting and clearing the table, cooking dinner, and washing dinner dishes. A chart divided into squares with their initials indicates who does which task on each day of the week. A New Mexico family rotates setting the table, clearing it, and making a salad each evening. A Colorado family with four children prepares a monthly calendar assigning nights to cook and to wash dishes. They make up weekly menus, post them for the cook of the day, and shop once a week for those menus. They do housecleaning as a group effort on Saturday morning. Each person is responsible for cleaning his or her own room plus one other assigned room. Chores such as planting the garden or stacking firewood are done as a team.

The chores that children most often do are setting and clearing the table, cleaning their bedroom and bathroom, vacuuming and sweeping, taking care of pets, carrying out the garbage, cooking dinner once a week (as young as age nine), doing the dishes, and cleaning up after dinner. They wash their own clothes or put them in the proper place for dirty laundry and check for holes or missing buttons. They fold and put away their laundry, prepare their own breakfasts and lunches, carry in firewood, mow lawns, wash cars, water houseplants, and help recycle glass and cans. A teenager makes his own barber and doctor appointments because he lives in New York City and can travel by public transportation.

Parents sometimes struggle with the fact that it is easier and faster to do chores themselves than to teach the kids to do them. "They love to help me cook and sometimes the help is more work," reports the father of two elementary school boys. Another father recognizes that he should be "more tolerant of imperfection" in his daughters' housework. Often when parents want their children to do chores the children resist, procrastinate, and "dilly dally around," making it faster for the adult to do the job. An insightful fifteen-year-old who cleans up the kitchen very well said to his mother, "I guess I shouldn't be this good at it, should I?" A parent educator,

Jane Bryan-Jones, explains that children learn to feel competent by doing tasks like dressing themselves, although it is faster and easier for the parent to do it and parents may be embarrassed if their child combines plaids and stripes.[7] Bryan-Jones advocates an "on-going process of letting go more and more."

Many parents feel that they do not ask their children to contribute enough to running the household. "We're not as consistent about getting them to do their duties as we'd like to be because it's such a hassle to get them to do them," two California parents noted. A Kansas couple said that their major regret as parents is that "we have not made our children more responsible. Every week, it seems, we resolve to do a better job of helping them." Teenagers are often away from home, busy with school activities, lessons, sports, and part-time jobs. Two brothers in Maryland, for example, have hours of homework from their special high school math and science program, are on a track team, and have paper routes. They have very little time to help around the house.

To get children to do their jobs parents remind them, yell, and threaten to dock their allowances or remand a privilege such as watching television—"It's a constant battle." Some parents attach allowances to work, while others believe an allowance automatically comes with being a family member, with extra chores bringing in additional money. A Washington mother relates that sometimes when she tells her son, Kyle, that as a consequence of not doing his chores he will not get his fifty cents for the week, he says he does not want it. Then she withholds sugarless gum. Since his toy purchases come from Kyle's bank, "I like it when he gets down to nothing so he's more motivated to do his chores."

Parents try to heed the advice of experts to apply logical consequences: If dirty clothes are not put in the proper receptical, they do not get washed; if possessions are left around the house, one couple confiscates them and puts them in a box that can be ransomed on Saturday for a small fee per item. Parents use behavior modification techniques of rewarding good behavior. For younger children, they post charts with points, stars, or stickers, with rewards for obtaining a certain number of stars. Use of the telephone and family car are rewards for adolescents.

In the long run, positive rewards for desired behavior are stronger reinforcements than punishment for undesirable behavior.

When Jed was being toilet trained, I bought a bag of small plastic space characters and gave him one as a prize each time he used the toilet. That was much more effective than the negative method I had read about and tried of having him clean out his dirty pants. One family who cleans up together on Saturday puts on energetic music to motivate everyone.

A Michigan mother is teaching her boys to be aware of what needs to be done, such as keeping track of their chores and keeping their clothes in shape. They will not grow up to be like the Indiana husband who told me he does what his wife points out needs doing. Administrative responsibility is burdensome when not shared.

Ten Basic Techniques for Coparenting

In summary, ten strategies for coparenting are:

1. Select the right partner to save much future struggle. Egalitarian spouses who can create new roles tend to have the confidence to be untraditional and face social disapproval. Often both of their parents were employed. Egalitarian spouses tend to be liberal politically and in their attitude toward sex roles, believing that women need their own career expression and men can be nurturant and do family work. A college education or involvement in women's and men's liberation groups helps to provide a framework for rethinking attitudes toward gender. Change is difficult unless we have words to define it.
2. Learn how to express feelings effectively, to listen attentively, and to negotiate compromises. Role sharers do not have many examples of equality to follow, so they have to negotiate frequently to decide who should do what in the family. Basic communication techniques include using "I" messages, rather than blaming "you" messages. An example is, "I feel burdened by being the one to always stay home with a sick child. I would like to have your help in figuring out a fair solution." A "you" message is, "You are so selfish, always putting your career ahead of mine." Active listening is nonjudgmentally feeding back to your partner your understanding of his or her feelings. This sounds simple but is rarely done. Most people give advice or inter-

ject their own experiences and thoughts, preventing genuine understanding.

3. Take advantage of what experts can teach about communication skills and creating optimal families. Go to a family counselor to learn to talk about feelings and listen to your partner. Most people do not think about these daily activities as skills and therefore lack them. We have been taught that expressing feelings is childish or feminine so we have to unlearn much repression. Books can also be useful. Forming discussion groups with other people with dual-career marriages, stepfamilies, and so on can provide necessary information and support.

4. Keep a time diary of each family member's activities for a typical week or two. List all the chores that are necessary to keep the home, yard, and car running smoothly. Include administrative jobs such as arranging child care and social secretary jobs such as writing greeting cards and buying gifts. Divide up tasks equitably, perhaps with a point system. Consequences may be attached to doing the tasks well or neglecting them. A job that is imperative, such as cooking dinner, may be given to a person who is likely to resist doing housework. The weight of disapproval from hungry people will be heavier than from people who dislike dirty floors.

5. Be aware that women often assume the administrative role in the family, remembering what needs to be done, making lists, assigning duties, taking care of social courtesies, and planning social events. Men often fall into the role of helping the woman with family work. If both spouses are working outside the home, this attitude of men as helpers needs to be eradicated. If the administrative duties are not shared, they should at least be recognized as time consuming, and the other partner should do more work in other areas.

6. Share child care from the beginning. Many couples are fairly egalitarian until the birth of their child. Parenting makes role sharing most difficult. Fathers need to take equal responsibility for parenting from the pregnancy, going to doctor visits with the mother, coaching the birth, and spending time alone with the infant. Time that the father spends alone with the baby gives

him the experience not to defer to his wife's mythical maternal instinct.

7. Develop a broad range of skills. Women quickly fall into the role of being the expert about family matters, since the culture has defined men as expert income earners. Women need to develop competency in dealing with repairs, cars, finances, and other areas regarded as masculine, just as men need to develop competency as coparents by parenting, reading, and talking with other fathers.

8. Establish family as a priority. That means being able to say no to overtime work and possibly to job transfers and promotions. Role sharers value family above work.

9. Establish a structure for sharing household tasks. Flowing along with good intentions does not work because of the counterthrust of society. Family work should be alternated; for example, one parent cooking dinner three nights a week and picking up the children from day care four days. Fun times also need to be scheduled for the couple and for the family. Times for sharing feelings and solving problems should be scheduled regularly, as should family meetings and times for the couple to go out.

10. Join with other like-minded people to share tasks such as child care, gardening, and cooking. Family life is very stressful due to the lack of supports for employed parents. Put pressure on local schools, government, and employers to face up to the needs of contemporary families and take action.

3

Democratic Discipline

Here is this other creature that you're responsible for and yet you don't want to be a tyrant or an authoritarian, you have to allow a lot of freedom. How do you live with somebody whom you love, and want to help, and yet recognize their autonomy?

— *Walt, father of two*

My daughter teaches me to be more assertive than anyone because she'll run over me if I don't set limits.

— *Vicki, divorced mother of one*

COPARENTS value shared decision making not only for themselves but for their children. Setting limits effectively and democratically for children is a challenge. In her book *Family Politics*, Letty Cottin Pogrebin observes that the American family is still hierarchical, based on a chain of command with the "big daddy model of dominance."[1] Pogrebin proposes as an alternative the democratic family, in which parents empower their children by giving them information and examples of "how to negotiate and reason with others." For a family to be democratic, parents themselves must share power and responsibilities. This means that the woman must give up her "domestic throne," and the man must not let work encroach on family time. He does not have the right to feel like a hero for being an involved father, Pogrebin states, and will need to learn his children's shoe sizes, their best friends' parents' names, how many quarts of milk are in the refrigerator, and grandmother's birthday.[2] Studies agree that autocratic parents produce children who are poorly motivated in school and have low self-esteem.[3] Parental rigidity is least likely to produce children who become sensitive and independent adults, according to a long-term study.[4]

As couples shape their new parenting style, discipline is a frequent item for discussion. An Indiana couple said that the main difficulty in sharing parenting is arguments over different standards about children's behavior, although "otherwise, I can't imagine raising a kid any other way," the mother noted. An attorney in New York explained that it is

> *tough maintaining consistent discipline when two parents are doing it. We sometimes end up countermanding each other, which results in difficulties. Our son Josh is very aware of differences in what Paul and I require and will or will not stand for, which makes him somewhat more manipulative of us than I was of my parents. I don't like it, but it may be a good survival skill.*

Often one parent is stricter than the other. In a Colorado stepfamily, the father believes that the mother is not strict enough with the children. She says that he does not watch them closely enough to catch them in the act and stop them when it is most effective. "We have had disagreements about that forever," she added. A father in Wisconsin observes that he tends "not to sweat the small stuff," while his wife gets upset about smaller infractions of rules. Another couple struggle over June's desire for her husband, Steve, to reinforce her in getting their son to do his chores. Steve explains, "I think I'm not quite so conscious of it as June is and if he makes a big stink about not wanting to do a job, I just do it."

Another father said their family's biggest problem was that he would jump in and take over, blowing his top, instead of sitting down to talk out a problem. He has changed since going to a family counselor. A physician said he feels "inadequate when my wife prods me and says, 'Well, are you just going to let this go on?' I feel like she's hit one of my weak spots. I react out of a need to please her and don't wind up feeling particularly good about the whole interaction."

In contrast, a traditional couple I surveyed divides the labor so that the mother has most of the care of the children, "so she does most of the disciplining," says the father. "If she needs help, I pitch in. When the kids get whiny or disobedient when I'm around, I give the authoritative word." The mother believes that the father should be the "law-giver and disciplinarian." She reports, however, that the children are more attached to her than to him. Although hierarchy is simpler than group consensus, the last-resort disciplinarian father is often left out of the real intimacy of the family.

Discipline Problems

A teacher of parent education classes, Jane Bryan-Jones, explained that too often discipline or limit setting is thought of as punishment, when it actually means to guide and to show. The parents' job is to guide their children into areas of acceptable behavior and set limits on the unacceptable areas of behavior: "If we're not willing to do that then they're going to come against it with others later in life who will not be as gentle, consistent and helpful to them."[5]

Parents agreed that discipline is a difficult area. Children may not respond to limit setting and children's peers may be a negative influence. Parents may not agree on the proper limits. An Ohio father of three children gave an account of his experiences:

> *Before we had children I had all sorts of philosophical observations about how to raise children. These ideas were based on what I considered to be inadequacies concerning my own childhood and my observations of the little monsters I saw my friends raising. I naively believed, as most childless people do, that I would have a great deal of control over what my children did—WRONG! I expected that if I kindly reminded them to say "thank you" to Grandma just once, gratitude would drip from their little lips forevermore—WRONG! I thought if I put up a cute little chart on the refrigerator with checks for cleaning up their rooms and flushing the toilets, those tasks would get done—WRONG! I even believed Spock when he said if we fed our kids all kinds of foods when they were small, they would greet anything other than tacos or pizza with hearty appetites—WRONG!*

South Dakota stepparents realize that discipline is one of their weakest areas as parents, especially since each of their children requires a different approach. One child is mouthy, one is whiny, and one regresses to baby talk. Parents report that babies have different temperaments from birth. "Some kids come out of the womb making demands," said Linda. One of her sons has "always been difficult, has had all kinds of allergies." If California parents yell at one son he "breaks apart and cries," while the other son "just looks you in the eye and keeps doing it." Often siblings fit themselves into different niches, such as the rebellious child, the academic child, the athletic child, or the social child.

Disciplining a willful child is clearly different from disciplining a child who aims to please. A pediatrician in Maine calls intense, bright, energetic children (whom he finds were often also colicky babies) "high reactors." The Maine mother of one of those high reactors reports that her daughter wants to "go out on the edge" of experiences: "If you're with a person like that a lot, like on the weekends, it wears you down." Another category of children described by child psychologist Janet Rausch are those who from birth engage in power struggles almost to the extent that if their parent says "go to the circus," the child will say "no."[6] It is encouraging to know that there are personality types, that your child's behavior is not solely the result of your mistakes as a disciplinarian or nutritionist.

Even an effective limit-setting technique may need to be changed as the child grows. Maryann compares herself to a batter trying to hit her child's wily pitch. She gets a discipline technique set, then receives a curveball and misses, gets ready for a curveball, and gets an underhand pitch. As an Indiana father related:

> *Every time that I think I have discovered how to do a fair job at it, the situations change, so that I feel I have to start over in learning how to be a good parent. It is difficult not to get discouraged sometimes when a child fails to respond to the type of help I try to give. Yet the important point is to keep trying to help him/her to grow up to trust.*

Ellen Galinsky observed that parents' process of changing their expectations or images for their children leads to growth.[7] Books about children's developmental stages are useful, as long as one does not expect that one's child will indeed conform to patterns such as that five-year-olds are serene and love to cooperate with their mothers.[8]

Parents also realize that their children behave worse with them than with anyone else. People save up their negative feelings for release when they feel safest, so parents are the natural recipients of their children's stored-up bad feelings. A few parents described children who responded well and consistently to a gentle statement of displeasure. More parents resorted to yelling out of frustration.

Today's children appear to be an especially confident and willful generation, one that will not need assertiveness training, Judy observed. A mother who supervises managers responsible for 35 million dollars worth of revenue reports, "Yet, when I come home, I sometimes feel I can barely hold my own with my six- and one-year-old kids." The mother of a five-year-old commented, "She's certainly obnoxious by my mother's standards, which are close to children should be seen but not heard." Another mother noted the difference in how she was raised, "I don't think we had any choices. My mom never asked me what I wanted to do or what I wanted for dinner. I ask my daughter what she wants to do."

Previous generations and other cultures offered more social supports for parents. A pediatric social worker in Denver whom I interviewed stated, "It appears to me that this entire city is going crazy. The schools don't seem to have any kind of control over what is going on, and even very nice parents don't seem to have their kids under control. When your kids are out of your sight you can't really tell what is happening."

Children are often portrayed as sweet, cuddly, and fun, but they are also uncivilized and selfish. They seem to go through an evolutionary process much like their primate cousins. Like other primate youngsters, boys engage in dominance struggles and rough-and-tumble play, while girls engage in more nurturant behavior. It takes time to civilize children. They can be loving and delightful, but are just as likely to disrupt their parents' needs for sleep, privacy, quiet, romance, sex, order, and getting a task done without constant demands and interruptions. One frank author confessed, "My son Eben has become an intruder in our formerly happy marriage. . . . I love him so much, but most of the time I can't stand him."[9] A Maine mother said she tries to appeal to her boys' reasonableness and decency, "when maybe they are not even reasonable or decent!" Often the needs of adults and children are in opposition and struggle seems inevitable.

The author James Dobson concurs, "I have yet to find a text for parents or teachers which acknowledges the struggle—the exhausting confrontation of wills—which most parents and teachers experience regularly with their children."[10] "The constant abrasiveness" of child rearing is described by authors Faber and Mazlish.[11] A divorced mother told me, "We're always negotiating and she usually wins." Another mother said of her gifted six-year-old, "He's had me figured out for years. I have to always be on my guard with him because he can outmaneuver me at any given moment. He's a sweet kid in many ways, but he's so in control sometimes that it's scary." The confrontation of wills is exhausting, as are seemingly simple tasks like getting a child off to school in the morning. One California mother has a positive way of looking at the struggle: "She teaches me to be more assertive than anyone because she'll run right over me if I don't."

Causes of Misbehavior

Common discipline problems are children dawdling and "lollygagging" while getting ready in the morning or at night, not doing chores, and "talking back." Jane Bryan-Jones observed that often the parent either feels that she or he has not spent enough time with the child or has not liked being with the child all day and feels guilty. As a result the parent is unable to set clear limits or to be consistent. The child manipulates the guilt feelings and the disharmony escalates. A Colorado mother circumvents being "guilt-tripped" by her children by saying,

> *My official position is that I'm just as selfish as anybody in the house and I'm just as entitled as you are to whatever. At least I'm not constantly being blackmailed like real nice mothers whose children say "You are really being selfish." I don't hear that one because I told them first—as I sit here in my eight-year-old slippers!*

Children are very perceptive about tuning into their parents' emotions and manipulating them. Children revealed in our interviews how aware they are of their manipulative techniques, such as getting one thing they wanted by begging for many things or being especially cooperative. Children seem to zero in on parents when they are concentrating and focused on a task, wanting to divert that attention to themselves. A Georgia mother, a recovered alcoholic, used to feel

> *wired for sound and raw, like somebody had stripped all the insulation off my nerves and I was exposed, like the feeling when somebody runs their fingernail over the chalkboard. Any sound or crying would do that to me; my son tapped into that and understood that if he cried I would do anything to shut him up. He was in some ways running me at my worst energy. Now I am more able to be consistent.*

Young children also misbehave because they are tired. Susan and Matt are very aware of the connection of misbehavior with fatigue, so they have a policy of not taking their children out when they are tired and hungry. Frequently that means quite a bit of juggling with schedules to deal with plane trips to visit the grandparents, for example. "Then my expectation is that they will behave on a plane or train, and it's generally worked out pretty well," Susan reported.

Some parents of older children report less conflict as children assume more responsibility. The main conflict for a family with a teenage son is planning when he is going to do homework and chores, along with his school activities and his paper route. Parents and children also mentioned conflict about children's reporting where they are going and when they are coming back.

Making decisions about a family activity can cause friction. Daniel gives an example of

> *driving somewhere with all five of us jammed into our little Toyota, when the usual happened. The kids all started screaming at each other and at us because (will we never learn?) their mother asked them where they would like to stop for lunch. It may have worked for the Waltons, but democracy has never worked in this family. So much for family decision making—it is a CROCK!*

Arlyn, a Colorado mother of four, has found that the need for discipline arises when children feel they are not getting enough attention. A misbehaving child is a discouraged child who needs encouragement, according to Jane Nelson, author and parent educator.[12] She summarizes Rudolph Dreikurs's observations of four common motivations for poor behavior: power, attention, revenge, and inadequacy. For teenagers, excitement and peer pressure are additional motivators. Nelson suggests four democratic steps for dealing with children's behavior: First, try to imagine what the child is feeling and check it out with him or her. Second, let the child know you understand, such as by telling about an incident in your childhood. Third, ask if the child would be willing to hear your point of view. Fourth, negotiate a solution to the problem.

Arguments between sisters and brothers are also a major cause of misbehavior. The biggest problem for the mother of two elementary school–age boys is "they're either loving each other and playing nicely or competing like hell all weekend. There doesn't seem to be any middle ground for them." An Illinois father, Don, reports that when his sons are separated, they're absolute angels, but when they are together, "watch out." His wife said it seems like the boys feel compelled to pick on each other when they are together, so the parents separate them.

Several children are more complicated than one. Another child is "that much less energy, more attention and space demand, and less privacy," remarked Susan. Parents try to cope with sibling rivalries, such as younger children striving to keep up with or be the opposite of the older sibling, or a first child feeling displaced by a new baby. You can take one child with you, but "you can't drag two kids around with you," notes a Washington, D.C., mother of three. She does not feel that a third child makes much difference, however. Another couple with three children worry that their youngest child gets lost between attention given to her oldest brother's activities and her other brother's physical handicaps.

Some parents believe that one child so radically changes parents' lives that additional ones do not make that much impact. One couple with four children explained that it took twenty-four hours a day to take care of one child and twenty-four hours a day to take care of four children. Their four children entertain themselves more than children in smaller families and "figure things out for themselves." In their large family, they establish firm rules; one child wandering around the house eating a sandwich might not make much of a mess, but four children eating outside the kitchen would create havoc.

Democratic Discipline

Parenting, said a California father, challenges our fundamental beliefs.

> *Here is this other creature that you're responsible for and yet if you don't want to be a tyrant or an authoritarian, you have to allow a lot of freedom. How do you live with somebody whom you love, and want to help, and yet recognize their autonomy?*

Parents should provide boundaries within which the child has freedom, resolved another father. His wife defines their role as parents as to help their daughter achieve independence as a functioning, productive, loving adult.

Authoritative parents provide direction and clear rules but not for the sake of blind obedience. Studies by Diana Baumrind show that authoritative parents have better results than either authoritarian or permissive parents.[13] Authoritative parents share their reasoning with the children, teaching them to solve problems by making their own decisions. A Texas father of twin teenage boys explains that when they come home with a problem, he talks it through with them, pointing out the possible consequences of various options. This process is "much more a scientific method than the traditional authority method" and gives them "personal pride in making the choice." Treating each family member with respect is a hallmark of his values.

"We have used authority and punishment but not with notable success," reported one Indiana mother. She and her husband went to a counselor to learn more effective discipline techniques, such as: "To listen with understanding, to share feelings, to find solutions to problems which come from all of us instead of being imposed by parents." Common sense indicates that any emotionally healthy person responds better to consultation than command. On the other hand, children test for boundaries and need to face the consequences of their behavior to learn responsibility. Warren noted that his partner's daughter will push for boundaries until "you get tough on her and it's astonishing: She's all nice and lovely." Children need limits as well as practice in decision making, responsibility, independence, and trust. They know and want this, as they explain in chapter 5. Studies show that high-achieving children are those who are given independence as well as authoritative limits by their parents and are not over-protected or dominated.[14]

Coparents who were raised by authoritarian parents recall that it was debilitating: "My father was so much an authority in our house we didn't say boo without his permission," Barbara reported. She vowed to raise her own children with love and to discuss everything. "That did not work either," she said, "because it is harder to enforce rules and regulations because there is such a struggle." Utah parents who get tired of negotiating with their children worry, as do others, "Are we patsies, getting run over?"[15]

Susan explained:

> *I've been really uncomfortable with the permissiveness that we've seen among friends who had kids before us. Their kids were little shits who seemed to be screaming for order, structure, and rules. Matt and I feel strongly that indulged children are unhappy children, insecure children. We feel that structure and standards are a fundamental parental responsibility.*

Their children have a consistent schedule and as a consequence, Susan feels, they are more relaxed and sure of themselves. Matt adds that he gets upset when he sees parents tell children to do something and then ignore it when they do not respond. Parents agree that consistently following through with discipline is crucial, or else children learn to whine and beg until their parents give in to their demands.

Coparents use strategies such as limiting the number of rules and enforcing them consistently to minimize power struggles. For small children, parents recommend rearranging the house to remove fragile objects that have a lot of "no's" attached to them. To prevent meal preparation from turning into a "no-no" confrontation, Massachusetts parents involve their young son by giving him responsibilities. He puts vegetables in the pot after one parent chops them and takes the silverware out of the dishwasher. Redirecting a child away from pulling the cat's tail to playing with a stuffed animal is another example of substituting an approved activity for a disruptive one.

Another way to limit power struggles is to include children in making rules and in deciding ahead of time on possible consequences for breaking them. The mother of a five-year-old says, "All the time I see people assuming that kids can't understand and aren't worth listening to. It hurts me to see that. That's my commitment to Whitney. I hope she will keep wanting to talk to me as she gets older." A Michigan mother also observes that many parents seem to forget that children are people, when in fact they have feelings and a native intelligence. Parents of West Virginia teenagers explain that they take their daughters' opinions on household decisions into consideration: "It would be pointless to go against the wishes of two strong personalities," said their father. Other parents feel it is important to let their children know that parents make mistakes too, and that children are only different from adults in that they have not had as much experience.

Children want to be trusted. One mother has always given her sixteen-year-old the benefit of the doubt, trusted him to make his own decisions after she explained the options, and found that "he has a reasonability that's uncanny." A California father summarizes,

> *I think in childraising as well as marriage, you basically get back what you put in. If there is trust and honesty, then there is a foundation on which children and parents can both grow. By respecting our kids, I think we get kids who tend to respect each other more, and are more democratic.*

The most influential discipline technique book mentioned by parents I interviewed was Rudolph Dreikurs' *Children: The Challenge.*[16] Dreikurs suggests that parents minimize power struggles, and thus the need for discipline, by allowing choices and working with natural consequences. Some of the choices that Liz gives to her toddler are, "Do you want to drink from the green cup or the red cup? Do you want me to brush your teeth or the ghost to brush your teeth? Do you want to eat your peas first or your mashed potatoes?" These kinds of choices allow children to feel that they have some control and to practice making decisions at the same time that they are complying with their parents' wishes. Ordering children to do something invites a power struggle.

Dreikurs suggests that parents *act* rather than talk, punish, or get angry. If the toddler drags her foot in the stroller, stop pushing it. If the child does not put his bike back in the proper place, tell him that he may not use it now but can try again in the afternoon. If the child is misbehaving in the car, do not drive, and sit quietly until she behaves. Consistency is crucial or else children will persist in their disruptive behavior, knowing that their parents will give in to silence them. Children reported that lectures are not effective because they tune them out. If parents or teachers frequently yell and scold, children stop hearing them. Instead of authoritarian demands, try a question, such as asking a child who spills a drink, "What can we do now?" or give information such as, "The paper towels are by the sink." If the child does not take appropriate action, lead him or her physically to clean up the mess. Action works better than words.

Another technique for correcting misbehavior is to use humor and fun, such as telling a child it is time for bed in pig latin, or putting little prizes such as pennies under the trash cans to be emptied. No one likes to be ordered about and children are no exception.

Parents should permit logical consequences of misbehavior to occur. If a child is late for dinner, it is cold, and if dirty clothes are left on the floor, they are not washed. If items left out of place are put away by a parent, a chore may be required to redeem them. If a child's request is whining or rude, parents need not respond. As one mother said, "I want him to start realizing that life is a series of causes and effects."

The most common consequence of undesirable behavior for young children, parents reported, is a time in isolation. Some use a timer so the child can watch the five or ten minutes tick off. One coparenting couple requires their children to think of three reasons why their behavior was in error during the time-out. For older children, logical consequences determine that if the car is used without permission, the teenager will not be able to use it again. Violation of curfew means the overtime has to be paid back from the next night out.

Parents stress the importance of positive reinforcement for good behavior. A Colorado mother realized that she and her husband were usually greeting their seventeen-year-old son with a reminder of what he had not done and that they should find welcoming comments to greet him. A Michigan family promised to extend their son's play territory if he was consistently home on time for dinner, in addition to grounding him if he was late.

Rewarding good behavior and ignoring undesirable behavior is the basis of behavior modification. The daughter in one Chicago household is given twenty stars a day with corresponding privileges and duties. Watching a TV show is worth two stars; complaining about her dinner or not taking a bath costs four stars. The parents started with a few least-tolerable misbehaviors so that she did not feel overwhelmed. The mother feels that it is important that the girl mark in her own stars on the paper so that she knows she has them. When children complete a job, they deserve praise, unqualified by criticism. Validations can be done routinely at family meetings and at bedtime. Useful exercises in building self-appreciation are described in *Self-Esteem: A Family Affair.*[17]

Dreikurs advises parents to stay out of siblings' power struggles and let them resolve their own conflicts. Arlene, a Minnesota mother of three, said her parents did her a disservice by settling her brothers' and sisters' arguments. She finds that children in her neighborhood carry their arguments further because they know their parents will step in. If Arlene's children start fighting physically, she tells them to go outside, and 90 percent of the time they stop. Arlene and her husband, Les, also use active listening techniques, reporting feelings back to the children, such as "You're upset about that, aren't you?" Encouraging expression of feelings and not acting as parental referees frees the children to express their affection for each other, Arlene reports.

Coparents learned to circumvent many authoritarian commands of "do this and do that" by putting effective communication skills into practice.[18] Clear communication includes a specific description of desired behavior, such as "Only ride your trike in the driveway," rather than "Don't ride in the street." Learning how to talk about feelings may require going to a counselor. An Oregon family went to a therapist when their son was having trouble at school, partly to gain insight about what to do and "partly to show him that if you had a problem you could go to somebody and talk to them, it is okay to talk out loud about how you're feeling."

Parents report that "I" messages are very effective, such as "I feel sad if you tear up your nice books," or "I'm too tired now to read you a long story," or "I'm angry because I was scared when you were late." A mother who was able to talk to her son about her anger and its origin in her childhood, found that "that talk with him helped because I haven't done my screaming number since." Adults' inclination is to give advice or provide solutions when what the child (or other adult) wants is verification that we have listened and understood. The simple statement, "You feel hurt that your friends don't want to play now," is more effective than a lecture on the joys of solitude. It is also less of a strain to listen actively than to try to solve your child's (or partner's) problems. This is one of the most helpful communication techniques with children that I have learned. If people want advice, they will ask for it.

Useful books on effective communication with children (and adults) are two by Faber and Mazlish: *Liberated Parents: Liberated Children* and *How To Talk So Children Will Listen and Listen So Children Will Talk*. Faber and Mazlish point out that logic and talking often are ineffective with children. If a child whines for a drink in the middle of a traffic jam, it is useless for an adult to explain logically why a drink is not available. An active listener responds, "You are so thirsty: Wouldn't a tall glass of lemonade taste wonderful!" This principle of responding with acknowledgment rather than logic or debate saves endless arguments. Another means of communication is writing notes. One note about a task can be more effective than constant verbal reminders. Parents help their children most by permitting them to work out their own solutions, Faber and Mazlish conclude.[19] This is especially important for girls, since they get helped more than boys.

Vicki, a divorced coparent, gave an "I" message to her elementary school–age daughter Gabrielle who was not doing her chores: "I need your help. I can't do it all by myself. If you had all this to do I would not want you to be by yourself. I would help you. In order to take from our family pot, to see that it is filled, each of us should give to the pot." When expressing her feelings did not reach Gabrielle, Vicki used consequences. When Gabrielle said she did not want to be part of the family, Vicki said, all right, "I'll serve you your food in your room. You can be a roomer here. I won't ask you to do anything. I also won't ask you to play with me." That worked.

A Maine mother, in hindsight, thinks she should have said a simple "no" more often to their son, rather than "always trying to appeal to his sense of reason. Sometimes I think that gets exhausting for a kid." In *How To Get Your Children To Do What You Want Them To Do*, Wood and Schwartz point out that sometimes clear demands are necessary.[20] To be effective, they advise, parents need to be emphatic and precise, without asking, reasoning, warning, punishing, or encouraging. Specific behaviors should be demanded. Parents may need to get angry and may need to physically reinforce the demand by turning off a TV or walking a child over to put her hand on a toy to be put away. They must also *expect* to be obeyed and focus on the specific behavior rather than analyzing why it exists or trying to make the child like doing the task.

A New York mother of a drug-abusing son said:

> *I almost lost my mind with it, but finally got him into a drug rehab. program that has worked miracles both for him and the interrelationship of the family. What I learned is that we have to take a strong stand as parents on being* the parent; *being wishy-washy and providing too much choice for the kid doesn't work! It is too confusing for the kid. He needs clear direction from us.*

Finding the middle path between permissive and authoritarian parenting is not easy. Parents can learn from experts, but experts have radically changed their advice for managing children over the years; clearly their wisdom is not absolute. A young, single father worries, "I am constantly afraid I am doing wrong." At some point, parents have to trust their common sense, their intuition, and their knowledge of their own child.

An altogether different approach to discipline problems that some coparents mentioned is paying attention to a healthful diet, limiting preservatives, and restricting sugar to birthdays and special holidays. Some parents reported that their children were calmer when their diet was limited to natural foods.[21] Allergies can also cause cranky behavior; finding their causes helped some children behave better, parents reported.

Coparents report that the best forum for working through limit-setting issues is a family meeting held once a week. The aim for one family with three children is "getting the people involved to sit down and talk about how they feel. The rule is that everybody has a chance to talk and everybody has to listen. You don't interrupt and you listen to what people are saying." A firm rule in family meetings is that people talk about how they feel and not blame others, that they use "I" messages rather than "you" messages. A Minnesota family rotates the leadership of getting the family together and facilitating meetings. An agenda is posted on the refrigerator and added to during the week. The two teenagers enjoy their turn to be the center of attention and have uninterrupted time to say what they want. The family usually starts their weekly meeting by taking turns sharing how the week has gone or how they are feeling that night, and then something they feel good about. The meeting ends with a fun activity, an important practice.

Another family, in Indiana, works in family meetings on how to get places on time, how to reduce disputes, and how to involve the two children in planning family schedules and shopping lists. Family meetings can be a place to work on feelings, such as discharging anger by pillow fighting or hitting inflated paper sacks; crumbling, throwing, and tearing newspapers; squirting each other with water guns; hitting a bed with a tennis racquet; or knocking down block towers. Meetings can also be spiritually contemplative times.[22]

Teenagers

Teenagers, as we remember from our own adolescence, can be difficult. Researcher Diana Baumrind suggests that girls may be more "reactive" than boys, "more easily stimulated to oppositional behavior."[23] Her studies of children who are parented in different styles show that some of the most traditional viewpoints are held by girls with active feminist mothers, for example. Yet she also found that competence and assertiveness in girls is tied to parental expectations of independence.

Adolescents undergo rapid changes. Their efforts to forge their own identities usually involve rebellion against their parents and turning toward their friends for acceptance. They can no longer be picked up and placed where their parents think they should be. This is a powerful incentive for parents to learn democratic, nonphysical forms of limit setting that continue to work as children get older.

A California mother of four children thinks that

> *Children, until they set foot in junior high school, are marvelous. Up to this point, they mind, they comply. They might get sticky, they might get dirty, they might take all the pans out of the cupboard, they might throw the dog in the creek. But at least you can*

do something with them. When they are teenagers they are more rebellious in wanting to be individuals, voicing their opinions.

A Colorado mother of three adds, "It seems that anyone you talk to with teenagers goes crazy. I really somehow thought that wasn't going to happen to me." She is surprised to find that after so many years of being a parent she is at a loss: "All these years I thought I knew what I was doing, now I don't know and I feel like a failure. I gave the children a lot of choices; I thought we were being so superior I guess; now we're having all these problems with my seventeen-year-old daughter and seeing how much she seems to hate us."

Any generation of teenagers is temperamental because of changing hormones, parents noted. Teenagers were described as not only moody but unpredictable: "Once you think you've gotten them pegged, they turn 180 degrees," said a frustrated New Mexico father. At thirteen, his daughter was impossible to live with, but then at fourteen she suddenly was fine. Teens are also very volatile with their friends, being close one week, splitting up the next, then coming back together again, observed a Kansas father of two daughters. A Colorado mother described her teenagers as seeming to be from Jupiter or Mars.

Children may try to shape their identity by being different from their parents. Arlyn asked me to pass on to readers that "no matter how good your home is and how reasonable you are, your teenager must find something wrong so he or she can leave the nest." In a New Mexico stepfamily, one son turned to drugs and staying out late, another son joined a wailing Baptist sect, a third son focused on making movies and his job at a television studio, and the daughter became a strict vegetarian. A mother in Minnesota explains that her daughter "measures herself against her mother to find out which ways she is different and at times that can be real hard. I think that is part of why she has more problems than our son." The teenage daughter of parents who are militant antismokers smokes; they are vegetarians and very concerned about diet, so "naturally she's heavily into junk food," her mother noted.

Young children tend to think their parents are terrific, observes a Maryland mother, but "teenagers begin to look at you as if you don't know anything and are desperately behind the times. They look down their noses and explain simple things to you as if you're a blithering idiot, so it's harder on the ego than dealing with younger children."

As teenagers separate themselves from their parents, they turn to their friends. One mother describes her sixth-grade girl as "wanting to be like everybody else," wearing the right clothes and makeup and owning the right stereo and computer. Talking on the telephone interminably is another teen activity. Parents of teenagers reported having a difficult time getting the whole family together for activities, even for dinner. Especially when they start driving and dating, teenagers have a separate social life. The mother of children of various ages noticed, "When they're little they are so aware of you and so wanting to be with you. It's nice when they cuddle up on your lap. Teenagers are much more standoffish and separate and involved with their own life."

One couple realized that they have started to argue more about their kids now that the children are in junior high school. Neither parent is sure what to do, whether they are too easy or too hard on their children, or what discipline techniques work, "and neither does anybody else." They thought that if they trained their children correctly from an early age this would carry through, but with their teenagers they find it difficult to see the results of their efforts. They worry more about their children going out now than when the kids were in elementary school; will they actually go where they say they are headed? In some ways, the parents feel more tied down now than when their children were little. Willa, the mother, adds, "It is really scarey because I've been a pediatric social worker for a while and it seems like all the stuff that used to work doesn't work anymore."

Sex, drugs, and other activities that teens would have been punished severely for thirty years ago are common today, observes a father. In a national poll, teens agreed (47 percent) that drug use is the worst influence on young people today, trailed by alcohol (11 percent), and peer pressure (9 percent).[24] Television ads convey the message that a substance you swallow, smoke, or drink can make you feel zestful, pain-free, sleepy, or energetic. Minnesota parents who found out their daughter was using marijuana turned to group therapy. They reported that their daughter learned how "to deal with your feelings, what is acceptable in terms of expressing them and how you get what you need." She participates in an ongoing group to provide a support system and a network to build her self-confidence. The whole family has learned how to talk to each other about their feelings as a result of the counseling.

Some parents offer a positive note in the midst of accounts of rebellion, drugs, and being treated like idiots. Some parents find teenagers are more enjoyable than a young child. A Washington mother of three teenagers explains:

> *For me what was harder was the many, many requests and demands that younger kids make. I like to sit and talk to my teenagers about their life and what is going on: I like to hear their ideas. When they want to think out loud, that's real fun for me. And when they challenge my values I kind of enjoy that too, because it's improving for me. It's been wonderful since my older daughter has been driving. And she's so responsible about it that we're not concerned. I think for me it got better each year.*

The mother of a twenty-year-old reported that their stormy time of rebelliousness occurred early, so that the teen years were "very smooth." A West Virginia mother says that her daughter had tantrums as a preschooler, but then she "learned to discipline herself and channel her energy and now is great. People used to tell me to really worry about her adolescence, but that has been pretty easy. Or else I've been trained to live with her!" Parents of an elementary school–age girl who had "a lot of social problems" were relieved that "she's in heaven in junior high." Getting older means an easier adjustment for some children and a harder time for others, without parents seeming to be able to predict future behavior.

Parents of young adults find that relationships improve. When Monica was a high school senior, she barely talked to her mother, but now that Monica is expecting a baby she and her mother are very close. Roger, a stepfather, believes that from age sixteen to eighteen teenagers think they know all the answers. As they get older they begin to back off. Roger likens the process to an apprenticeship to adulthood. At the journeyperson level young people realize that they do not know everything after all.

Parents who feel that they are doing well in raising teenagers stress the importance of honest and open sharing of feelings and consulting with them in setting of limits. Carol, the stepmother of two teenage boys, observes that "they can be pretty honest about who they are and say what they really think and not have to do so much rebelling. I credit Dave with an ability to be really open and human and setting limits for them." The same comment was made by a Texas stepmother of outstanding achievers, who reported that her husband is very honest with the boys. He says what he really feels, so they trust him. Teenagers still need parents' love and attention, says a Colorado mother: "You have to listen a lot. Mine usually come in and flop on the bed in the evening and we'll talk. They need a time for you to listen to them."

Gary, a social worker, reports that parents who relied mainly on physical discipline have the most trouble with teenagers: "Fear doesn't keep working when the kids get as big as you are." On the other hand, Debra, his stepdaughter, does not want to listen to guidance. Gary and his wife have turned to restricting her time away from home as the most effective method of controlling her behavior. If Debra studies two hours an evening, she gets Friday evening out. If she makes her weekly appointment with her mental health counselor and goes to exercise classes twice a week, then she gets Saturday, too. Gary emphasizes that if parents do not feel they are communicating effectively, it helps to go to a counselor.

Coparents can also provide independence training. A Colorado family makes sure teenagers of both sexes learn how to fill out an income tax form, change the oil in a car, cook, do laundry, mend, balance a checkbook, and open a savings account. Each child in the family was told at age fourteen that he or she had four more years to learn how to live independently so the child had better get busy. When the children turn eighteen they are free.

Teenagers can be rebellious creatures from another planet or interesting companions. Their needs for structure, attention, and love are not less than small children's but take different forms. Instead of physical care they need emotional support. The painful possibilities of struggle are an incentive for parents to establish early nonphysical methods of limit setting and habits of shared decision making.

Schools

Home and school are where children spend most of their time. Coparents are concerned and frustrated about the schools their children attend, which do not teach children to think for themselves, a skill 50-50 parents value. "The education system is bankrupt," concluded a California father. Academic standards have declined, said a father in Utah. Parents of bright children were especially critical of schools, which can be a "graveyard." They observed that teachers have to focus on the average students, not addressing the student who is bored because she understood in the first five minutes or the child who is slower. Teachers have too many pupils and not enough resources. Too many interruptions such as pep rallies and announcements interfere with learning. Some teachers just "rigidly teach them factual information," another father observed. The teacher of a bright, New York, elementary school–age child would be happy if she was a "finely tuned multiple choice robot," her father complained. A Texas stepmother of teens agreed that students are not taught "enough thinking about life."

Some parents found trying to change schools for the better frustrating, and characterized school personnel as unresponsive to parents or community interaction. Parents of a hyperactive child who had a history of problems in elementary school saw him fall apart as he entered the more complex structure of junior high. When they went to talk to his teachers and counselors, "every one of them acted like we were over-concerned parents," they reported. "'Leave us alone, we'll take care of it' was their attitude." The boy ended up being expelled from school. If their son had received help in adjusting to junior high, the parents felt, the blowup could have been prevented.

Wisconsin parents noted that their sons got an excellent academic education because they live in an upper-class suburb, with parental pressure for schools to provide college preparatory training. As a consequence, the students grow up to be well-educated and "terrible snobs." Parents I talked with who were most happy with schools often had their children enrolled in academic high schools or in alternative classrooms. Progressive programs such as elementary school "open" classrooms providing children with choices encourage parent involvement. California parents said that their child's open classroom uses the same discipline techniques that they do (such as time-outs), shares feelings in a group setting, combines age groups, and includes children in decision making. Utah parents also send their children to an alternative public school, because "we want our children to learn for their own sake. We didn't want an elementary school where curiosity and the desire to be different are pounded out of the children." Some parents send their children to private school, but worry about the lack of diversity of the student body. An Alabama mother's solution is to not leave education to the schools but to push for special programs her son needs: "You have to constantly keep on them."

Fun

The bond between a couple is heightened by the shared memory of good times,[25] and the same is true for the bond between family members. In a fast-paced, TV-oriented society, many families lack cohesive time together talking, playing, learning, and cuddling. Many 50-50 parents structure and plan for family goals, having regular family meetings, study hours, and fun times. "You really have to work to fit in the fun," since housework and shopping have to be done on the weekend too, one parent noted. Linda, an Indianapolis professor, tries to do some special activity with her preschool daughter every day, such as play a game, have a picnic, or go on an outing to a children's museum.

Families may go on a weekend excursion to the beach or a lake; they may picnic in the park, visit a zoo or museum, go hiking, fly a kite, rent a paddle boat, go sailing, walk around town, play video games, or go shopping. Some families set aside Sunday as a day to go to church and to be free from housework, or celebrate the Jewish sabbath on Friday evening with a special meal and ritual. An Ohio family with adult children congregates with their dates at Sunday dinner, then plays cards and talks afterwards. Meals can be special times, whether children choose a favorite restaurant, help cook a special dinner at home, or make breakfast pancakes together. Some families insist that everyone be home for dinner. Otherwise, with teenagers, the home turns into a hotel, said one father. Dinner time is earmarked as free of both criticism and TV.

Other at-home activities parents mentioned are playing cards and board games such as Scrabble or Monopoly. A game called "Life," about families, helped unite a stepfamily with two children. Family members combine reading and snuggling, or lying on a couch "playing footsie." One couple reads ghost stories aloud in a darkened room with candles. More active at-home group pleasures are roughhousing on the floor or dancing to the radio.

Talking at the dinner table and family meetings were other favorite pastimes parents mentioned. "I want them to know me—to not be a cardboard mommie," explained one mother who values family time together. The drive home from school is a time to talk without household distractions such as the television set. While Dave transports his sons, "we sometimes talk, we sometimes argue, we do a lot of punning. There's a lot of verbal play, we tease each other a lot." Some coparents have done away with the TV to keep it from monopolizing family time. A New York mother says that she enjoys her teenage son's company immensely, so they have fun just sitting around at home.

In summary, creating a democratic parenting style is demanding and certainly requires the best thinking of at least two adults. But it is definitely worthwhile. Research shows that children develop best with two nurturant parents who are authoritative rather than authoritarian or permissive. Shared decision making and negotiation, important skills for children to learn, are modeled by egalitarian parents. Children thrive in the atmosphere of respect, understanding, and reasonable boundaries that coparents can provide.

Techniques for Authoritative Parenting

1. Take regular time to talk with children about family dynamics. Together, establish clear consequences for violating family rules. Make sure children understand the reason for limits and your feelings about issues, including your own childhood experiences.

2. Set positive limits—which are clearer than negative limits—such as "Ride your trike in the driveway" instead of "Don't ride in the street." Praise and reward good behavior.

3. Stick to a limit you set for a child; do not reward a temper tantrum by giving in to the child's demands, even if it occurs in a public place.

4. Give children choices and responsibility whenever possible. Include children in problem solving and negotiation of family disputes.

5. Avoid lectures and nagging—enduring the consequences gets the message across much more effectively. For example, if a child is late for dinner, the dinner is cold.
6. Recognize that children are clever at manipulating and pushing "guilt buttons." Use active listening skills to acknowledge their remarks, such as "You're angry that the other kids get to stay out later than you do," rather than engaging in a debate.
7. Use active listening to avoid arguments. This saves an enormous amount of strain.
8. Treat your child with the same courtesy and respect you would show someone who is not a family member.
9. Let children resolve differences between themselves. Stay out of their squabbles.
10. Instead of yelling and hitting, give children time outs, ground them, or withhold privileges.

4

Raising Girls and Boys with Options

> My daughter (age six) is a blatant example of social conditioning—she loves Barbie dolls, playing house, putting on makeup and fingernail polish. At a certain level it freaks me out, but she's really having a good time doing it. It's not my fault—it's television and her friends.
>
> — *Bruce, divorced father of two*

> I think the only way to counter society's sex roles is for the kids to see a different model. How you act is much stronger than what you say.
>
> — *Karen, mother of three*

Gender Development

Gender roles and discipline are the two parenting responsibilities most frustrating and bewildering to the parents I interviewed. Coparents want their children to have options, to be fulfilled, and to achieve. "Equal parenting leads to whole children," observed a Texas stepmother. Many parents gave examples of their children's wholeness:

> Amanda, age sixteen, from West Virginia, stands up vigorously on issues like whether the football coach is giving her a challeng-

> ing learning experience in the world cultures course he teaches. She runs cross-country, has an intellectual boyfriend, and is outgoing and dazzling.
>
> Jonathan, age thirteen, from Colorado, goes to school in cowboy boots and hat, jeans and a jean vest, and a NOW shirt proclaiming "A man of quality is not threatened by women's equality."
>
> BJ, age six, from California plays with a girl and doesn't expect any less of her and won't let her pretend to be weak or lapse into feminine stereotypes. His brother, Daniel, is in nursery school and says girls are smart and can do anything.

Yet coparents frequently reported frustration in their attempts to give their children a full range of choices. "I don't know if anything can ever be done with a society that manufactures Rambo dolls for children," said Earl in Maine. Some boys of egalitarian parents played war with guns made of sticks, and some girls wanted to wear frilly pink dresses that make it hard to play actively. Some girls raised by egalitarian parents predicted less future success in their math grades than boys and expressed less interest in careers involving math and science. However, the girls that Margaret Ferrin Cieslikowski and I surveyed were as high in self-esteem as the boys.

Many parents saw boys as more active, engaging in rougher play and having less control of their energy. "Nate runs around and zooms around a lot more than Lynn does. She's more into playing with Barbies and small detail things," her father Clark observed. A Utah mother who did her master's thesis on four-year-olds observed that boys were more active and aggressive. Her stepsons physically act out their feelings, while her daughter is more verbal; the boys draw military airplanes and jets, while her daughter is not at all interested in planes. A Michigan mother was thrilled when the friends of her eight- and nine-year-old sons each brought a stuffed animal to a slumber party. She interpreted this as a sign of nurturance and affection in the little boys. But an hour later, when she took popcorn in to them, she heard the sounds of "pow wow, bang bang." The boys were playing war with the teddy bears. A five-year-old girl was puzzled by her boy friends' interest in guns and *Star Wars* games, and asked her father why boys were like that. He told her that it puzzled him too.

Dr. Benjamin Spock maintains that the most crippling disease for boys and girls today is sex stereotyping.[1] According to Letty Cottin Pogrebin, rigid sex-role scripts are a prison predestined by gender, even though these restricting roles may feel "natural."[2] Traditional gender roles are neurotic, inflexible, defensive reactions against being thought unmasculine or unfeminine, Herb Goldberg explains.[3] A Washington father concludes that traditional sex roles developed out of a former necessity but now are relics of an outmoded system that no longer functions well. We are clearly either male or female—no special proof is required.

Parents' fears of producing girls so feminine that they do not become achievers are valid. Children with "typically masculine characteristics" make gains in their intelligence scores, while children with feminine traits—passivity, shyness, and dependency—lose points.[4] High masculinity scores are connected with self-esteem, especially for high school girls, and are tied to women's career success and even with housewives' good adjustment.[5] Girls who perform well on problems requiring complex reasoning "tend to reject a traditional feminine identification," while girls who identify with their traditional role tend to have lower self-esteem.[6] Independence seems to be necessary for analytical thinking. Girls who receive too much parental warmth, comfort, and protection (or, at the other extreme, rejection) are less likely to be independent and to achieve. However, boys who receive high levels of parental warmth tend to achievement.[7] The more "sharply the mother is differentiated by sex," the poorer the girl's analytical ability and the lower her IQ scores.[8] Children of authoritarian parents have less academic success than children of authoritative parents.[9] These findings indicate that girls need independence training to achieve their potential.

Girls' academic interests need to be encouraged early, because by age thirteen girls typically begin a decline in achievement, especially in math and science. Barbara Powell suggests in *How to Raise a Successful Daughter* that a girl should be a tomboy at some stage in her life. She should be given toys such as puzzles and Tinker toys that require skills and be encouraged to participate in sports.[10] She should see role models such as a working mother or women professors—which is probably why a high percentage of achieving women attended women's colleges. Ideally, Powell reports, the girl should be in a small family and not born too early in her parents' marriage. I have often found a majority of firstborns in groups of professional women, but a recent study found no correlation with birth order and academic achievement.[11] The researchers did find that both girls and boys perform better when they are from small families.

Fathers play a large role in sex-typing daughters. Having a highly involved father increases a girl's scores on tests of masculine traits, though not beyond the feminine range, according to Abraham Sagi's Israeli study.[12] A recent Colorado study found that fathers who shared most in child care were more flexible in their sex-role attitudes.[13] (Higher education also correlated with fathers' flexibility.) Other researchers have found that successful women had fathers who respected and encouraged them, while daughters of dominating fathers often developed traditionally feminine traits, especially if their mothers were satisfied with their homemaker role.[14]

Developmental psychologists give coparents useful insights into the formation of sex roles. Children "self-socialize," that is, they formulate and reformulate "social rules" appropriate to themselves and they fit their behavior to these rules.[15] Children at four and five develop gender stereotypes independent of their parents' attitudes, often ignoring breadwinning roles of working mothers. In elementary school children's peers and the media are the main teachers of gender roles.

A hopeful note on the developmental process is that children, especially girls, have less rigid ideas about gender roles as they get older. The greatest conformity to peers occurs from ages eleven to thirteen. Teenage boys often believe in and identify with a masculine stereotype rather than creating their own definition of maleness. Boys' self-esteem correlates with their personal competence, including academic performance, while girls' self-esteem often stems from social approval. Boys have less flexibility in their sex-role development, but girls are expected to be less competent.

Unfortunately, much child development research has used boys' development as the standard of normal behavior. Carol Gilligan's book *In a Different Voice* describes girls' moral development as different from boys'.[16] She begins with Nancy Chodorow's and Dorothy Dinnerstein's thesis that masculinity is defined through separation from the mother, while femininity is defined through continued attachment to the mother. Gilligan concludes that men tend to have difficulty with intimate relationships, while women tend to have problems with individuation. Gilligan found in studies of college students that males often worried that intimacy could lead to entrapment or betrayal, while women worried about being left alone. In Gilligan's five-year follow-up study of her former Harvard students, men defined themselves in terms of achievement and women in terms of relationships, similar to other findings.[17] In their moral development, boys and men think more in terms of abstract principles of justice while girls and women think about relationships, with an "ethic of care," Gilligan maintains. By fifth grade, for example, boys play competitive games in larger groups than girls. Boys frequently argue about the game but continue playing. Girls' disputes tend to end their game, indicating their priority for feelings over rules. Gilligan's discovery of different moral development explains that involved fathers may be able to help sons learn to form intimate attachments. Involved fathers make it possible for boys to define themselves without having to make the wrenching separation from their primary parent.

In her long-term study of gender differences, Carol Nagy Jacklin found that researchers have exaggerated the differences between boys and girls.[18] She followed 225 children from birth to the first grade and found that birth order had more influence than gender on children's development. First children received more pressure to achieve, while later borns received more warmth and praise. Amounts of sex hormones were very similar in boys and girls. Parents did not treat boys and girls very differently, except for infants. Parents used many typical stereotyped characteristics to describe newborns, but by the time the baby was six months old, this stereotyping diminished greatly as the parents came to know the individual personality of their baby. Jacklin did find that fathers were more likely to give children sex-stereotyped toys and to do rough-and-tumble play with their sons more than daughters. Girls tended to be more timid and boys to express more anger and aggression. However, most children fell in a common middle range.

An earlier study by Fagot and Hagan discovered that 80 percent of the parents of two-year-olds tried to encourage equality. In most areas they treated boys and girls the same, although they were more encouraging when girls asked for help than when boys did (which is independence training for boys) and allowed boys to explore more objects.[19] As children got older, however, parents began to treat them in a more traditional fashion.[20]

Although most parents, especially mothers, do not treat their preschool daughters and sons very differently, by the time they are in school children have very stereotyped attitudes about males and females. They are biased in favor of males, viewing them as more important, more skilled, and more adventurous. The West Virginia mother of two daughters said that at kindergarten age boys "turned on them and started treating them as 'girls.' The sexist teasing, showing off, and innuendo were very hurtful. We encouraged them to wait it out, told them that it would pass."

In general, children see women as less competent, less punitive, and more nurturing than men.[21] Donovan, a Utah coparent, was with his five-year-old son Andrew when they saw a woman police officer drive by. Andrew observed that his dad could drive faster and get away from her. Donovan does not know "where he gets it. It's discouraging." As early as kindergarten boys tend to overestimate their future success relative to their ability and girls to underestimate their success. In a fifth grade class in San Francisco, half the girls wished they were smarter, while only 18 percent of the boys did, assuming they were already smart. When asked what offices they would like to hold, 63 percent of the boys wanted to be president compared to 21 percent of the girls.[22] Cross-culturally, girls have less sense of control over their lives than boys, especially if they are not of a high socio-economic class.[23]

In general, boys are more content with their gender than girls are. When children in Colorado were asked to imagine how their life would be different if they were to wake up as the other sex, girls liked the idea, feeling they would have more freedom, a better time, and exciting careers as athletes, pilots, and other jobs usually held by males.[24] Some girls also felt that their parents would value them more if they were boys. Boys did not relish the idea of a gender change. They speculated that if they were female they would have to be beautiful, dress well, and work in jobs such as secretary and nurse serving others.

Stereotyped job choices were evident even in a group of gifted adults with intelligence scores of over 151. At age forty-four, 69 percent of the men and only 11 percent of the women were in professional and managerial careers.[25] Many of the parents I interviewed were horrified when they heard their daughters aspire to be nurses instead of doctors. A New Hampshire mother, who heads a health department with many female doctors, heard her preschool daughter proclaim her younger brother the doctor and herself the nurse in their play. Their mother said she "intervened but fast to clear that one up and then sat there shaking my head!" A father reported that although his kindergarten daughter has memorized her book about *Moms Can Be Anything*, she too wants to be a nurse. As children get older, however, girls become more nontraditional in their career plans, especially if they have female role models.

Sources of Stereotypes

If parents do not teach children these traditional attitudes, who does? Peers and media are two of the strongest influences on elementary school–age children's sex-role attitudes,[26] according to coparents I interviewed. One eleven-year-old boy who wanted to take creative dance at his New York summer camp "got ragged and bullied and people were really mean to him about it. Now he chooses his battles very carefully and does not stick his neck out for something unimportant," his mother reported. A preschool boy, Pete, enjoyed dancing and playing dolls with his sister along with two neighbor boys, until their father declared Pete's house "off limits" for his sons.

A Pennsylvania father explained,

> *I used to think that if you set up things right, you could counteract the stereotyping. But I don't believe that anymore. I'm a psychologist, I really wanted to counteract the sexist-type stuff. I bought her trucks, I cook. . . . My daughter (age six) is a blatant example of*

social conditioning—she loves Barbie dolls, playing house, putting on makeup and fingernail polish. At a certain level it freaks me out, but she's really having a good time doing it. It's not my fault, it's television and her friends.

The peer pressures continue on into high school. "I never knew how much courage it takes to survive male adolescence without being flattened," said the mother of a thirteen-year-old boy. A sixteen-year-old boy reported that other boys scorn a girl who worries about her grades and that it is not sophisticated for girls to excel academically in traditionally male areas. As a result, few girls in his Wisconsin high school earn math and science awards; most stick to excellence in English. Seryl, the mother of a high school senior, feels that her daughter defines femininity as having a sugar daddy to take care of her, even though her mother is employed. Seryl is a draftsperson, but "somehow when she went out in the world she just didn't see the need to be financially independent. She didn't believe it or want it."

Coparents are critical of elementary schools and teachers who divide up girls and boys in lines and activities or tell them that girls should act like little ladies and boys should not play with dolls. In junior high counselors still channel boys into shop classes and girls into home economics. A boy who played with a girl on the playground at school and who admitted to liking Wonder Woman was beaten up by other children. His school principal was not supportive because "he wasn't the right type of little boy. The principal thought he was a pervert," his mother said. His parents sent him to a private school, but many parents cannot afford that alternative. An Ohio mother with a "frilly" daughter who reads *Ms.* but loves *Seventeen* magazine feels "so alone with the responsibility" of presenting options to her daughter, because schools are traditional and do not support equality. Teachers may think they encourage girls as much as boys, but observers find that boys dominate the classroom, getting more attention from teachers.[27] For example, when girls call out comments they are told to raise their hands, while boys' comments are acknowledged. Boys also receive more praise, feedback, and instructions about how to accomplish a task by themselves. Teachers are more likely to do tasks for girls, teaching them dependence rather than independence. Schools also mostly teach about what white males do, providing few role models for girls, although nonsexist resource materials are available.[28] The result is that although girls start school ahead of boys in academic skills, by high school graduation boys have higher SAT scores on both English and math.

Coparents named "Dukes of Hazzard" and "Popeye" as examples of the powerful sex-role stereotyping presented on television. A Washington father thinks that the Dukes's cars are power symbols for men. He gets tired of hearing his seven-year-old stepson recount stories of the destructive things the cars did. Children spend more hours watching television than they do in the classroom, and a study found that children who frequently watch television are more traditional in their sex roles than children who watch occasionally.[29] Television presents few female characters worth emulating, and cartoons have even fewer females. Even "Sesame Street" has few female characters—and Miss Piggy is laughable. Both the boys and the girls I surveyed picked mostly males as their favorite characters on television.

A single father who raised his daughter from infancy thinks she gets her cues from TV. He is amazed that although he is very casual in his dress, his daughter, now six, is fascinated with clothes and appearance. He recalls:

> *I can remember walking downtown with her when she was two and it was the first warm day of Spring. Somebody was walking along with shorts that covered about half her buns and she had high heels, very tan. Erin turns around and she smiles and says, "Who is that, Miss Sexy?" She kind of dips her shoulder; my son wouldn't even have noticed it.*

He feels that if he gave her a choice between going to Disneyland or to a department store, she would pick the store.

Television shows and commercials show successful women as young and sexy. As they get older, television women get approval by cooking and cleaning for their families and getting the dirt rings off their collars. Television usually shows women at home with few career options. Even Wonder Woman works as a secretary. A single father observes that his eleven-year-old daughter picks up "real feminine roles" from family shows such as "The Brady Bunch" and "Eight Is Enough." The authorities in the commercials telling women how to clean are male voice-overs. Children's fairy tales such as Sleeping Beauty, Cinderella, Snow White, and Rapunzel, in which the hero selects the passive young girl solely because of her physical appearance, are prototypes presented in a sexier manner in TV shows and commercials.

The speech patterns of adult men and women reinforce the messages that it is better to be male.[30] Women's speech and body language is that of subordinates, while men's is that of superiors. Women seek confirmation and are reluctant to make declarative statements. They frequently use a questioning inflection or end sentences with a tag question such as "don't you?" "isn't it?" or "okay?" Interrupted and ignored more than men, they use intensifiers such as "Listen to this!" Like children, they are more apt to disclose personal information, smile, cock their heads to the side, and hunch their shoulders up. Women and children get touched more and get called honey, babe, chick, and girl. The fact that words like *he*, *man*, *chairman*, and *mailman* are supposed to signify both genders also loads the deck against women's self-esteem. Girls need to be taught to speak more declaratively, drop childlike speech patterns, look directly, not feel compelled to smile or agree with male speakers, and interrupt long monologues. Speech is a subtle area but a powerful evidence of ingrained sexism.

Attitudes toward gender may vary across regions, classes, and ethnic groups. Utah parents who moved from a "culturally diverse" neighborhood to a white, upper-middle-class neighborhood observed their boys adopting more competitive and rough behavior. Julio, a coparenting professor who grew up in Puerto Rico, explained that it was difficult for him to get involved in child rearing because in his culture the male is considered incompetent with children, hopelessly unable to wash or feed a baby. His own mother "would elbow me out of the way" when he tried to diaper his first infant. A Puerto Rican mother is considered the disciplinarian, Julio said, and the father is expected to be playful. Boys are pampered and spoiled, while girls have to start fending for themselves early, getting food for themselves and their brothers. On the other hand, Julio never hesitated to take his little boy to his office and to class, because ethnic minority children are often integrated into adult activities.

Children's grandparents were faulted as another source of rigid sex-role stereotyping. One grandfather refused to kiss his four-year-old grandson, stating, "Boys don't kiss. Boys shake hands." These same boys are somehow expected to grow up and be affectionate lovers, after so many years of not being hugged, kissed, and cuddled. Girls are protected by grandparents. One grandmother insisted on baiting her granddaughter Amy's fishing pole and taking the fish off the hook. Amy's stepfather explained that "she is an especially attractive child. Grandma can't bear to see this kid unhappy, so she is going to bait the hook each time." Some grandparents were critical of mothers working outside the home. "Are you going to work and leave four kittens at home? Those poor little kids," said the paternal grandparents of a stepfamily in San Francisco. These same grandparents were also critical of their son's active role in the kitchen.

Parents' Attitudes

In addition to the obstacles to nonsexist child rearing outside the family, coparents are surprised when their own biases and limitations crop up. For example, a father finds himself handing a drill to his son, but not to his older daughter. A mother concluded that stereotyping, such as being overly protective of her girls, is "so subconscious that it's going to take years for things to really equal out. You only do a little bit each generation."

A blue-collar worker in Indiana explains why it may be more difficult for fathers than mothers to free their children from sex-role stereotypes. More pressure is put on men to conform to a narrow role, but "if you take a man aside, he might talk about sensitive things, like music or flowers." In general, there is a lot of pressure on men to "put on this masculine face." A Missouri physician (married to a woman who coparents with her first husband) described himself as a male chauvinist, raising his children with a double sexual standard. He talks to his sons about "the dominant role the male has in sex" and shows them pornography to encourage their heterosexual activity. He expects each of his daughters to "marry, be a housewife, and be happy ever after." Given the high rate of both divorces and home mortgages, he is not being realistic.

Being overly protective of daughters is an issue for many coparents. A father commented that his wife got angry when he played roughly with their toddler daughter. An Ohio mother of two twin boys and an older girl notes, "Sometimes I treat them differently. I try not to, but one does. I know I worry less about the boys playing in the woods or being gone for periods of time. I have more fear for my daughter. On the other hand, I expect more of her—maybe as a projection of me." Mothers mentioned that they found themselves talking more with daughters and playing more actively with sons. The mother of two teenagers observed, "I certainly can't talk about as many things with Bob that I talk about with Jessica. I realized that his head works differently." Another mother who finds herself talking more with her daughter and being more physically active with her son said, "I know this is out of a textbook but that's the way they are." However, a stepfather finds his daughters "more straightforward, confrontive. They lead me a merry chase."

A California father said he is harsher with his son than he would be with a daughter. "There are times when fears about him being a sissy come into my head." Another father agreed that he was harder on his son and expected more out of him, while he gives in to his two daughters more easily. Girls learn "appeal strategies" to get adults to do things for them. A father said, "I certainly don't push macho, but I got nervous when one of the boys painted his fingernails gold as a joke. I must admit that I would have a harder time dealing with the choice of a hairdresser career for my boys than an auto mechanic career." A reporter observed that he is more casual with his son, calling him his buddy and treating him in the "male way that men have of interacting with each other." He thinks it inevitable that he will treat a boy differently than a girl and fears creation of a unisex child. Letty Cottin Pogrebin believes that this fear of creating a unisex or homosexual child is groundless, since sexual preference is firmly rooted in a child's nature: A child needs access to a wide range of behaviors.[31]

Some fathers were relieved to have daughters and not sons. A West Virginia father explained, "I feared having sons, because I remembered father/son relations as very difficult. Having daughters was a delightful relief. Being surrounded by women is a very comfortable feeling, too, and they supply all the energy any boy might." A New York father of a daughter is also delighted because the desires he suppressed as a male child can be vicariously experienced through his daughter's activities. He mentioned "dancing, expressiveness, and making myself vulnerable." His daughter knows that he expects her to do well in school and that he thinks she could be as good a president as any child in her class. She knows that her family is going to celebrate her womanhood when she begins her menstrual cycle. He states, "I have consciously worked at making my daughter happy that she is a girl. She knows she has choices." Steve, a father who grew up with all brothers, enjoys the new knowledge he gains from his daughter about "female anatomy, needs and desires." He feels he can make a real contribution by raising a nontraditional girl. It is fun to help a daughter to be as full a person as she can be and not have constraints put on her, says a Georgia father who has "always really liked women as people."

Some mothers mentioned power struggles with their boys who want to "do it my way and now" and who have a tendency to blame their mothers when something goes wrong. It is easier, however, to explain the hazards of stereotyped sex roles to boys than to girls, explained one mother. "Some of the older kids come over and are macho to them, and they really hate that and it is so obvious. Whereas, Leila, who is a very assertive little girl, is getting very interested in frilly things and makeup kits. It's much harder for me to explain to her why that is harmful."

Parents were concerned that their boys avoid some of the pitfalls of masculinity. Sports was one of the danger areas. Boys fear being the last one picked for a team and associate losing a game with a loss of masculinity. Too often a boy who loses feels that "he has been castrated, like he's less than a man. It has far-reaching effects," says an athletic father. Having to fight is another worry parents have about their sons. Fighting "can be real horrid, especially for boys," said a father who got in his share of fights in junior high school. A California mother worries that life is harder on men, putting pressure on them to set the world afire and be tough and unemotional. She confessed, "Sometimes I wonder if I'm doing my son a service or not, letting him express feelings. Chauvinism is still so subtle."

The differences between boys and girls appear so early that some parents wondered if there is some genetic basis for these differences. A Colorado couple with adopted and biological children concluded that the children would have been very different no matter what the parents did. Their adopted daughter, Mia, is physically coordinated and artistic, while none of the other children are. When Mia was three and her brother was four and a half, their father bought them each a set of tools. She put hers in her drawer and continued to play with dolls, while her brother started using his tools right away. All he ever did with his doll was to draw on its face. They had very little contact with other children at this time, and their parents concluded that there was something innate about their son's and daughter's interests.

Bob, a single father who did most of the child rearing since his son and daughter were little, believes "I have not raised them one ounce differently and have not encouraged them in different ways. I was just as protective of Tim when he was a baby as with Erica. She is not fragile at all. She is more of an athlete than he is by far, but she is the classic little girl. She's pin perfect all the time. She does her own hair. I don't think Tim has ever combed his own hair."

Sue and Matt try to raise their preschool children in a nonsexist way, but others describe their girl as very feminine and their boy as very masculine. Matt said that he has always been physically active with his daughter, playing ball and throwing her around, probably more than with his son because she was the first child. Their toys and many of their clothes are shared and their parents have been careful in their selection of children's books. But their son is more independent, seems to need less reassurance, and plays by himself with trucks and riding toys longer. Their daughter is more interested in her appearance and in housework, and is more eager to please them. She is less active and more interested in sitting to do puzzles or to read. By the time her brother was age one and she was two, he was already hitting her and she was afraid of him.

Susan and Matt agree that they treat their children differently, but think it is in response to their personalities. "They've been so different, literally from birth. I don't think that's based on anything we have done. I think it reinforces the way we relate to them," says Susan. Matt adds, "I can't separate to what degree I treat them differently because they are such different personalities, and to what degree I treat them differently because the personalities are tied to gender."

A mother points out that even though we think we do not treat boys and girls differently, we do. We "can't fathom the influence that society has on the young." Her former husband believes that since boys and girls are physiologically different, they take different paths to arrive at a similar end, that is, their nurturing abilities as adults. Scholars conclude that most of the differences between boys and girls are "well-established social myths"[32] based on what society expects and rewards. The fact that masculine and feminine behavior are defined so differently in various cultures indicates the impact of our differing expectations for girls and boys.

Parents observe that improvement occurs with time. Two little girls who once asked their parents not to buy "boy things" for them at Christmas now bring up their own objections to gender stereotyping. For example, they began discussions on the playground to get the gym teacher, who students feel is unfair to girls, to "change his ways."

Parents' Goals for Their Children

Since egalitarian marriages produce children with higher self-esteem than traditional marriages, I asked egalitarian parents to describe their goals for their children, so that I could understand their values and philosophy of child rearing. Their responses fall into four major categories. The largest number of responses has to do with emotional traits and relationships with other people, such as being happy, caring, and confident. The next three categories are about evenly distributed. One goal is preparing for college and career, such as being self-supporting in an enjoyable job, or being excited by learning. Another goal is having the opportunities to develop full potential, like "be all she can be," "come into his own," and "no closed doors for her." The final goal is being socially responsible: aware of others' needs, feminist, liberal politically, questioning, and standing up for one's beliefs even if in a minority.

Parents' goals for their children are sometimes shaped in reaction to their own upbringing; parents want something different for their children. Some parents aim for better communication—"I grew up with the pretense that everything was wonderful, and learned not to make too many waves," said one mother. Some hope their children can enjoy their childhood as long as they can, not get married too early, and not feel too pressured to achieve. Parents want to treat children like people rather than possessions, for children to feel good about what they are doing. A surgeon said, "I feel anxious about who I am and what I'm doing," and does not want that anxiety perpetuated in his children.

Many parents want to give their children options they did not have, especially women who felt they had no choice but to marry and have children in their early twenties. Parents were often reluctant to state any specific goals for their children, wanting above all for them to make their own choices about how to be happy and fulfilled. Overall, coparents highly value providing options for their children, in reaction to pressure they felt from their own parents.

In comparing the various family styles, married couples stressed activist social values more than the other groups of parents. Married coparents want their children to act on behalf of "those whose rights are abused," have a social conscience, do service to the community, and have the courage to stand up and be different. They want their children to be strong, independent, and confident, as well as sensitive. These goals reflect middle-class values; blue-collar families are more likely to stress obedience and conformity to authority.[33] The divorced and lesbian coparents put more emphasis on survival skills, such as being able to find a satisfying and well-paying job and a supportive relationship.

Coparents reveal their egalitarian values in that they made few distinctions between their goals for their sons and daughters. They specifically want girls to develop self-esteem and boys to be caring. Few focused on marriage for either gender, although one father hoped his stepchildren would fall in love as he had with their mother. In another survey, 102 fathers tended to say that their daughters should do whatever they wanted to, but their sons should get good jobs.[34] Egalitarian parents' values are not typical compared to an analysis of the American consumer, but are becoming more widespread.[35]

Techniques for Nonsexist Child Rearing

Letty Cottin Pogrebin, an expert on nonsexist child rearing, has reared three children and written parenting books such as the indispensable *Growing Up Free*. In the 1970s, when Pogrebin was having feminist consciousness-raising meetings in her living room, her daughters were upstairs dressing like Carmen Miranda and Cinderella. Now they are Ivy League university students. They were simply experimenting with imitation of adults, Pogrebin explains, "which doesn't mean the child is going to become Phyllis Schafley, a Total Woman of the Marabel Morgan school."[36] This same sort of curiosity makes children want to use hammers even though they do not become carpenters, and plant seeds when they do not grow up to be gardeners. "We've invested these particular role investigations with too much baggage and worry too much about it," Pogrebin believes.

The parents' job is to give their children stimuli, Pogrebin states, so that the children can discover what they like and are good at without the parent prejudging their choices. Providing the child with visits to museums and different kinds of lessons such as how to grow plants and use a computer are examples of activities that encourage children to discover what they like, she suggests. If parents make choices possible for children of both genders, "you don't have to worry and feel guilty. Whatever the child ends up being is fine. You don't have an investment in the child not wearing a dress or liking makeup. Who cares?" she asks.

Naming is important, points out Gloria Steinem, who is amazed at all the feminist mothers who have retained their last names and given their children the father's name. Other alternatives are: (1) giving a girl her mother's name and a boy his father's name, (2) using one parent's last name as the child's middle name, (3) hyphenating the parents' names, encouraging the child to drop the hyphen at age eighteen and keep just one name, so that marriage will not result in four last names, (4) creating a new family name (such as Suntree), or (5) joining the parents' names into one, like McKatz.

A father says that his job is to teach his children how to decide intelligently for themselves. "The most enlightened thing I realized is that we can't control them ultimately and they're going to make their own decisions, and not to feel responsible because they didn't do what we wanted." Steve decided to have fun raising his children rather than worrying about the outcome.

Other parents provide "counter pull" to give their children the freedom to decide what they truly want to do. Part of the balancing process is to teach children to question what they see on the television and at school. A British study of nonsexist child raising reported that parents "raise children's awareness" by critiquing stereotypes and encouraging them to be autonomous and to have power over their own lives.[37] Coparents feel that if they give their children information about social issues, "they are not helpless and it makes them feel like they should and must do something" about the possibility of nuclear war or about ill-treatment of ethnic minorities and women.[38] Being considerate, kind, and fair means giving girls and boys an equal chance, explains a father who is the primary caretaker of sons. A lesbian mother agrees that the root issue is values, and that sexism is a cruel way of debasing people.

Clarifying the family's values requires discussing them. A Minnesota woman in her late forties noted that when she was growing up, parents did not talk to children about sex, money, or death. She makes a point of frequently talking with her son and stepsons about these issues. Discussing values also includes confronting children on sexist remarks, and pointing out appropriate information to counter stereotypes. Practicality can also motivate nontraditional behavior. One mother told her daughters that if they want a nice car, house, and other possessions, they have two choices—they can marry it or earn it. "If you earn it you keep it. If you marry it you could lose it," she pointed out.

Parents must work to bring out awareness of "hidden messages" on television. Not only does television teach role stereotyping, it teaches apathy to the misery of others, states a father in New York. Some parents have removed the family TV set. Others limit viewing hours and watch with their children, discussing stereotyping as it arises. One family started with editorial comments on the Flintstone cartoons. New York coparents make comments such as "That's silly. We don't know anyone who acts or looks like that," or "I don't know why that woman in that commercial is acting that way—maybe her parents didn't bring her up well." "Boys do so cry—Daddy does and so does Grandpa!" Writing to advertisers to object to stereotyping on the basis of gender, age, and ethnicity can be a family project. Some parents have turned to showing videotapes, which can be carefully selected.

In reading children's books, coparents change the pronouns so that they are not always "he" and invent more activity for the female characters. They read books like *Tatterhood*, a collection of folk stories about heroines, and books about options for boys like *William's Doll*. They substitute genderless words, using fire fighter instead of fireman, mail carrier instead of mailman, and police officer instead of policeman. If they read sexist books, they explain that people used to think that way.

Boys need practice at nurturing so they can learn how to be good fathers. One family got their son a Kermit the Frog doll because it can be dressed by the child. Taking care of pets can also develop nurturing skills; Jed walks around the house with a cockatiel on his shoulder calling her his honey baby. A mother whose daughter loved to play with makeup got her clown face paint instead and told her, "I don't like Barbie dolls. I don't think that girls should go around standing on their toes. What does she do besides get dressed and wait for Ken to give her things?" Another mother figured the best policy was not to make a fuss about the Barbie makeup kit her child got for Christmas. She told her how she felt about Barbies and after about two or three weeks her daughter put the kit aside.

Most girls' games do not involve teamwork, negotiation, and leadership. Jacks, hopscotch, jumping rope, and playing house do not teach the same kinds of organizational skills that team sports do. Parents who introduced their daughters to sports like long distance bike racing, including learning how to change tires, find that this increases girls' confidence. Assigning girls chores such as mowing the lawn and other yard work, and paying them for it, are other ways to prevent a girl from being "a shrinking violet hothouse flower type." A girl who declared that snow shoveling was boys' work was told, "Fine, then you can wash all the dishes and set the table for your brothers because that is girls' work." She got the message.

In dealing with schools, parents point out gender biases to teachers and ask them to change, but they report uneven results. A father in Indiana finds that most teachers are sympathetic but feel that there is little they can do. Coparents work for change, with fathers volunteering to lead Girl Scout troops although only mothers were asked, and others organizing feminist Brownie troops. Parents praise aware teachers who encourage girls to do well in math and use inclusive language in the classroom. When his daughter brings home a school assignment written in all masculine gender, an Alabama father asks, "What's this, Erin? You don't want 'he,' 'he,' 'he.'" Some parents require their girls to take math and science courses and participate in athletic programs.

The national organization Girls' Clubs of America makes the following suggestions for change in education:[39] If women are not included in textbooks, create a committee for change and consult with the board of education. If girls do not spend equal time learning to use computers and other high-tech equipment, ask administrators to develop programs to encourage girls' use of computers. If teachers and counselors suggest that girls prepare for traditional jobs, develop an advisory board of working women to supplement the guidance program. Encourage field trips to nontraditional jobs. If there is not equal emphasis on sexual responsibility for both boys and girls in human sexuality courses, talk to teachers and administrators about necessary changes. Write to your congressperson to support equal access for girls in vocational programs, athletic programs, and scholarships. Girls' Clubs of America recommends the magazine *Equal Play*, which covers nonsexist education, reports on new research, reviews children's resource material, and suggests classroom activities and ideas for nonsexist teaching and child rearing.

Parents agree that the example they themselves provide speaks loudly, as Karen explained:

> *I think the only way to counter society's sex roles for kids is to see a different model.* How you act is much stronger than what you say. *The kids have seen me work, pay bills, carry garbage cans, do the income tax, etc. They've seen their father cook, clean, launder, and arrange flowers for party tables.*

In a coparented home boys and girls learn that there is nothing they cannot do around the house. Phillippe, a computer programmer, says that he makes sure that his sons periodically cook, clean, and dance. If his son says that only girls do something, Phillippe does it to show him that men do it too. A Washington father thinks it is important for his son to see that his attachment to close male friends includes hugging them, "so Kyle's not going to have a hard time touching his buddies and women." Fathers' participation in family work is one of the most important steps toward presenting children with options and flexibility.[40]

Parents set an example of mutual respect in the family. The boys in a Texas family are shocked when they see their friends' fathers ask their wives to jump up and get them something at dinner. "We're best friends, we all do everything together," their stepmother explains. A divorced mother in New York says that her son has "watched his father's respect for me and the peer relationship with both me and his second wife. My son watched me grow and become independent, strong, and happy. He believes that women are capable of that." The struggle to counter the prevailing gender limitations is easier as children mature and are able to critique irrational stereotypes for themselves. When given encouragement and a variety of choices, children can develop into fuller beings unfettered by the restrictions with which most of us were raised.

Checklist for Providing Children with Options

1. Do you discuss media stereotypes of women as either young and sexy or older and preoccupied with feeding and cleaning and of men as tough, alone except with their horse, competing with other men, and emotionally unexpressive?
2. As you read with your children do you point out how often the active main characters are male and the females are just pretty and passive?
3. Do you provide your children's teachers with resource suggestions for information about open options for boys and girls?
4. Do you provide role models of women in nontraditional professions by, for example, taking your children to a female physician? Do they see men like their father in nurturing activities?
5. Are decision making and work shared equally in your family?
6. Do you take time to encourage boys to talk about their feelings and check over girls' math and science homework?
7. Do you hold weekly family meetings and rotate leading the meeting?
8. Do you encourage girls to play team sports and boys to develop their creativity?
9. Do girls and boys get equal attention for their appearances and activities?
10. Do both girls and boys understand the likelihood that they will be employed for most of their adult lives and that they need to prepare for an interesting and well-paid career?

5

Children's Views

> If kids realize why their parents do things, instead of just thinking that it's stupid, it makes everybody a lot happier.
>
> — *Fifteen-year-old girl*

> We really care for each other and understand each other. Even though we get mad sometimes, we both know we're going to be there for one another.
>
> — *Fifteen-year-old boy*

STUDIES about parenting observe children, but rarely consult them about their views. This is a loss because children's frank and uncensored comments are "reality checks" for parents, and the advice children give in this chapter is sound. Margaret Ferrin Cieslikowski interviewed 42 children of truly egalitarian married parents and 41 children of traditional parents; the children were about evenly divided by gender. The egalitarian parents were among those interviewed for this book and for *The 50-50 Marriage*, and the traditional families were recommended by the egalitarian couples. Couples were selected on the basis of their division of family work. (See appendix 2 for additional information on these families.) We compared the children's gender development, self-esteem, and future goals; how they evaluate their families; and their advice for parents.[1] The children reared in egalitarian families (22 girls, 20 boys) are referred to as the E children; children reared in traditional families (18 girls, 23 boys) are referred to as the T children.

One E child, Elizabeth, is featured in this chapter for several reasons: she is twelve, the mean age of the children; she reports that "everyone has an equal say" and does equal work in her family; and she suggested that she give a child's views on role sharing. Elizabeth was a sixth grader in New York when I interviewed her in 1987. Both of her parents are teachers. She loves dancing, singing, playing the piano, school, sports, and reading good books. She hates homework. She is considering becoming a child psychologist, dancing on Broadway, or working in advertising.

Overall, E children confirmed that their parents are in fact egalitarian; E children were significantly more likely than T children to say that both their parents are involved in family roles. The E children intend to duplicate role sharing in their own future families. They are also more likely to support women's rights than T children. One of the most important findings is that E children have higher self-esteem than T children. A reason for this is that their parents include children in decision making. T boys do not appear to do as well as the E boys emotionally or academically, perhaps because they do not get enough attention from their fathers. Childrens' self-esteem and successful sex-role development have been tied to both maternal and paternal involvement and warmth, and adolescent self-esteem to fathers in particular.[2]

Power and Control Issues

Who has power in the family? Three-quarters of E children viewed both their parents as boss, compared to a third of the T children. A nine-year-old E girl said that both her parents make decisions. If they disagree, they have a talk. Elizabeth explained that when a decision is being made in her family, the three of them take turns explaining their reasoning and then the rational choice is clear. Her mother, Nancy, often gets ideas and her dad, Seth, says, "Okay." It helps that Nancy teaches about decision making in her home economics classes. Each year as she gets older Elizabeth is given more choices and freedom; for example, when she learned to be careful crossing the road she could walk by herself. She observes that her parents are unique in treating her so maturely and that they have reacted against the lack of responsibility entrusted to them in their own childhoods. A Texas sixteen-year-old observed that, although his dad is six feet and four inches, his mom shares authority. His older sister Kathy observed, "I have a quarter input into family decisions. It's all very democratic. Other parents think kids are totally illogical and stupid. No one is as happy as we are." Her comment puts equal parenting into a nutshell and explains the origin of the E children's high self-esteem.

Of the few E children who saw one parent as boss, boys were more inclined to see their father as dominant, as is common.[3] An eleven-year-old who was unhappy with his family (and has lower self-esteem) explained, "Dad doesn't always take charge, but he just seems like the boss and he makes most of the punishment. He says what we can and can't do, but my mom does that a lot too. We listen to my dad more because we are afraid of him." An eight-year-old girl had similar views about her mother's role: "She tells us what to do, and holds all the money and doesn't let us spend it unless it's really important. She makes us do the right thing around the house and gives us directions."

One way of determining who has power in the family is to look at who does the housework. This is a bottom line indicator of shared power. Elizabeth says that her father, Seth, does most of the cleaning in their house. Because his father was in the military he likes order; not a speck of dust is left anywhere when he is done. Seth makes macaroni and cheese and microwaves food but Elizabeth and her mother do most of the dinner preparation. Most of the E fathers were very involved in cooking, cleaning, washing dishes, and doing laundry. Only two of the boys reported that their fathers did mainly traditional outside jobs. Five of the girls reported that their fathers only did jobs such as repairing, building, working on computers, and paying the bills. A sixteen-year-old girl in Colorado said, "When he does work inside the house, it takes him forever, so my mom never asks him. He does yard work." In contrast, T children described their fathers as usually working in the yard. Some did the dishes: "Sometimes he even cooks," said a twelve-year-old girl. The T children viewed their fathers as mainly responsible for the yard, the car, and earning money. "He is never around," one T boy complained.

What housework do children do? Elizabeth gets a $10 allowance each week if she feeds the cat, makes her bed in the morning, cleans her room, does her homework, and picks out school clothes by bedtime. If she misses a day her allowance is docked. Her room has to be cleaned by Sunday if she wants to watch television the next week.

She also does the dishes sometimes. Seth keeps track of her job completion and Nancy pays her. In general, E boys and girls do dishes, clean their rooms and bathrooms, take out the trash, do laundry, and babysit for their younger brothers and sisters. Girls did not mention yard work as often as boys. Boys in egalitarian homes do child care and housework, as well as mow lawns. Actually, parents seemed to do most of the housework. "I don't do much and feel guilty. I do the dishes every once in a while and clean the bathroom," said an eighteen-year-old girl in Washington. "I do a little bit of everything, but I would like to cook more," volunteered a fifteen-year-old boy. One girl explained that her mother wants her to have fun while she is a kid before she gets old like her mother, who is forty-four.

Power and money are often connected, so we asked the children how they get money. Most of them get a weekly allowance ranging from 25 cents to $10.00 a week. A little more than half of the E boys and more of the girls see their allowance as being tied to specific chores. "They say I get it for being part of the family," said a thirteen-year-old girl, "but that is just a cover-up because I think I have to work for it." Most T children said that their allowances hinge on doing chores.

How do the children go about getting something extra they want to buy? They mentioned wanting items such as gifts, food, stuffed animals, stickers, baseball cards, and movie tickets. The largest number of E children felt free to ask for something in a direct and straightforward manner. They presented good reasons for why the purchase was necessary, talked about it, and asked how they could get it by doing extra work around the house.

Some children had indirect and rather manipulative strategies for getting something. A few of them resorted to begging for something: "I ask them and beg and plead and say please, please," said a twelve-year-old girl. A seventeen-year-old boy reported, "I beg them; I try to control the situation." One nine-year-old girl's technique was a "sweet, convincing tone," and one thirteen-year-old threw fits. Children seem very aware of the strategies they use. An E boy who wanted to spend the night at a friend's house said that he "put on a guilt trip," by truthfully telling his parents that the friend had tried everyone else and he was the only one left. "I'll be quiet and behave myself" is the approach of a twelve-year-old boy when he wants something. Another boy, sixteen, tells his parents what he would like to do many days ahead of time and just keeps asking them. "I have to work up to it," stated a thirteen-year-old Ohio girl: "I have to be nice for a while and get them in a real good mood." A nine-year-old uses a shotgun approach, telling her parents many things that she would like. They usually chose two of them. However, the majority of the E children feel that they do not need to be manipulative to get what they want, more evidence of democracy in coparented families.

Children were asked to define important family rules. By far the most important parental concern in E families was that children do their chores. The second major concern, mentioned by more girls than boys, was getting along in the family. This included not talking about "gross stuff" at dinner, not interrupting, having good manners, and "being nice to one another." T families were more evenly divided in emphasis on doing chores and proper behavior. T children mentioned that they were not supposed to fight, curse, yell, talk back to their parents, or lie. Concerns about not fighting and cursing were much more prevalent in T families. One boy wished that his parents would "try to tolerate rowdiness to a small" extent. A lower priority for E parents is obedience. "Don't tell Dad off," said a boy, sixteen. "No screaming when he tells me to go to bed on time," remarked a girl, nine. Most of the concerns about obedience in E families were expressed by boys. Keeping parents informed of comings and goings and being on time was a little ahead of obedience issues on the E priority list of rules. A boy, seventeen, said the kids were supposed to let everybody know where they are going. Other family expectations for both E and T children were being honest, getting homework done, and getting good grades.

E children felt that both parents were interested in their schoolwork, and many girls saw their fathers as most interested. Since Elizabeth's parents are both teachers, it is important to both of them that she get A's and B's—too important, she feels. She wishes they would not be so "drastic" in threatening not to allow her to babysit or take dance lessons if she gets less than a B. In T families, fathers were seen as less interested than mothers in schoolwork. Only four of the T girls and two of the boys viewed their fathers as more involved. Girls in T families were more likely to see both parents as interested in schoolwork, but four said neither was involved. T boys were divided between both and neither parents interested in their schoolwork. Children was involved fathers receive more academic stimulus and excel on various achievement tests, another argument for coparenting.[4]

Next we looked at what causes conflict in families. Since neither Elizabeth nor her parents are "morning people," their conflicts are likely to occur as they are getting ready for school. When they are angry with each other and say something mean, they give each other the "black look" and say, "You shouldn't have said that." Elizabeth has the advantage because she gives the nastiest look. They ignore each other for a while then sit down and have a talk later, explaining how their feelings got hurt.

A number of E children felt their parents' disappointment about school grades was a source of difficulty. Conflict in both T and E families was also caused by disagreements between brothers and sisters. Chores left undone, watching TV, and deciding on places to go caused disagreements too.

Children mentioned arguments between parents as another source of family conflict. One E mother reorganized her husband's filing cabinet, and "he got all mad because she did something nice for him which he didn't think was too nice," her ten-year-old son reported. Another couple argued over blurry photographs taken by the wife, according to an eight-year-old girl in Texas:

> *My father always gets mad at her and they get in a big argument. Finally they both settle it by saying they will throw away the camera and it goes on forever. They start talking about the people who got in the way of the picture and that takes their mind off the subject.*

Who resolves these family conflicts? The majority of E children reported that their parents compromise. They sit down and talk, take a vote, or flip a coin. Some of the girls said their mothers resolve conflict and some of the boys said their fathers do. Both E and T children were more likely to regard the same-sex parent as more of an authority. The majority viewed both parents as problem solvers, although less so in T families.

Most of the parents interviewed for this book reported that their main discipline technique was "time outs." The E and T children agreed that being sent to their rooms and being grounded were frequent punishments. Some had their allowances docked. Many reported their parents' yelling at them. A twelve-year-old said his father "gives us the eye. He looks." T children were more likely to be spanked than E children. They also reported some mothers who used their husbands as disciplinarians, in the "wait until your father gets home" tradition. No E children reported this tactic.

E kids feel that being hit is not an effective disciplinary technique. A fifteen-year-old boy said his parents ground him or restrict his activities. He believes this lasts longer than spanking: "Some kids get spanked and they don't care, they're over it in five minutes." Children dislike not being listened to by their parents and hearing long speeches or lectures. They value dialogues rather than hearing long repetitive monologues. "My parents go blah, blah, blah," said a four-year-old E girl. A counselor's son reported that in a disagreement with his father, "Sometimes he doesn't listen to what I say and I get mad. I'll let my children tell me what they're going to say, then see what I think." Children want limits, seeing them as evidence of concern. A sixteen-year-old said scornfully that other parents do not have as much control as his parents: Other parents do not mind if their kid goes driving at fourteen, he observed critically.

T children advised parents to listen to their children, give them a chance to explain, trust them, "give them more of a say," and "let them be the boss sometimes." Their families seemed more authoritarian in their power structure than E families. One T boy even said that "usually the parents are the happy ones, unless the parents are really kind. You just can't have the whole family completely happy."

E children had definite ideas about what forms of discipline are effective and fair. A sixth grader appreciated her parents' explaining their standards for her and talking with her. In contrast,

> *My friends' parents always say, "Do this." "Why?" "JUST DO IT." It seems like it would make the kid want to do the opposite, just to get back at the parents. My parents seem a lot more reasonable. A lot of my friends' parents don't talk to kids or their friends either. They'll say 'uhhh' or don't say anything. My parents always talk to my friends, as well as me.*

E children who think their parents are doing an excellent job report that parents explain what they want and how it can be done.

E children appreciate directness in resolving conflict. A sixteen-year-old boy complains that his mother will not sit down and talk with him directly. "She has ways to let me know that I'm messing up, like maybe being in a bad mood, or beating around the bush, and talking to me about things until I get the picture. Then we usually get in an argument and I'll say, 'I'm sorry, I'll try harder.'" Another teenage boy gets upset because his stepmother withdraws emotionally when she is angry. He reported that their family counselor suggested to his parents that they not just get angry but rather establish consequences: "Either you can do this or that. If you don't do it, then this or that will happen." He did not think they had really tried it: "The way they do it, it's a threat, anger is involved. It's different the way they do it."

E children observed that their parents' moods affected their disciplinary styles. If one father was in a good mood, he would ask his child to do something in a "nice way." If he was grumpy, he would not let them play with him. Another father was described as "sulking" when he was interrupted. Another criticism of some E parents' disciplinary techniques was that they did not follow through. They would say that the child was grounded for a week and then ground for only two days, for example. A four-year-old said her parents repeat, "We will clean up your room tomorrow. They just keep saying that because I don't clean it up tomorrow. My hands get kind of tired," she rationalized.

Parents use the behavior modification techniques of giving rewards to reinforce good behavior. The parents of a six-year-old Indiana girl have something fun for her to do after she finishes her work, the girl reported. Raising children is like training horses, a fourteen-year-old girl believes: "You praise them a lot for what they do well."

Identification with Parents

Studies show that children tend to identify with the parent who is most nurturant and effective.[5] We asked the children how they were similar to each parent. Interestingly, E children's responses were much the same for both parents. Elizabeth feels close to both her parents, saying, "I love them both equally," although when one parent is angry with her she stays near the other. In contrast, other children at her school view their parents as dworks, dweebies, total spazs, and space cadets. She said she is friendly like her mother and is like her father in being able to confront an issue, to tell someone they did something wrong and unkind. Feeling similar to both parents may be unusual, for a study found that few children chose to be like the opposite-sex parent and were influenced most by same-sex examples.[6]

Some E boys said they are similar to their mothers in that they like to listen to other people's problems, are hard working, like animals, and are not talkative. They said they are like their fathers in being caring, getting mad easily, and being irritated by the same things. Some E girls felt similar to their mothers in that they both yell a lot, have the same taste in clothes, and are stubborn and enthusiastic. Girls felt similar to their fathers in being adventurous, nice to people, forgetful, lazy in the mornings, and lighthearted.

T girls gave different types of answers from E girls for how they are like their parents. They are like their mothers in enjoying cooking, shopping, sewing, and collecting dolls, and in being stubborn. T girls' similarities with their fathers revolved around active pastimes like sports and travel. Some mentioned character traits like being patient or having a temper. Boys identified with their fathers in liking sports and being hardworking, energetic, organized, and logical. T boys said they were like their mothers in attitudes such as respecting education and liking reading, or in ways of being with people such as being outgoing, nice, or quiet. T children seemed to view their fathers as more active outside the home and their mothers as more active inside the home.

When we asked E children which parent they spend the most time with they answered "both"—closely followed by "Mom" for the girls and "Dad" for the boys. With her father, Elizabeth goes ice skating, sleighing, and cross-country skiing in the winter. Her mother likes warming them up with a hot drink. Seth and Elizabeth also like to go to New York City to shop and see museums or a Broadway show. Elizabeth spends time talking with her mother. A few E boys expressed the wish that they had more time with their fathers. A four-year-old said he felt sad because his dad was always at work, so he acts more like his mom. He said he likes her and helps her. An eleven-year-old complained that his dad spends too much time reading the paper, but these complaints were infrequent.

T girls and boys were much more likely to report spending more time with their mothers than with their fathers: 52 percent of T boys reported spending more time with their mothers than with their fathers, compared with 18 percent of E boys. This may be the crucial factor explaining why E boys have higher self-esteem and are more likely to aim for professional careers.

With few exceptions, E children felt close to both parents. An example of the warm feeling a fifteen-year-old son had for his mother was his statement, "We really care for each other and understand each other. Even though we get mad sometimes, we both know we're going to be there for one another." Another boy, eighteen, said he enjoys making his mother laugh. A girl his age said, "Daddy and I are very much alike. We're hard workers, systematic and thorough, and like to discuss politics." But when her father was elected to a local political office that took up much of his time, he asked about her activities "in a token way; out of habit. It feels awful," she said. Over half of the T girls feel close to both parents; the others feel close to their mothers. T boys feel close to both.

E children felt they could talk to both parents. This is unusual; in a national survey over two-thirds of adolescents reported that they discussed problems with their mothers.[7] Many E girls found it easier to talk to their mothers and slightly over half of E boys to their fathers. Elizabeth finds it easier to talk to her mother about relationships at school, such as if she likes a boy or if someone is making her feel badly. It feels strange to talk to her dad about these topics because he went through the things a little boy went through, not a little girl. He is so wonderful, he understands this, she said. Elizabeth talks to him about other topics, such as what is going on at the center where he works out and she takes her ballet lessons. The majority of T girls found it easier to talk to their mothers. The T boys found it easiest to talk to both parents, followed by Mom, and then Dad. "A happy family cares about what other people are interested in and is sensitive to what is important, like what hurts them," a female high school senior concluded. Talking with their parents is one of the valued family activities.

Children in both egalitarian and traditional families largely agreed that they were proud of both parents. Sixty-five percent of T boys, compared to 11 percent of E boys, viewed their fathers as more interested in their activities, perhaps because their families tend to do more sex-typed activities. However, the T boys report that they spend more time with their mothers. Boys in traditional families are between a rock and a hard place when they are expected to have sex-stereotyped interests, but don't spend much time with an interested male model. Overall, traditional children are less likely than egalitarian children to see their parents as similar, and T girls and boys are less similar to each other in their views than E girls and boys. E children replied "both" parents to thirteen questions about family roles significantly more often than T children.

Birth Order

E children had fewer brothers and sisters than T children (1.3 compared to 2). While children reported that disagreements between brothers and sisters were a major source of tension in their families, most children liked having siblings. "I think people with brothers and sisters and animals have much richer lives," said a fifteen-year-old with a brother, a sister, a horse, and a dog. Firstborns liked the responsibilities they are given in their families. They liked to watch their younger siblings grow up and liked their companionship. Firstborns felt they had "broken in" their parents so that parents know more about raising their later children. Some firstborns complained about getting the blame because they are expected to be responsible for the others. They viewed the younger children as having more freedom. Having seniority also means more jobs and work to do, firstborns reported.

Firstborns felt they had more authority: "Sometimes you can order the younger people around," a boy of twelve remarked. A seventeen-year-old E boy reflected many of these firstborn views in his comments about his brother:

> *We can be good friends and I have somebody to talk to. Sometimes we have whiz bang fights. It's nice to watch him follow in my footsteps, but I seem to have higher standards for him than he does. I get jealous because he seems to be performing a little better than I did at his age.*

Firstborns sometimes see younger children as a nuisance. "My brothers are always on my back," a Utah girl, nine, stated. A boy her same age complained, "You'll be reading and the little kids always jump on your back, and try to throw pillows at you."

Younger children agreed with their older siblings that their parents treated them differently: "They had a couple of tries and by this time they are probably doing right," declared a Texas teenager who has two older brothers and a sister. He gets a lot of help from his siblings, he added. Younger children agreed that firstborns have more responsibilities, are treated more strictly, and teach them. "You don't make as many mistakes because you learn from what your brother did," said a thirteen-year-old boy. A twelve-year-old girl observed appreciatively, "You can ask your sisters what it was like when they were your age."

Middle children had some complaints. A T girl felt that she is not given as many things as the youngest and is not favored as much as the oldest. Another middle child said that someone over her is telling her what to do while the youngest is complaining about her not playing with him. But her role is "kind of neutral so mom can't say anything to me."

Last-born girls felt they were babied more. "They all think I'm spoiled, protected, and get a lot more things at a younger age than my brother and sister did," said a girl who likes being the youngest. According to an eight-year-old girl, when she gets hurt, she gets cared for: "Someone will comfort you, they don't just leave you." But sometimes younger children feel left out of activities like sports that they are not big enough to join. Older siblings tell them to "bug off" or pick on them. Younger children also did not like being compared to the older children. They did like having a companion because "when you are little you are just trying to survive; even going to church, it's a big advantage to have another person. Now, I go out with my friends," stated a Wisconsin boy, seventeen. Overall, although fighting occurs, siblings like having someone to play with.

Fighting was the reason that an only child, ten, was glad he did not have a brother or sister. Another only child, eight, would like to have an older sister. She was glad she does not have younger kids in the family to worry about or to keep track of as a babysitter. An only child who is very tidy was happy she does not have to share her room. Sometimes Elizabeth wishes she had a little sister or brother, but generally she is glad to be an only child because she gets all her parents' attention and they have more money to spend on her. She would like to have two children herself. Firstborns who were only children for many years remembered they got more attention before the next child arrived. A twin, eleven, said he did not like having to share a bedroom with his brother. They never agree on anything, and he feels older than his twin who is the "class clown." But in general children seemed to focus on the advantages of their birth order.

Differences between Girls and Boys

In general both T and E children described themselves as outgoing, friendly, and active. "Friendly" is the word they most frequently used to describe themselves. Elizabeth is lively, happy, never down; "If I am, I don't take it out on other people." People at school say she is stylish and preppy. She has "a jumpy jumpy personality," which means that she is nice to everyone. A few negative self-descriptions were used by E boys. One said he was argumentative, another got in fights, another was moody, and one said he does not like to work. As well as being outgoing, mellow, groovy, and funny, some E boys mentioned being caring, helping people with their problems, enjoying discussing feelings, and being thoughtful. These traits, not usually ascribed to American boys, are an important result of being coparented.

The E girls also saw themselves as people-oriented. They commented that they enjoy meeting people, smile a lot, are understanding, like to talk and joke, and are easy to get along with. A few described themselves as being "weird," not liking to be around a lot of people, and being obnoxious. One girl gets a little "uptight." Having a disability loomed large in some children's self-images. A ten-year-old in West Virginia mentioned having to use a kidney machine, and another related that the poor hearing in one of her ears is getting better. T girls also described themselves as friendly, as did T boys, and funny, or nice. One girl described herself as weird, and another as shy. One girl, age fourteen, said she was "defiant, rowdy, and smart."

When asked what activities they did well, a large majority of E and T children selected sports. Playing a musical instrument and arts and crafts activities were also mentioned. One E girl said she did well at looking at bizarre guys, and a twelve-year-old T girl said she did well at talking to guys on the telephone.

We asked the children to fill out the Rosenberg measure of self-esteem,[8] and found no significant differences between the girls' and boys' scores. (See appendix 2 for the data supporting this discussion.) "I'm never bothered by what people say," said Elizabeth. If someone says something mean, it may bother her, but then she thinks, "They're so low, I don't care what they say." She likes to look good, she said, but she does not care if her clothes are the Esprit label from Macy's the way many other girls do.

Children of truly egalitarian married parents had significantly higher self-esteem scores on the Rosenberg measure than children of traditional parents. The difference between E and T boys, but not girls, approaches statistical significance. (The mean score for E boys was 41.1, compared to 37.9 for T boys; mean score for E girls was 41.2, compared to 38.7 for T girls.) Other studies have found that boys with high self-esteem have fathers who are involved in their lives, although dominant fathers are correlated with lower levels of self-esteem.[9]

Of the 66 children surveyed whose parents were interviewed for this book, the children in stepfamilies were most likely to have high self-esteem (46 percent of them), probably because they were older than the other groups of children. The only noticeable difference between high and low self-esteem scorers was that a third of the low-scoring children had divorced single parents, although they made up only 14 percent of the children surveyed. Low scorer's fathers were not less involved in child care than other fathers.

Among the children of egalitarian and traditional parents surveyed by Margaret Ferrin Cieslikowski, most of the low self-esteem children were from traditional families. A few more were boys than girls. The five E children with low self-esteem scores had clearly identifiable problems. A ten-year-old girl was on a kidney machine and a sixteen-year-old boy had experienced a divorce as a preschooler, after which his father and stepmother, with whom he lived, had moved frequently, and his mother was unstable. The other three E children were two boys and a girl from the same family. They all complained more than other E children about not being able to talk with their parents, not having frequent family activities, and being "ordered around," especially by their fathers. Their parents divided family work evenly, but the children felt left out of making decisions.

To find out more about children's attitudes towards gender, we asked them to describe their favorite television characters. Both girls and boys used humor as the criterion for picking a favorite. The E children picked all male favorites, except for one girl, who picked the female dance teacher on "Fame." One T boy and one T girl picked Crissy on "Three's Company." The T girls more often selected female characters: Mary Poppins, Brooke Shields, Jeannie, and Nancy Drew. The lack of female favorites says something about the appeal and quantity of leading female characters available to viewers. The children's parents monitored TV viewing, so that the E children watched an average of one and one-half hours a day, much less than the national average of three hours a day for teenagers. The T children watched more television than the E children.

Because math skills can be an important gateway to professions in the sciences and other technical areas, we asked girls and boys to estimate how they would do on a math test at school next week. All but the T boys had similar predictions. A's were the most common prediction, followed by B's, and then C's. Among T boys, B's beat A's by one. When asked how they thought they would do in the future, the majority of the E girls and T boys thought they would drop one grade down, while the majority of the E boys and T girls thought their math grades would stay the same. Typically, boys rate themselves as more competent in math and future successes in general than do girls.[10] However, we found that T boys are less confident about their abilities than E boys. This seems to be connected to their report that they spend less time with their fathers than do E boys. Also, 39 percent of the T boys said that neither parent was interested in their schoolwork, compared to 19 percent of the T girls and 14 percent of all E children. T girls seem to be thriving, although their self-esteem scores are not quite as high as E girls'. Are T girls doing well because they have attention from their same-sex parents (mothers), and their brothers not doing well because they lack contact with their same-sex parents (fathers)? Other studies indicate that fathers spend more time with sons than daughters, although girls do benefit intellectually when fathers spend time rearing their children.[11] The plight of the T boys shows that boys need time with their fathers: Stantrock's finding that boys do better in father-custody families rather than mother-custody families confirms this.[12]

Most of the E boys picked math and science as subjects in which they do well. A little more than half of the E girls picked language skills and social studies over science and math. The T girls were divided between those who picked math and science and those who picked language skills and social studies. The T and E boys differed again; a few more T boys picked language skills than math and science. Predictably, when we asked about goals for their future jobs, over half the E boys selected science-oriented professions such as engineering, medicine, geochemistry, computer programming, and science. Only six out of the 23 T boys had these types of scientific goals. Scientific careers were not generally selected by girls. Only three out of the 22 E girls said they wanted to be doctors; one wanted to be an ornithologist. Three out of the 18 T girls picked careers in the sciences, although none have mothers with full-time jobs. Nine T girls picked traditional jobs such as nurse and teacher.

The majority of the E girls planned to be professionals such as lawyers, veterinarians, architects, or Elizabeth's first choice, child psychologist. Some picked traditionally female careers such as teacher, dancer, gymnast, writer, reporter, physical therapist, toy store owner, clothing store buyer, and interior decorator. E boys who did not plan to have professional careers named traditionally male jobs like pilot, disc jockey, restaurant owner, athlete, or actor. Almost half of the T boys mentioned jobs as athlete, policemen, truck drivers, or other nonprofessional careers. Five of the T boys had fathers in blue-collar jobs and did not plan for professions, compared to one E boy with a father in a blue-collar job; he plans to be a lawyer. All the other fathers were in professional or managerial careers. This consistent difference between T and E boys is striking, indicating that sons need to spend time with their fathers to be high achievers.

What do children think about differences between boys and girls? We asked them to imagine that, as adults, they could only have one child and could select the sex of the baby. All but two of the boys, six of the E girls, and five of the T girls wanted a boy. Elizabeth would like her first child to be a boy because it would be fun to see what boys are like; she already knows what it is to be the little girl: "sweetheart and cutie." The one E boy who preferred a girl said simply that he likes girls (he is nine). The T boy explained that girls are not as rough. E girls preferred boys because: "You don't have to worry about them so much. They'll get in trouble, but they can take care of themselves." Girls added that boys are easier to raise because they get along with their parents better. Boys are more of a challenge because they get into fights and do not obey anybody. It would be a challenge to bring up a boy who was interested in the arts, another girl said.

The E boys preferred to have a male for the same reason that many girls chose females: They would be able to understand a same-sex child better. A fifteen-year-old boy explained, "I would know more what is involved in taking care of him, because of thoughts I had as a boy. I could do more with a boy." A ten-year-old said he was not used to what girls like to do, such as play dolls: "I'm not too sure about them, but boys . . . I know what they want to do." Boys looked forward to playing sports with their sons. T boys thought boys have more fun and can do more sports activities; they will also carry on the family name and have more opportunities in general, they said.

Boys in both groups thought girls would be harder to raise. E boys noted the following concerns. "You have more worries, especially in the teenage years," said an E ten-year-old. Girls have their monthly period and worry about getting pregnant, noted a high school senior. They have a harder time using the toilet, said a fourth grader. They have to worry about putting on makeup and looking good. They are expected to be pretty and slim, and "they have to work on their bodies," observed a tenth grader.

Boys also saw girls as more restricted by peer pressure. A Missouri boy, nine, worried, "My Mom said girls are smart until they're about sixteen and then they're just not smart at all." A fifteen-year-old boy noted,

> *If you're a girl, you can't really be free, especially at the age I am. I see a lot of girls that form themselves to what boys want and I think that I would do that too because of peer pressure if I were a girl. Girls don't have baseball, football, or soccer teams at school, either.*

Even a four-year-old boy noted the inequalities between the sexes: "It's not fair that men can show their nipples and women can't." A T boy viewed girls as "talking about their problems while boys are in the mud, slapping their dogs and running." Girls worry about getting raped or pregnant, said another T boy.

E girls were as critical of the male role as boys were of the female role. Boys are hyper and wild, said a nine-year-old. Another girl her age said the boys in her class are rambunctious and "go bang, bang, you're dead all over the place. They're interested in sports and don't even like the word 'art.' But if they have to draw, it's a ship blasting other ships, blowing them up with ray guns." Boys experience group pressure too, according to the girls, but not to appeal to the opposite sex. Boys are supposed to be "macho." They have to compete in everything, and prove themselves more than girls do. Boys have to prove their masculinity in sports and by drinking and smoking, said a West Virginia teenager.

Some of the qualities E girls liked about their own gender were that girls can be closer to their families, especially to their mothers. Girls can spend more time with children and can stay at home more. A boy, fifteen, agreed that girls feel comfortable talking to their parents about their problems, while guys do not. Girls are "less hung up," said a Washington girl, eighteen: "It's alright for girls to laugh, giggle and scream in the school hallways. I'd die if I couldn't let that out. I can get away with more than boys, by being nice and sweet and charming." Girls also liked the fact that females can wear pants and dresses and nail polish, engage in sports activities, and sew and cook, having a wider range of expression open to them. E girls thought girls have more fun, and some that it is easier to be a girl: "I like to have some decisions made for me," said a seventeen-year-old girl. T girls observed that girls do not have to ask guys out, prove themselves in sports, or have as much responsibility as boys. They live longer too.

When asked about their current problems, E girls and boys shared concern about relationships with friends. For example, a girl worries about a friend next door who bothers her when she is playing with another friend. Boys were also concerned about school. They voiced anxiety about preparing for college or not having started on a school project. Girls were more concerned about their families and their friends than school. They mentioned worries such as interrupting parents or fights with a brother. Children's other concerns reflect the violence that permeates American society, in the media, on the streets, and in our homes. One boy, eleven, said he was afraid of nuclear war, a common concern, because "the more you get to know about it, the more you are afraid of it." Another boy, ten, said he dreaded someone coming into his room and pulling out a knife. A girl, eleven, feared being kidnapped. Some T boys worried about getting killed, "getting nervous," or waking up at 3:00 A.M. in the dark.

The main problems for T girls were, first, school, then friends, and then family. One girl worried over a history test; a fourteen-year-old was concerned about friends drinking and using drugs. Another worried because "when Dad says not to do it, I do it." T boys did not focus on their parents, again different from the other children. They were more troubled by fights with siblings and friends. One sixteen-year-old had trouble going up to talk to girls he liked. A few were concerned about their lack of achievement, laziness, procrastination, and "doing well in life."

E and T adolescents reflected typical teenage concerns. One sixteen-year-old girl felt that she could not trust guys, and a fifteen-year-old girl wanted to lose weight. A fourteen-year-old boy was trying to cut down on his cigarette and marijuana smoking. A major adolescent issue is sex, a national problem for the million teenagers a year who get pregnant. Crystal, a sixteen-year-old girl who was having intercourse with her boyfriend, said that sometimes they use foam and condoms, but more often they do not use birth control. "I block it out of my mind most of the time. I know that it is a dangerous and stupid thing; I've been thinking about that a lot." To get together, Crystal's boyfriend sneaks into her bedroom or sometimes they go over to his house when his mother is asleep, telling Crystal's father they are going to a movie. Crystal has not discussed her sexual activity with her mother because her mother has not asked and does not want to know. Her divorced father has dates spend the night when the children are visiting him, but both her parents "totally disapprove of me or my brother having sex with people." Her dad asked her if she had made love and she told him no. She felt guilty: "I have never in my whole life told lies. I said 'I would tell you if I did have sex.'"

A boy, fourteen, explained that sex is a lot easier for guys. As teenagers start to date, some in the eighth grade, girls won't have sex,

> *unless they're really in love with a guy. More don't than do. The girls want a commitment. It's always the guy that is being the aggressor. The girls never like try to take the guy's clothes off. I can't*

> *figure it out, except that they are more scared than a guy. But after something like that happens, people start being more committed.*

Nationally, about half of teenagers are sexually active, as are about 80 percent of college seniors.[13] Both sexes believe that boys have stronger sex drives. By the sixth grade some children are "going" with each other, although a California girl reported that this mostly consists of telephone conversations, with girls doing most of the calling. Before sixth grade, boys and girls do not have much to do with each other. A sixth-grade girl said that other girls thought it was really weird that she had male friends. She was in a club with boys who fixed up a barn as a club house. Her friends were "boy crazy, so they say 'he's cute' instead of 'he's nice.' They just care a lot about what the boys look like."

As another way of understanding the children's attitude toward gender roles, we asked what they thought about the women's liberation movement. E children were significantly more approving of women's rights than T children. All the E girls were approving. One fourteen-year-old said that although it is the twentieth century, men still "feel threatened because women might be as good as them, so they can't be such hot-shots." "Women may look dumber," said a nine-year-old girl, "but they are still about the same. I don't think its fair that we don't have equal rights." Elizabeth thinks that feminism is wonderful; it is great that men and women can be equal. When a male chauvinist pig of a boy asked her to tie his shoelace, she retorted, "Didn't you learn to do that in kindergarten?" She would like her future husband to agree with her on the importance of the feminist movement and other progressive groups like the Hunger Project.

Some girls had reservations about feminism. A ninth grader said she was sort of for the Equal Rights Amendment, but not as much as her mother. Another girl, fourteen, said she was not a strong feminist because she did not like to be in a radical position, or be a "big pusher of ideas." But the ERA is very important to her, as it is to her mother. "Women should be treated equally," said a recent high school graduate, "but I don't think they should be masculine. Men should still open doors for them." Many of the egalitarian girls have feminist mothers who are dissatisfied with traditional female roles. Mothers' dissatisfaction with the female role often spurs daughters to be less traditional.[13] The T girls split between being neutral or disapproving of the women's movement and being approving.

All but two of the E boys approved of feminism, with the two exceptions both neutral about it. This is a man's world, one boy said critically. Another boy agreed that it is hard for women. Women's liberation is great, believed a sixteen-year-old, who views any individual as deserving equal rights. A woman can do anything he can do, said a nineteen-year-old in Texas. Boys expressed several qualifications of feminist ideals. If women want to be liberated, they should carry equal responsibility by being drafted into the military. They have also gotten carried away with changing the language, one high school boy believed, by deleting words like chairman. Female sports reporters in lockers rooms are also too extreme for him. About half of the T boys approved of the women's movement. This is an area where T and E children clearly differ.

All of the E boys except three who were neutral approved of mothers working outside the home as their mothers do. Less than half of T boys approved, probably because none of their mothers work full time. "It's not fair for them to have to sit around the house not doing anything," said an E ten-year-old. One of the E boys, seventeen, who feels neutral explained that he was very disapproving at age ten when his mother went to work. He felt jealous that she had "something more important than me to take care of." He viewed himself as selfish, but he did not want to go over to the babysitter's house: "I remember an intense love for my mom, or maybe more of a need for her." The general sentiment, however, seemed to be that it is "cool" for mothers to work. All the E girls approved of working mothers: "It's enriching for the family," observed a seventeen-year-old. A tenth grader said it made her angry if husbands do not let their wives work. The T girls were about evenly divided between those who were neutral or disapproving and those who approved of mothers working outside the home.

Overall, girls and boys often seemed to be in separate worlds: they had separate leisure activities, interests in school, and attitudes about family, and they viewed each other as foreign creatures who draw boats being zapped by ray guns or who have strange monthly problems. Some feel nervous about having the other gender as friends. As one boy said, "I can't figure girls out." An indicator of future change is that the girls plan for careers as well as marriage and family, as is typical today. Only two T girls did not have career plans. Many of the E boys (but not the T boys) said they value talking about feelings, helping people, and supporting equal rights for women, skills which will help them succeed as future role sharers.

Children's Goals for the Future

E girls and boys shared the common goal of going to college and having a career. One Texas girl, eighteen, qualified this by saying that she would not be "one of those women who dress in a suit and go to board meetings with a hundred executives." She would like a job more on her own, with time at home to read and do research. She also expressed reservations about extremists in the women's movement.

Most of the E children planned to marry and have two children. Some were not sure. T boys and girls wanted more children, again reflecting their own family situations. Children whose parents had divorced were especially wary of marriage. "I know I'm a brat," said a fourteen-year-old boy who wasn't sure he wanted to have children. "I'll never quit my job just to have a family," a twenty-three-year-old female college student observed. "Maybe just because that's the way it was in my family."

We asked E children what they were looking for in a spouse and if their opposite-sex parent was a model. About half wanted a spouse like their parent and about half did not. The boys who wanted a spouse like their mothers appreciated independence and intelligence. A twelve-year-old boy said his wife would have to be "kind of smart" like his mother because she would be the one to balance the checkbook. A seventeen-year-old hoped for a wife like his mother who is "real independent, takes care of herself, and is assertive." He also hoped she would be "very lady-like, feminine, compassionate, and intelligent." A boy, fifteen, described his mother as pretty and intelligent and would also like those attributes in a spouse. A boy, six, added that his wife should want babies and be a good reader, as well as be pretty. E boys who wanted to marry a woman different from their mothers wanted someone better looking, mellower, not so motherly, more aggressive, more helpful in explaining things, and more active.

T boys were also about evenly divided between wanting to marry someone similar to their mothers or different. Those who wanted someone different wanted a wife who would be more outgoing, affectionate, and interested in sports; not be bad tempered or pushy; let the kid be the boss sometimes; not "spaz out as easily"; "not always pointing out my mistakes"; and have a job. A fifteen-year-old wanted to marry someone like his mother because she is outgoing, energetic, and helps in the community.

While the E boys seemed to want an independent and pretty wife, the E girls were interested in a future husband's involvement in family life and in his expressiveness. An eight-year-old said that her husband

> *would be more expressive and would talk better to other people. My dad just keeps it to himself and it gets worse and worse. Whenever I get mad at my father, my mother says, "Don't do that to your father," and he just makes me so mad. He never gets yelled at a lot.*

A girl, twelve, compared her prospective husband with her stepfather. "He will not be grumpy, he will be much more active and will not sit around the house and watch TV a lot." Some girls were concerned that their future husbands not smoke or drink. Elizabeth would like a spouse as understanding but not as protective as her father. He says, for example, that she cannot go out on a date until she is sixteen, has a driver's licence, and learns karate. She would like a husband as loving, caring, and sweet as her father but not as demanding that everything be right—such as her A's and B's in school.

A thirteen-year-old E girl appreciates her father who "cooks a lot and doesn't expect my mom to be the ideal housewife," and a nine-year-old likes men like her father who are "very helpful around the house." Some of the girls realized that their parents are unusual and were afraid they would not meet men as "nonsexist" as their fathers. "I've been raised to think that everyone is equal and there aren't too many kids that appreciate that. There aren't too many guys that I know who cook and clean," observed an eleventh grader. She added, "Boys just get up in the morning and relax and have everything served to them. A boyfriend and his dad sat on the couch and asked for beers while his mom and I cleaned up after dinner. It made me furious." Six of the T girls wanted to marry a man much like their father. Others explained that their ideal husband would help more around the house, would do more things with his wife, would express himself more, would not be so spoiled, would not be out having a beer until 9:00 P.M., and would not yell or be so strict.

The E children plan on doing family work equally, because it is not woman's work but people's work. The E boys expressed a sense of fairness. Sharing responsibilities is necessary because "I wouldn't want her stuck home as a housewife. I wouldn't imagine that she would like that." They also recognized the economic need for both spouses to work. Some boys made some qualifications with respect to the demands of their jobs. Some also seemed to have a sense of being magnanimous and doing their wives a favor: "I'll *let* my wife have as much free time as I can give her." None of the girls mentioned *helping* their husbands with family work or allowing their husbands to have leisure time. Some boys intend to put more energy into their careers, and some girls will put more energy into their families. Not one E child pictured a traditional family with a breadwinner father as the boss and the mother as the homemaker. A girl, age twelve, concluded that families get along better when both parents have a job, "so the woman doesn't have to do all the housework and the man do all the outside work." In contrast, many of the T girls assumed that they would be doing more family work and their husbands more paid work. The T boys agreed with this assumption, although a few said they would cook or do most of the housework.

Advice to Parents

The majority of E children liked their parents' child-rearing practices. The 175 Texas and California college students that Katherine Pope and I surveyed also rated their parents' effectiveness in child rearing highly, with more A ratings given than B's, and only a few C's. Almost half the E children would modify their parents' child rearing somewhat. They would give children more responsibility, be nicer and more agreeable, and spend more time playing with children. The advice Elizabeth gives to parents is to try and teach your kids ideas they will always remember, such as if somebody does something wrong, do not do the same to them and do not yell back. Talk to your children about when you were little, what you felt like.

Be open with your kids: "Our family is great—if I ask them something, they'll tell me." Tell them about God, but they will find out for themselves why God exists, states Elizabeth.

"Give them freedom to do things and let them make mistakes. If they don't, they can't learn from them," said a California boy, fifteen. Let them take care of themselves, but also help them "correct anything they are doing wrong," advised another fifteen-year-old boy. Give children self-confidence, recommended a girl, seventeen. Being kind, not "cutting them down," and not yelling at children helps to establish cooperation. "Always show children that you love them, no matter what," suggested a female high school senior. Praise is more effective than punishment. "Don't make a child feel like she is not good. Nourish their goodness," concluded another senior girl.

A fifteen-year-old T girl said, "Communicate more with kids. Tell them all the good reasons why they should do it; don't just say . . . 'Do it.'" "If kids realize why their parents do things, instead of just thinking that it's stupid, it makes everybody a lot more happy," explained a girl, fifteen. Children asked for enough information to understand their parents; parents should listen to children to be able to understand them in return.

It is important for children to be given their share of work, children believe, to learn responsibility. Kids should not be allowed to "goof off." "Respect your children, even though you might not agree with them," advised a T girl, age sixteen. One sign of respect is for parents to knock before they enter the child's room. Studies back up the children's assertion that independence is good for them. A Harvard study of outstanding preschool children found that their mothers encouraged their children to explore, were usually busy, and were not authoritarian.[14] Children's self-esteem is linked with both parents' acceptance and warmth, clear but not authoritarian limit setting, and respect for individual differences, just as children suggest.[15] Parents should create trust so that children can come to them with questions: "Any question, you'll answer it. Parents have to remember when they were children and how they handled themselves," advised a girl, eighteen.

Children also suggested that parents read to children "until their ears fall off" and restrict television viewing. Expose them to many experiences and places, but "when they want to go to their room and curl up in a corner, let them do that, too," said an eighteen-year-old girl. Take them to church, suggested one girl. Another girl, fourteen, believed children should be allowed to make their own choice about religious beliefs. Parents should not impose their political beliefs on their children either, added another girl. And parents should not impose their unrealized ambitions from childhood on their children. They should not make their child play the piano or play baseball because the parent did not get to play as a child.

Parents must also take into account the stage of the child's development. When children are two, for example, "you have to bear with them, and remind yourself that they haven't gone through the world yet, and don't know what they're doing," observed a boy, fifteen. Do not be a perfectionist, a thirteen-year-old boy advised. Do not be ashamed if you learn about children from your firstborn, added another boy.

Children were concerned that future parents should not marry young. The children of divorced parents stressed the importance of a good marriage. "If I get married I don't want to make it in vain," said an eighteen-year-old girl. She continued, "If I ever get divorced, I want to be friends and not enemies that fight. My mom talks about my dad in a bad way." A nine-year-old Indiana girl advised:

> *Before you marry, be sure that the guy or gal is the right person. A lot of kids are really upset since their parents have separated. Some feel like they don't get to see their father or mother anymore. Some feel like ping pong balls, pushed back and forth. Some of them don't like their stepparents: It makes them unhappy just to know that they're together. I am glad I was two when my parents separated, because I didn't know what was happening.*

Before a couple has children they should make sure they have a happy marriage, so they "won't ruin a kid's life," said a boy, sixteen.

Children suggested that prospective parents should carefully discuss whether they really want children and how they plan to raise them. If after these considerations they decide to have children, they should talk to experienced parents about what works with children. Make sure one spouse does not overpower another, because that does not work, observed a nineteen-year-old boy. Do not give in to your husband if he gets grumpy, a girl, nine, advised. Do not have too many children and do not put them in the same room because that causes arguments. Never favor one child over another or blame one another if things get rough. Stay home together, play games, and have fun together, they advised.

Who knows effective parenting principles better than children? They give the same advice as adult experts, to be authoritative rather than authoritarian or permissive. Their advice applies to effective employer/employee relationships as well. The essence of their ideas is that parents should take time to talk with children, be encouraging rather than punitive, and allow children to risk making errors by being responsible for their decisions.

Children ask to be treated as human beings, with respect and kindness. They want to exchange information and feelings with their family. They do not want to be spoiled or to have their mistakes ignored. They are not asking for permissiveness but fairness, for parents to remember what it is like to be a child. Children living in egalitarian families enjoy the democracy in their homes and plan to duplicate shared roles in their adulthood.

6

Coparents' Perspectives

> We are closer communicating friends than more traditional families because we have more characteristics and interests in common.
>
> — *Will, father of two in his second marriage*

> One of the most important things we do for our children is to treat each other with respect and kindness.
>
> — *Arlene, mother of three*

Equality in Marriage

Marital happiness usually drops with the birth of a couple's first child. This common problem leads to the central question of this chapter—How does coparenting affect couples' marriages?

Most Americans report that they have equity and satisfaction in their marriages, but the reality is often different.[1] Something is wrong when half of recent marriages end in divorce. Marriage usually pulls couples into traditional sex roles,[2] and becoming a parent often increases role differences between spouses. Couples' happiness declines as new parents assume more traditional roles, new fathers increasing their work hours and mothers decreasing theirs.[3] Conflict increases, usually about "who does what." Also, parents may discover that they have differing beliefs about child rearing. "It is not change per se, but increasing differences between partners that leads to marital satisfaction and dissatisfaction," researchers Carolyn Cowan and Philip Cowan recently concluded. They found more marital happiness among parents who participated in a couples' group where they learned how to cope together with the changes a baby brings. The implication is that role sharing is conducive to marital success.

In studies of "optimal" families (those judged to be functioning well), the adults have an equal distribution of power.[4] Families judged "adequate" are much more unequal. Yet in a 1985 opinion poll, only 15 percent of women and 23 percent of men reported that household chores were evenly divided between them, despite the fact that over 50 percent of the respondents stated that they believe in shared responsibilities.[5] In a large national survey, 68 percent of the dual-earner couples reported that their marriages were equal, but "the idea of shared responsibility turned out to be a myth."[6] Even among couples who believed in equality, the women did much more family work. Seventy-two percent of the husbands who advocated equal division of labor did less than ten hours of housework a week. Also, the more housework husbands did, the more they fought about it. Researchers Philip Blumstein and Pepper Swartz concluded, "His work gives him a great deal of influence. The assumption that they should be indulged shapes the lives of heterosexual men." "I often feel disconcerted and even angry about sharing more than is expected from the vast majority of men," author Donald Bell explained in *Being a Man: The Paradox of Masculinity*. As a consequence of their sense of "entitlement," men in dual-earner families have more "pep and energy" than their tired wives.[7]

The coparents I interviewed did better than couples in national surveys at sharing family work and responsibility. Of the 67 married couples who returned my written surveys, 73 percent were either within ten hours of each other in time spent each week on child care or housework, or the man did more child care. (This is similar to those couples I interviewed for *The 50-50 Marriage*, 66 percent of whom were equal in practice.) A father in Oregon explained, "It's very exhausting; one of the most difficult things is not having any precedent or friends who share what we're doing." But role sharing has its benefits as well, such as enhancing intimacy. Will, a Texas coparent, explained, "We are closer communicating friends than more traditional families because we have more characteristics and interests in common."

I compared 84 role-sharing individuals from this study and *The*

50-50 Marriage with 22 couples around the United States who were recommended to me as happily married after at least twenty years of marriage. The groups had similar scores on the Locke-Wallace marital satisfaction questionnaire. On this questionnaire, a score below 100 is viewed as a predictor for divorce.[8] The mean score for the role sharers was 115, for both men and women. The score for the group specially recommended as happily married was 114, with wives reporting greater happiness (119) than their husbands (108). These findings suggest that role-sharing couples are happily married, the egalitarian men a little more happily married than the comparison group. One of the fathers explained, "Sharing and consideration are nearly synonymous. It would be inconsiderate for me to expect Paula to watch the children all the time or for her to expect me to earn all the money." There were no significant personality differences between the couples who were most happily married, least happily married, or in the middle, except that the most happily married individuals were likely to score androgynous or masculine on the BSRI personality test.[9]

Reasons for Role Sharing

Equality is good for marriages and families, but there is a gap between what most couples say they value and what they actually do. What causes role sharing among pioneering coparents? The profile of the 291 coparents I interviewed shows that they are highly educated: Around half of both men and women have advanced degrees and professional jobs. They are liberal politically, approving of feminism and disapproving of traditional sex roles. Almost half of their mothers worked outside the home, and a little over half had a Protestant upbringing. They are least likely to live in the South. Their mean age is thirty-seven, their youngest child's mean age is six and one-half, and they usually have one or two children. (See appendix 1 for more information.)

Couples have similar attitudes and values, but some are more equal in practice, according to their written surveys. More truly egalitarian parents are likely to be in a step- or divorced family rather than in a first marriage. Men spend equal hours in housework, but women do more child care. Even in families where the father is considered the primary parent, wives do just 10 hours less child care a week than their husbands. The most equal coparents are likely to have older children who require less care (8.4 was the average age for the youngest child of the more egalitarian couples, compared to 3.5 for the less equal), professional jobs (63 percent for the more egalitarian couples compared to 42 percent for the less egalitarian), and high masculinity scores. These three determinants remained constant in the couples interviewed for *The 50-50 Marriage* and this book. It looks as though couples become more equal as mothers do less child care, professional jobs provide more flexibility, and masculine traits are necessary to formulate new gender roles.

Individuals who score masculine on the Bem Sex-Role Inventory are most likely to be egalitarian (71 percent), while those who score feminine are most likely to be in the more traditional group (68 percent). In contrast, several other studies found that men with high femininity scores were more likely to share housework and decision making.[10] The crucial factor is that high masculinity scores are tied to high self-esteem,[11] which is needed to resist pressure to conform to traditional sex roles. Other studies found that husbands with higher levels of self-esteem are more involved in child rearing and that wives with power in their marriage have higher self-esteem than those with less power.[12]

So few role sharers exist that scholars only began to study them in the 1970s (see Appendix 3). The main influences on shared parenting seem to be reactions to our parents' example, having a working mother, being part of a dual-career couple, and belief in fairness. Liberal attitudes about gender are often associated with sharing equally, and the wife has to be able to give up control of "her" kitchen and nursery.

Our relationship with our parents is an important influence on how we organize our own family lives. I advise my students that in selecting a mate, the first factors to look at are that person's parents' marriage, and how the person related to their parent of the opposite sex. Parents influence our behavior either when we react against negative patterns or duplicate positive patterns. Letty, in New York, explained that her husband's parents expected him to work around the house: "He came that way, without a sense of masculine privilege. I don't think there is really much changing we can do if they don't come that way. Otherwise, you are on a battleground." An intriguing finding is that reaction to parental behavior we disliked may have most impact on role sharing.[13] We compensate for our parents' inadequacies by using different approaches with our own children. Many of the men I interviewed vowed not to be as distant from their family as their fathers had been and were determined that their wives be equals. The most egalitarian husbands were likely to perceive their mother's lives as unfulfilled.[14] Women vowed not to be dependent like some of their mothers, who did not know how to balance a checkbook, gave up their career aspirations, and leaped to the refrigerator when a man lifted his glass.

Forty-nine percent of coparents I interviewed had working mothers, with a higher percentage among the married couples, including 73 percent of the families where the father was the primary caregiver. Other studies of role sharers found a similar pattern.[15] A major influence on role sharing is economic: Having job flexibility also contributes to shared parenting.[16] In one study, men who changed to flexible working hours increased their fathering time by 18 percent.[17] Role sharers are often dual-earner couples. Bert, an attorney who is married to a writer, explained:

> *It's more comfortable not to have to do that [housework] stuff. You can rationalize if your wife doesn't work, but if both people work, there is no way you can rationalize if you care about the other person. I couldn't come home and lie down and see her working. I'd be conscience stricken. It's part of basic fairness.*

Wives reported that men's sense of logic and fairness is the best way to approach them when seeking equity.

Practical considerations, rather than beliefs, motivated nontraditional families studied by Norma Radin and half of those studied by Smith and Reid.[18] Linda Haas found that her role sharers' main motive was a "practical way of obtaining certain benefits in their family life." The husbands studied by Haas had a relative lack of interest in work: Over half expressed an interest in part-time work. Complementary findings are reported by William Coysh, who discovered that involved fathers are likely to have a wife who views her work as demanding.[19] The less his satisfaction derives from work and the higher his self-esteem, Coysh found, the more likely a man is to be an involved father. Many of the men in my two studies also said that family took priority over work, critical for role sharers.

A key factor for role sharing is that a woman's education and earning power give her bargaining power at home and make her less attached to being the sole nurturer in the family.[20] When her sources of satisfaction are varied, she is less likely to exclude her husband from the kitchen and nursery. The closer the amount of the spouses' earnings, the more likely they are to role share.[21] Haas found that couples shared child care more equally when the wife had the greater income. Arlie Hochschild, however, was surprised to find in interviewing dual-earner couples that the wife's income did not have as much effect as the couples' beliefs about proper male and female behavior.[22] Hochschild concluded that belief in fairness is the most crucial factor in sustaining role sharing. My studies and others, like Diane Ehrensaft's, have shown that feminism has influenced many role sharers' belief.[23]

Spouses must believe that men are nurturant and wives must be able to give up control at home. Linda noted, "If a woman gets past the sense that she is ultimately responsible for the house and kids, she'll be more likely to part with half the responsibilities and not feel guilty as a result." From a husband's point of view, a Wisconsin father explained, "We have had many fights about me tending not to stay tuned in and take responsibility when all four of us are together and I use my exclusive time with the children to run errands and do my things. I'm working on putting energy into fun and projects with the kids." Two factors are necessary for equality: The wife's bargaining power, usually generated by her ability to contribute a significant income to the family, and the couple's beliefs about gender roles.

Family structure also influences coparenting. Couples in second marriages are often more egalitarian after experiencing the limits of a traditional first marriage. (81 percent of stepparents compared to 52 percent of parents in intact marriages spent within ten hours of each other on child care, or the man did more.) Remarried spouses have both had a period of time when they were single, independent, and the heads of their household. Being past their twenties helps equalize roles, as men are likely to be more nurturant after age thirty when they have established their careers. The majority of parents in both my studies are in their thirties, while few are in their twenties. Having sons may also predispose a father to be a more active parent, as men do more with their sons than daughters.[24] The full-time fathers I interviewed were much more likely to have sons than daughters, while in other family types the children's gender was about evenly distributed (see appendix 1). Generally, fathers do more family work when their children are under twelve but beyond infancy, and less when teenagers are able to do housework.[25] In summary, some couples share roles because of their job demands, some because of their beliefs about equality issues, some because they want to be different from their parents, some because the man is more easy going and nurturant, some because of reaction to a traditional first marriage, and some for combinations of these reasons.

Advantages of Role Sharing

Before the 1960s the dominant belief about marital satisfaction was based on Talcott Parson's theory that the best marriages are composed of two complimentary opposites. The husband is "instrumental," active in the world outside the family where he earns their living; the wife is "nurturant," responsible for keeping the family well adjusted. In contrast, newer findings about happily married couples show that similarities in partners' backgrounds, values, expectations, and roles are conducive to marital satisfaction.[26] Marrying one's best friend is the clue to marital happiness, according to the couples I interviewed for *The 50-50 Marriage*, and a best friend usually has similar interests and values.

Sharing power and family work are characteristics of happily married couples,[27] although couples who agree that traditional roles are best can have high marital satisfaction too.[28] Working mothers who feel overburdened by their responsibilities report lower marital adjustment. Women are less likely to think of divorce when their husbands do housework, although men may not be as happy about sharing child care.[29] Stereotyping and rigidity are characteristics of unhappily married couples.[30] Respect is a key factor in marital satisfaction, just as it is a basic component of any friendship. Husbands may say that they have as much respect for a wife who is a homemaker as one who earns an income, but "they in fact do not," according to one extensive study.[31] The conclusion we can draw from this research is that marital happiness is enhanced by the similarities and understanding associated with role sharing. The consensus among coparents was that role sharing is hard but worth the effort. A Massachusetts coparent explained that sharing "requires an inordinate amount of time spent discussing, planning, strategizing, scheduling, negotiating and sharing information. We both enjoy our child so much that we don't particularly miss any of the activities we gave up."

Marital satisfaction seems to be the main determinant of an individual's happiness, with job satisfaction as the second influence.[32] Dual-career couples are crowding therapists' offices, according to a *Time* article, "The Perils of Dual Careers," because they have difficulty combining the demands of two careers and a marriage.[33] Arlie Hochschild reported that she saw "a war going on" between about a third of the dual-earner spouses she studied because of the strains of the "second shift." One hundred and seven randomly selected dual-career spouses we surveyed reported that the most common sources of stress in their marriages are time conflicts, followed by finances, and then work. Their most effective coping strategies are to communicate and to spend quality time with their spouses.

Despite the time pressures in dual-earner marriages, "the bulk of the research seems to indicate that working women are generally more satisfied with their lives than housewives."[34] Working wives have more sense of mastery over their lives, except possibly lower-income women in subordinate jobs.[35] Sara Yogev found that when both partners were happier as a result of both working, the woman was usually working by choice and both spouses had a positive attitude about her job.[36]

Studies on the causes of husbands' satisfaction are more contradictory. A recent study concluded that men feel they should be the main breadwinners, and therefore, they are less satisfied if their wives need to work outside the home.[37] Men with liberal attitudes about gender have higher marital satisfaction when their wives work than men with more traditional attitudes.[38] Men are less prepared for role juggling than women: Of dual-career parents who both had MBA degrees, the men reported more anxiety about their lives than the women.[39] Recent studies showed no difference or found greater marital happiness for husbands with employed wives.[40] Typical of men we surveyed, a teacher, happy his wife has a career, explained:

Having known my wife for many years, some when she was "at home" and some in a career, I can attest to the fact that being married to a career woman is terrific! She is more interested and interesting, vital and alive when she is doing significant work outside the home. We may not see each other as often but we are happier together now.

A multitude of studies about marital happiness suggest that the most important needs in marriage are to feel understood, listened to, cared about, and able to disclose one's true feelings.[41] This requires time to talk and have fun as a couple. A Pennsylvania minister is concerned that "in being functional and effective do we forgo courtship skills? Intimacy is our major weakness as a couple." Hundreds of individuals in Ontario and northern California that Doug Beckstein and I surveyed responded that intimacy was associated with 1) open communication, 2) trust and acceptance, 3) sharing common interests and activities, 4) going through a hard time together, and 5) sex and cuddling. That was the order of frequency for women. Men were the same except that numbers one and three were switched. The only difference between men's and women's views, then, was that men put a little more emphasis on shared activities while women emphasized communication.[42] People who disclose their feelings are likely to have high self-esteem; especially important are disclosures about child-rearing beliefs and careers.[43] Self-esteem is clearly an important characteristic to look for in an egalitarian mate.

Commitment to compromising and negotiating problem areas is also essential to the longevity of a marriage. Steve explained, "I found I can't take my relationship for granted. If it is going to continue it is because we work at it. Honesty, commitment and communication are cornerstones. Being a proud partner in marriage encourages me to take chances and explore non-traditional parenting roles."

Other general factors determining marital satisfaction are the age at which couples marry, the ages and number of their children, and how long they have been married. A recent intriguing study of employed wives found that the gender of children has a major impact on marital satisfaction: Having two male children leads to decreased happiness, while having female children is similar to having no children in terms of mothers' marital satisfaction.[44] The authors speculated that "young boys demand more diligent monitoring which may influence the wives' perception of the amount of support they receive from their husbands." Abner Boles concludes from his survey of many studies that marital satisfaction is tied to the quality of couples' communication, self-concept, parenting stress, and expectations compared to actual performance of family work.[45] It follows that role sharers are likely to have happy marriages since they understand their spouses' roles, gain self-esteem from work, and share parenting and other responsibilities.

Case Studies of Divorce

Problems with role sharing and dual-career marriages were described by ten couples who have divorced since I interviewed them for *The 50-50 Marriage* (one of the stepparent couples and one of the first marriage couples interviewed for this book have divorced since I interviewed them). Four case studies of the divorced couples are reported here, with an emphasis on the effect of children on their parents' marriages. The views of divorced parents about causes of marital satisfaction seem especially revealing because, while married parents might not speak out for fear of offending their spouses, divorced parents have nothing to hide. I interviewed the divorced individuals from 1984 to 1986. The four couples represent long-term, middle-term, and short-term marriages.

Peg and Rick were married for twenty-eight years, live in the Northwest, and have three daughters. As a couple they had difficulties understanding each other and nurturing their relationship. Peg believes that one reason she married Rick is that he was placid and agreeable, in contrast to her yelling and screaming mother and sister. Peg's parents were divorced, and Rick's stable family looked ideal to her. His placidity later became repugnant to her; commonly, needs that draw spouses to each other get outgrown and become irritants. Peg also thought Rick would be a capable business partner, and she was attracted to him sexually. As her generation did not believe in sex before marriage, her sexual feelings influenced her decision to marry. Rick liked small, cute women like Peg. He had fun with her, enjoyed dancing with her, and felt they were of similar intelligence. Peg thinks he was attracted to her because she is like his mother—strong willed and dominant.

They waited eleven years to have children partly because Peg was frightened by the stories her mother had told her about childbirth. Rick had mixed feelings about having children: "I felt a loss, they're separators, yet they're the greatest thing in the world. I'm more interested in the children than she is today." Both agree that he is an excellent father, but in hindsight he believes he could have started out on a better foot if he had been present at the births and prepared to be a father by reading parenting books.

Peg agreed that having the children was a separating influence. Being at home with them meant "I was under the guns twenty-four hours a day and he was under the guns twelve hours a day." She could not stand housework, although she liked being with her daughters. She felt more distant from Rick after the children were born because, although he tried to be empathetic about how she felt, not being at home all day he could not really understand. She reported that he was very fair, never thought of parenting as exclusively her job, and did his share when he came home from work. Their daily activities, however, changed sharply: "Before, we were two equal partners. It was different being at home, where I felt isolated. One person stays back and the other goes forward," she observed.

Peg thought everyone else in their suburban neighborhood was happy as a clam until she got involved in a women's consciousness-raising group and realized that other families had similar tensions after children arrived on the scene. Peg's involvement in the women's movement crystalized her dissatisfaction with their division of labor. When they went to parties, Rick was frequently upset because someone would engage Peg in an argument about feminism. Rick felt he represented all men to Peg and that, although he made a lot of strides toward "knowing where she was," he could not progress far enough to please her.

Other problems in their marriage, according to Rick, were the many hours he spent in business and going out after work with business associates—generally not being considerate of her needs for companionship. "When I woke up, it was too late for her," he said. Sex was another problem. Peg had tremendous fears about it and he observed that together they had a lot of hang-ups. Rick thinks Peg "gunny sacks," or withholds confronting problems.

Peg found Rick withdrawn, even in sex, and says she never got enough touching from him. "He is from the John Wayne school of not revealing feelings," she said, "so he even felt guilty when he cried at his mother's funeral." She thinks he is passive-aggressive, blaming her but at the same time wanting "to make nice," so that he does not confront issues. Peg describes his combination of anger at her and withdrawal as "crazy making," because she could not resolve their conflicts when he retreated emotionally. These comments illustrate a fundamental characteristic of disturbed families, that they are unable to make straightforward descriptions of their feelings and instead rely on indirect statements.[46]

The children prolonged the marriage but led to divisions in their roles that made Peg resentful. Would their marriage have survived without children? "No," Peg says, "he never understood me." Her statement reiterates the theme that spouses need effective communication leading to understanding and intimacy. When Rick finally went to a counselor to work on communication, it was too late for Peg. In their generation mothers were expected to stay home, but if Peg had worked outside the home she might not have been so resentful.

Julie and Bob live in the South, have four children, and were married for twenty-seven years. Like Peg and Rick, they dated when Julie was still in high school and married in their early twenties. Like Peg, Julie was looking for a more harmonious home life than she had known in childhood. She spent a lot of time with Bob's family even when he went away to college. It was a "jailbreak marriage" for her, Bob reports. He was in love with her, wanted to take care of her, and still thinks she is a beautiful, sexy woman. His paternal feelings were welcome at first, but Julie grew to resent them, just as Peg grew to resent Rick's placidity.

As Bob climbed the career ladder in the ministry, he was "quite a workaholic," he noted, so the babies were pretty much Julie's responsibility. If they woke up during the night, Bob said, "I didn't worry about it because I knew she would hear them crying. I could do what I *wanted* to, but Julie *had* to do it. I left most of the parenting up to her until they were maybe three years old, until they were ready for rough housing." Like other men, he thought his career was supposed to be the husband's major responsibility.

His minister's salary and Julie's paycheck for part-time work as a school aid did not bring in much of an income to feed four children. They did not have money for babysitters so that they could do activities Julie wanted to do, like square dancing. Julie felt confined: "Sometimes I'd be at home with the children and just start crying." Being a minister's wife was like living in a glass house, but she had been trained by her southern mother to always be sweet and nice, even if she did not feel that way. "We gunny sacked a lot, avoided issues," Bob said, as did Peg and Rick.

Although the children restricted their leisure activities, they "made us close when they were little, when the family was together most of the time," Julie observed. As the children got older, their son's soccer matches were a focal point for enjoyable family activity, but in general the children had activities of their own and the family did not spend as much time together. "Then you've got to look at yourself, at what you two have going," Julie said. At age forty-five Julie had time to look at her marriage to Bob and ask herself, "What do I really want to be doing with my life; who am I?" She felt she was losing herself with Bob, "like I was dying. I couldn't get out from under it and I had to get out."

Bob seemed almost perfect, Julie admitted. As their children grew out of infancy, he did his share of family work and was an excellent father. When I first interviewed them as a married couple, Julie said that their marriage was wonderful and growing. Bob worked on communication skills with her by attending personal growth conferences. Ironically, Bob's virtues were part of the problem. Bob explains that Julie thought he was always right, always in control, although that was not his intention. "I may have been more of a daddy than she knew," he explained. His higher paying job, status, and educational level did not help her sense of confidence, he believes.

Bob's dating experience since their marriage ended has taught him that "Women are better than I thought they were sexually and intellectually." His statement indicates that he did feel superior to Julie in some areas and that the disparity between their self-esteem was too great. He was satisfied, but Julie got tired of feeling inferior to Bob. Just as Peg turned to a lover, Julie did too. When Julie's children graduated from high school, she decided after much soul searching to do what *she* wanted to do. She left Bob and married her lover.

Children tend to divide the worlds of their mother and their father, although young children also hold the family together and provide a nucleus for activities and love. Children may act first as unifiers and then as separators. As children reach adolescence, the bond they provided earlier in the marriage weakens. The lesson is that parents must take enjoyable time to be alone together as a couple, especially when the children are young. Also, if a woman wants equality in the family, an outside career may be essential.

In their late thirties, Paula and Jim represent the more recent generation of dual-career couples. Unlike the older couples, both had a college degree and a career goal before marriage. Their interest in church work first brought them together. But like the other couples, they found that the need that originally attracted them to each other became offensive later. Paula said that one reason she married Jim is that she met him when she was twenty and had just moved to Detroit from her parents' farm to attend college. She was excited about the new vistas open to her in the city but afraid of the freedom. She was also frightened that she would be a spinster like her few women college professors. Sex was only for engaged couples, she believed. By the time she realized that their personality conflicts were deep-seated, their wedding invitations had already been sent out and they had engaged in sexual relations. She saw no way to back out. Jim said he got married because of teenage puppy love, as well as parental pressure and the expectation that a minister should have a wife.

Jim and Paula shared a church job in the Midwest. When they recalled this experience, they reported a painful lack of support from their colleagues and families who expected Jim to be the breadwinner and Paula the main parent. An additional source of stress was competition between them for recognition of their work. While they were job sharing, she received the praise and he received more of the criticism, Jim reported. What made it hard for her, Paula explained,

> *was that we were in the same field. He wasn't being asked to do as many things. He seemed to resent me having a life of my own, like*

> *having friends that weren't also his friends. He wants someone that will say he and the family come before their job. I didn't see that I had to say one was more important than the other.*

The birth of their two sons was a strain on their finances. Like many other couples I interviewed, they did not have much money in their twenties to hire babysitters. "Kids restricted the freedom that either of us had, and there had to be a lot more negotiating. We tried to make it work because of the kids," Jim recounted. Paula was only at home full time with the boys for a year, but during this time she built up some resentments. Overall Jim was equally responsible for child care, especially of their firstborn. Jim thinks that the media and books make marriage and parenting sound easy; if you just follow the authors' instructions you are not supposed to have problems with your kids. But having to work out new ways of organizing a family can be stressful as well as exhilarating.

Jim feels that he was doing 75 to 90 percent of the giving in the last five years of their marriage. An example he cited was that the money he earned was shared, while the money she earned was hers. He felt he did more of the family work as well. Their situation illustrates that although dual-career couples may say they are not competing with each other, they do tend to keep score and be single-minded and, as a consequence, may not feel encouraged by the other spouse.[47] Jim and Paula each thought that the other gave career more importance than personal needs. Jim's desire for Paula to put the family first and her unwillingness to do it are reasons for their divorce. Men's dissatisfaction with the role performance of their wives seems to have more impact on marital satisfaction than wives' evaluation of their husbands', although women are usually more dissatisfied with their marriages than men.[48]

For thirteen years of their marriage Paula felt she moved where Jim needed to go for his career, helped smooth over the damage done by his abrasiveness with their colleagues, and did what she hoped would make *him* happy. Yet she was not happy and development of her job skills was held back. She grew up in a traditional home so, she said, "It's hard not to trip into guilt, or hook into the 'I really should be doing this for him' syndrome, so that's my piece of it. I always had a fear that he would wish he was married to a traditional woman." Jim's perception is that her reaction against her traditional family made her an overachiever. She did not have the example of parents who were equally involved in family life as his were.

Like Peg and Julie, Paula used a short affair as an impetus for breaking up her marriage. She and Jim are currently immersed in graduate studies on the East Coast and are painfully working through a custody settlement. One of their greatest difficulties will be locating professional jobs near enough to each other to permit them to share child rearing. Jim would like custody of his first son, and ideally of his second son as well. Paula wants joint custody.

Ted and Kate were married for five years. When they married, she was twenty-four and a nurse, and he was thirty, in wildlife management in the Rocky Mountain area. He was ready to be married, "longing for roots." She was attractive, intelligent, a good worker, and shared his appreciation for nature. She got pregnant soon after their marriage. Kate viewed lack of spontaneity as the biggest impact of their son's birth on their marriage. "A child puts a big crimp on you," Ted explained:

> *You have to plan ahead. For example, when we went on a trip to photograph big horn sheep, he screamed and cried the whole way, an incredibly bad ordeal. It creates friction that you have to deal with. He can be tremendous pressure, and I just want to take off, but it wouldn't be fair to Kate. Until a little while ago it was impossible to do anything in the evening because you had to give him all your attention.*

Ted was a very involved father, but he and Kate grew apart; they didn't even know each other's friends, he said. He thinks that the underlying problem is that he and Kate did not build grounds for communication. They were equal in their division of labor but they did not talk or argue. They were so comfortable that there was no "hard edge." He does not think that Kate was ever able to be "up front, honest with me." Since they did not keep each other informed of their changes, they became like strangers who share a bed. Good communication is the first requirement for a healthy family, according to a survey of family therapists.[49] Role sharing is not enough to insure a happy marriage. Couples need the communication skills and the ability to disclose feelings that lead to intimacy. Kate went to another state for advanced training, became involved with another man, and asked Ted for a divorce. She moved in with her lover, taking their elementary school–aged son with her. Ted is heartbroken about the infrequency with which he sees his son.

The common thread in these accounts of divorce is that marriage, like a plant that needs watering or a car that needs lubrication and tune-ups, eventually will fail without care. Among older couples, the women felt that their husbands gave priority to their careers, even though they did much more family work than most men. Among younger couples, the demands of both spouses having careers and role sharing at home meant they felt shortchanged and unsupported in their marriage. The egalitarian couples who survive these demands on their energy insist on nurturing their relationship. Their intention is to live together always, recognizing that their children will leave home at age eighteen. As another woman who divorced observed, "Maybe we got so into shared parenting, we forgot to share the relationship." Children can be like sponges soaking up their parents' energies, as well as a bond and commitment that holds them together.

Coping Techniques for Employed Parents

Coparents are usually both employed; this creates time pressures that require considerable role juggling. Coparents agreed that their working role consumes most of their time, followed by parenting, being a spouse, and last of all time for self. Marital satisfaction is higher when couples learn to establish priorities, delegate work, and say "no." In a Catalyst survey of dual-career couples, women reported that their main difficulty was too much to do, while men disliked not having enough time with their spouses.[50] A production supervisor said, "It's tough to be married to a wife with a career. It's more demanding and she has less time to spend at home. Hopefully, the added inconveniences and duties required by having a working spouse is worth her fulfillment and the extra financial income." Men are more used to being nurtured by women than are women by men.

The dual-career couples I surveyed (see appendix 1) agreed that finding time for the demands of career, spouse, children, health maintenance, and personal interests is very difficult. A male librarian succinctly summarized a common theme: "I have no free time." Negotiating how tasks are divided "requires a very high level of love and trust between my wife and me, and we consciously work to maintain it," he said. A male architect, 37, added, "I have struggles of conscience in allocating time and personal resources to work, spouse, children, and recently, myself."

Other men in dual-career marriages explained that special skills are needed: "Combining a career and family offers a challenge in patience, cooperation and time management," said a nurse/respiratory therapist. A consultant added,

> *It means learning to negotiate all sorts of decisions that involve careers and lifestyles that otherwise would be simply decided based on the career needs of the single worker in the family. We have no role models or past experiences to learn from in the face of rapidly changing values.*

To cope with the stress of balancing many roles, men I surveyed in dual-career marriages rely on good communication with their wives. A teacher explained, "I talk to my wife, retreat into my family and get a great deal of comfort. I know that I am loved." A computer programmer said, "I spend a lot of time just with my wife. It feels good and strengthens our marriage. She is my best friend." Men said that it is important to communicate honestly, perhaps to learn communication skills from a marriage counselor, and not to let friction develop. "Learn to share your time, resources, expectations and goals. Confront conflicts before they become intense interpersonal problems," advised the architect.

Women also mentioned the importance of relieving stress by communication. A nurse said when she comes home, "I talk, talk, talk with my husband." "Being in a family, being loved, helps me cope," explained an office manager. A university registrar said, "Open and honest communication helps tremendously." She also feels that it is important that a couple consciously reevaluate their goals every year so they do not find out too late that they are moving in opposite directions. Because "there are still those people who believe a woman should be home with her family and some are quite vocal," a veterinarian surrounds herself with a support network of friends and family who believe in combining motherhood and a career.

Some men mentioned being tolerant and accommodating the other person as ways to help balance the demands of a dual-career marriage. An architect advised, "Both parents should accommodate the other first, then negotiate conflicts of scheduling, finances and time." Another husband said,

> *Tolerance is vital. I'm finding that one can try to provide an environment for the other person to be their best. If we're feeling good about ourself then it's easier to feel good about the other person. So we take the time to do that each day. Both of us often take some quiet time to meditate or commune with the "inner voice" to make sure that we're doing what is "right."*

Women also mentioned the need for patience. An electronics researcher said, "I'm learning to be more patient with myself and my partner and to realize it's not worth it to get overstressed." She asks, "How important will this problem be six months from now?"

Some men assumed a rational approach to coping with stress. "Take time to work things out in your own mind, then return to face them," advised one twenty-nine-year-old. "Make things facts. Once facts or history is established certain things can't be changed, therefore there's no sense in fretting over them or wasting any more energy on them," said a thirty-three-year-old. Priorities and choices must be made rationally, suggested a professor: "We must choose between marriage, reproduction, house size, career demands and rewards, health maintenance, friends, relaxation, travel, reading, and saving for the future. We have limited time and energy. We cannot have it all."

When establishing priorities, Roger, a professor, advised people not to confuse what *has* to be done with what others say *should* be done. For example, rather than sitting through a meeting, send a statement with someone else. Roger also suggested doing the most unappealing task first and quickly taking care of routine chores such as going through the mail. Another professor said he focuses on the most important problems over which he has some control. "Coping primarily involves identifying the problems I can do something about," said the architect. "Establishing priorities and structuring time for top priority items is essential." A male educator said, "We build a play time into our schedules and make each other and our children the central focus of our lives. Everything else is secondary."

Women also recommended establishing priorities and scheduling regular time with their spouses. A teacher's family saves each Friday evening free "to relax and unwind." Having their sons spend the night with their grandparents and taking time off at least once a year from her family helps a child care professional. A manager walks out of work meetings when they run overtime, "feeling guilty, but virtuous." Susan also has cancelled guests and parties, and stayed home with sick kids and "forgot what I've left hanging at work. It all comes down to remembering we've made family our priority, and that means doing just that. Sometimes it's tough."

A female veterinarian stressed the importance of attitude. "It's essential to not let feelings of guilt engulf you because you can't be home all the time, but instead dwell on the positive aspects of combining the two. Ask "'Is it worth getting upset about?'" An administrator with a ten-month-old son says she refuses to feel guilty about not being able to do it all, although it is a humbling experience for her to change her image of herself as the competent woman with briefcase in one hand and smiling baby in the other. She talks to herself about how she made the choice to combine a career and a baby, reminding herself that it is absolutely exhausting but enriching. It helps her maintain a positive attitude to have friends to share "horror stories" and laugh with.

Taking time for sports and recreation is important. Some couples have an established time every day for exercise or meditation. "That block of personal time becomes my relief valve," explained one man. Women mentioned the relief of walking, aerobics classes, and sex. Yard work is therapeutic for some, especially pruning when angry, and escaping into a novel was mentioned by others. An instructor takes a "mental health day" away from work and does something she enjoys when she feels stressed. It is easy for workaholics to lose perspective about what is of primary importance, notes a dietician. Planning a special treat like a trip helps.

Women professionals suggest the following techniques for coping with conflicting demands. Give up feeling indispensable and striving for perfection, and live in the present. Take a stress management class, listen to relaxation tapes, write in a journal, hit a ball or pull weeds to discharge anger. When late, instead of being frantic, call ahead to inform the other person. Pay for help when possible, and delegate work to others. Unplug the telephone.

Other researchers have found that the most effective coping strategies are to negotiate real change with others rather than trying to work harder or be more efficient by yourself,[51] yet another argument for coparenting. On one hand, role sharing and coparenting lead to intimacy. On the other, they create a time squeeze for both parents and require negotiation of new solutions for how to organize family life. The couple relationship must receive regular nurturance and attention; it must not be allowed to slide to the bottom of the list of priorities. If these principles are followed, coparenting can enhance closeness and understanding in contemporary marriages.

7

Involving Fathers

> If I had to choose a single, recurring incident that might symbolize some of the social frustrations of shared parenting, it would certainly be the numerous times people have said to me, "Oh, I see you're babysitting today," upon seeing me with my child.
>
> — *Earl, father of one*

> Leave for a while and let your husband know what the whole picture is like.
>
> — *Mary Kay, divorced mother of two*

A Fathering Identity

Attitudes toward fathering have changed in recent years; most fathers are now present at the birth of their babies and can be seen carrying their children in backpacks. "I continue to grow personally and share in the delight and wonder of our children as they grow. I am committed to involvement with each of my family members," said a California father of two. Men are also increasing their share of family work, although actual "change is much smaller than is generally realized": After a review of many studies, Joseph Pleck and Michael Lamb concluded that fathers do about a third of what mothers do if "narrow" measures of involvement are used, and about half when "broad" measures are used.[1] The media features the new father both positively and negatively. *Newsweek* writes about "the new fatherhood."[2] In the comic strip "Cathy," Andrea and her husband are equally fanatic about talking to and instructing their unborn baby.

After she is born, both change the diapers. Gary Trudeau poked fun at the new father in his comic strip, "Doonesbury." In the strip, Rick writes an article on his computer about the joys of fatherhood while his child tries in vain to gain his attention. Advertisers like Kodak use the father and child image, and social scientists are starting to write more about fathers. A dominant theme in new books about men is that missing their "lost fathers" is a major influence in men's lives.[3] Fatherhood is in vogue.

Yet the institutions surrounding the family seem oblivious to change. Employers, for example, lag far behind in making work place changes to accommodate involved fathers and employed mothers. Fathers take care of their children more when they have flexible or alternating work schedules and also when they focus less on work.[4] In addition to job constraints, a major reason for men's lack of equal parenting is that our society has not expanded an identity for fathers beyond that of the good provider. President Ronald Reagan summarized the mainstream definition of fathers' roles in a Father's Day proclamation in 1982: "Fathers are family founders. As traditional breadwinners, protectors of wives and children and models for character development and behavior, they contribute to the nation's strength."[5]

Reagan's view of fathers' contributions is rooted in the industrial revolution, when the existing form of the nuclear family was created. Fathers left their family farms to work in factories and commerce; women focused mainly on child rearing for the first time. By the end of the nineteenth century men did not openly weep.[6] Robot-like, punctual, obedient workers maximized profit without allowing compassion or conscience to interfere. Our polluted rivers, lakes, oceans, soil, and air remind us of the consequences of such dehumanized behavior. Now the atmospheric ozone is depleted and budgeting for school lunches takes second place to "Star Wars" military spending. Men who have been taught to distance themselves from their feelings can neither weep nor be very joyous with their children.

Since the nineteenth century, parenting has been defined as mothering. The good father is absent because he is away at work providing for his family and being a leader in his community. Boys do not learn fathering skills; in fact, we often think of fathering as a one-time act. As a result, psychologist Michael Lamb observed, many men feel incompetent with young children.[7] If a father spends much time at home he is considered lazy, unmasculine, and unsuccessful, and therefore not a good example for his children. "The rediscovery of fatherhood offers the greatest promise for the human parenting of our children," maintains Robert Sayers, who teaches classes for fathers in the San Francisco Bay area and edited *Fathering: It's Not the Same.*[8] When working with a group of fathers, Sayers's first task is to help the men develop an identity as fathers. Their fathers were usually the traditional breadwinners described by President Reagan. Contemporary fathers know they are different from their parents and wives, but they lack models of an active male parenting style.

Information about parenting has no male core on which to stick, Sayers notes. Discussion of fathering, child development, and family life falls on deaf ears if a man does not know what it means for him to be an involved father. Sayers leads the search for an identity by asking men to think about their own fathers. Often they feel angry, wounded, and betrayed because of their fathers' emotional absence, and know that they want to be more active. Sayers gives men in his classes the Meyers-Briggs personality test so they can see that there are many different personality styles and gain clarification about their own approach.[9] Being intuitive or rational, judging or sensing, feeling or thinking, introverted or extroverted are constellations that combine in different possibilities—which is also useful information for family members in comparing and understanding their personality types.

Fathers are first trained to be the "mother's supporter" in birth preparation classes, explains Sayers. After the birth, the mother can become the "expert" parent, because she feeds the infant and spends more time with it. Some men then withdraw to the good provider image. Sayers reports that often fathers placate and accommodate the new mother while developing underlying resentment: They either want to be mothered or to compete with the mother to be the most nurturing parent. As a consequence, the father often becomes an outsider in his family.

Sayers helps men in his classes define the ways that fathers are different from mothers and value the masculine contribution to child raising. In the two day-care centers he founded, Sayers observed that the male staff workers are funnier, rougher, and less preoccupied with details and cleanliness than the women workers. He believes that mothers' love is unconditional and embracing, while fathers' love is more conditional: It pushes the child and has a rough edge that helps the child define his or her identity separate from the subsuming mother love. Fathers help give children objectivity, ambition, forcefulness, competitiveness, and assertion. The symbols of these masculine traits, as described by the poet Robert Bly, are the hero, the warrior, and the wildman.[10]

Studies find that babies love the rough housing, the tossing them in the air that men do.[11] Men play more with their infants, talk less, do less containing and limb-holding and more poking than mothers.[12] However, when men become primary caretakers of their infants they are similar to female caretakers in smiling more, imitating facial grimaces, and repeating the baby's high-pitched sounds.[13] Fathers teach children a sense of independence and responsibility in being in control of their lives.[14]

Sayers believes that contemporary culture denigrates masculinity by focusing on the negative aspects of male sexuality and forcefulness, such as rape, battering, incest, and sexual harassment. Women as well as men are wounded by the emotional absence of their fathers, mistrust the male side of themselves, and project their fear onto the culture. By pushing aside masculinity and the positive contributions it can make to children, we have become lopsided, Sayers believes. Both genders are deficient because of the lack of intimacy with our fathers. The positive masculine qualities we have ignored can provide structure, form, purpose, the teaching of tradition, ritual, ceremonies, customs, rites of passages, challenges, and responsibility in the family, Sayers believes.

Warren Farrell adds that men learn in sports and at the office to take risks and challenges, to face the consequences of their actions, and to work with rules and trade-offs.[15] All these skills are valuable in dealing with children. For example, Farrell made trade-offs with his partner's daughter: "If you sit quietly at my public talk, I will go to your Little League game." He used the conditional, less protective love described by Sayers—in a positive sense that is conducive to growth. As masculine qualities in the home are valued, men will be better able to shape their parent identity and teach their children.

After reading this chapter, psychologist Joseph Pleck agreed that many fathers may view themselves as providing something uniquely masculine to their children, perhaps as a way of making themselves feel comfortable with being so involved. But, he added, many fathers do not make this distinction, nor is there any conclusive proof of a male parenting style.[16] "What is needed is a shift and broadening in the nature of men's fathering identity from being only an economic breadwinner, not the creation of an identity which is totally silent," he recommended.

Since men are primarily defined by their work functions, work is the part of their identity that most needs modification. Bill, a part-time professor in Arizona, observes that he would be "more of a person" in his working-class family's eyes if he had a nine to five job. "You grow up with expectations that you are going to support your family," notes Mark, a full-time father in Oregon: "At times, I don't feel like a man. I feel odd, like I have to explain myself." When men get home from work, they often tune out, while women want to tune in.[17] Fatherhood may become a side issue in men's pursuit of financial success. For men, becoming an involved parent is a conflict in a way that women cannot understand, Sayers notes, since women's main identity is their relationship with other people, not their work.

Warren Farrell explains that the main security men have is their earning power. Work success is men's best defense against female rejection, he believes. Farrell's theory is that men depend on women for emotional support and sexual gratification and attention.[18] Men have the burden of being the initiators of sexual interaction and are the ones who get rejected. They cope with this hurt and dependency by diminishing women to objects (body parts, "chick," and so on) and by turning to success at work as their area of control. Work is their insurance policy both for personal gratification and for attracting women. However, by concentrating so much on work and competition, men lose touch with their sensitivity, warmth, tenderness, and ability to listen.

Studies show that involved fathers focus less on work and put less premium on work success than less involved fathers.[19] Robert, a Minnesota professor, stated, "I would love nothing more than to stay home all day." At age twenty-nine Robert went through a work crisis, deciding to leave his lucrative law practice to become a professor. He realized that his identity did not need to revolve around becoming a dean or the president of the university. He became more expressive, realizing that he was bright, charming, and articulate, and that his personality, rather than his job success, was his identity.

However, he still likes to excel, and he is one of the top table tennis players in his state.

Involved fathers may prejudicially be considered henpecked. Men alone with children may be viewed as temporarily relieving the primary caretaker, incompetent in their parenting skills, or deviant, perhaps sexual perverts. Earl, a Maine photographer who works at home, is the primary parent for his young son. He explains,

> *If I had to choose a single, recurring incident that might symbolize some of the social frustrations of shared parenting, it would certainly be the numerous times people have said to me, "Oh, I see you're babysitting today," upon seeing me with my child. The message seems to be that the child with father is in some kind of family limbo, and the real stuff won't begin happening until Mom gets home. I'm absolutely positive that many of my friends wonder at my motives in spending so much time caring for a child. You cannot hope to explain to many men that being a parent is something more rich and complex and emotionally involving than the care and feeding of a good dog or sports car. I've had a number of men ask me, "So what do you do, hang around with the kid all day?" There is this sincere feeling that men have, that they're out there where the action is, doing the important stuff while their spouses are just fooling around with drool and diapers. The priorities are so screwed up.*
>
> *It is also a little annoying to realize that the thirteen-year-old girl who is helping me out for a few hours a week feels that she is more adept at handling children than I am. I find that her mother actively supports her in this belief and they are both amused by my notions about parenting.*

Other fathers I talked with are amazed at the number of people who instruct them when they are with their babies in places like the supermarket. They get unsolicited advice about whether the baby is correctly dressed and held. They are considered not only incompetent but possibly deviant. Michael, in New Jersey, described attending a babies swim class at the local YMCA with his three-month-old son. During an exercise that called for swapping children, the mothers avoided switching babies with him, not wanting to entrust their babies to a man. He felt that either his sexuality or his employability was in question.

Some fathers are recognized by their wives as being more patient, easy going, and less goal oriented than their wives are. In Montana, Pat explains that she will come home from work and be with the baby, and then take on bill paying or some other goal-directed activity. Her husband, Cory, will come in and remind her to pay attention to the baby. Another goal-oriented mother finds that she tends to read her son educational books, while her husband is more relaxed with him. Ron's baby has a fan club at the university where Ron works made up of people who come out of their offices when they hear him coming. Sometimes being an extraordinary father can fulfill some of the need to excel.

Fathers find that spending time with their children opens up a whole dimension of life. Bill, in Arizona, explains that it is part of "my human life experience." When his child is sick and he sees him start to sleep and breathe well, it "means so much more to me than anything in the world. Other fathers miss out on that." Bill found that parenting "awoke emotions of love, created an emotionally intense experience." John discovered that his caring, compassionate nature needed to be developed when he was a medic in Viet Nam. He now puts it into practice as an involved father. He reports, "I'm proud of my baby, I love to show her off, I'm proud to be the only man in the swim class. I loved going to the store with Sarah in the Snugli. I get so much positive reinforcement from Sarah." Fathers have fun with their children, enjoying activities that they would not otherwise do, such as visiting a train station. Dick explains that it is pleasurable to hug his son: "His nice little body feels good. I learn a lot about life and human nature by seeing how they develop and recalling how I did."

Men in their thirties are more likely than younger men to have established an identity secure enough to allow them to become involved in what has been considered a feminine activity. Being a real man has to do with maturity, explained a forty-year-old new father. One study comparing couples who became parents in their early twenties, in their early thirties, and in their forties showed that the men most involved in the daily care of their children became fathers in their thirties.[20] "If I were in my twenties again under the influence of all the usual male identity problems," Earl observed, "I don't think I would be able to see our social structures with quite the same amusement that I feel now." Robert explained, "I'm much more patient, less in a hurry," than he was in this twenties.

Wives as Gatekeepers

Often a major reason why a man is distant from his children is his wife's gatekeeping stance; that is, his wife views herself as the primary caretaker of the children.[21] As more women enter the work force, their identity is less likely to rest entirely on their nurturing role; the economy thus leads women in the direction of shared parenting. If child care is viewed as the major role for women, a wife notes, you want the child to depend on you, more than on anyone else. Dr. Debra Klinman of the Fatherhood Project talked with a father who went to a father-baby class where he was asked to take full responsibility for the baby on the day of the class—dress it, pack its things, and so on. The mother said the outfit did not match and redressed the baby, reasserting her role as primary parent. They talked about the incident later and it became a joke between them. Many other women feel threatened about giving up their centrality at home because their husbands have more external power, Klinman notes.[22]

A male professor explained,

> *I am currently more involved in the parenting process primarily because my previous wife felt very strongly about maintaining traditional role differentiation. She didn't want me to trespass the conventional bounds of fatherhood because she felt that was undermining her own territory. Her presumption was that child care should* not *be shared equally and that it wouldn't be a good thing if it was.*

Studies show that a predictor of paternal involvement is the attitude of the wife about how involved men should be in child care.[23] Norma Radin discovered that mothers who felt loved by their fathers but wished they had spent more time with them were likely to have husbands who were involved fathers of preschool children.[24]

A technique to involve a father is for the mother to leave him alone with the child regularly or simply not do certain tasks he has agreed to do, such as bathe a child. The editors of "Father Earth News" commented, "Most men throughout history have learned the sexist strategy of the 'strategic delay.' . . . we know that all we have to do is wait long enough and our women will ultimately break down and clean up any messes that exist on the floors, in the sinks and on little bodies."[25] The editors suggest that women not succumb to this tactic.

Fathers in a workshop I led on shared parenting, at the 1986 California Men's Gathering, reported that being left alone with their child was what enabled them to gain a sense of competence. Jed Diamond's wife went on a trip for five days, so "no one was there to bail me out." He learned he "could do things I thought I couldn't do." During a separation from his wife, Russell found, "I didn't realize how dependent I was on my wife to arrange things like the babysitter until she left home." Fathers also reported that it was sometimes easier to learn parenting skills from a man friend than to rely on their wives.

Rational discussions of fathering responsibilities, couched in terms of logic and fairness, work with many of the men I interviewed. This approach requires presenting data, such as detailed lists of the chores required to care for the children and maintain the house. A time diary can be kept for a week to see who has more leisure time. Coparent's requests need to be specific, not just "I can't raise these children all by myself," but "These are tasks that I would like shared." Once the necessary work has been agreed on, a structured division and alternation of child care is imperative, as described in chapter 2.

The sooner fathers assume responsibility for their children, the better, or else the mother quickly becomes the expert and the father defers to her parenting know-how, handing her the child when it cries. The mother must not accept the flattering role of the parenting authority or take the child every time it is distressed. The mother should refrain from correcting her spouse if the diaper is not put on perfectly or if he puts clothes on the child that she thinks are inappropriate. When he is "on" with the child, she should respect his decisions and not undermine them to perpetuate her role as the parenting authority.

How difficult it is for the father to assume equal responsibility probably depends on his own parents' division of labor. If his mother waited on family members, his internal scripts will feel violated if his wife is different. His wife will seem like a poor mother if she expects their children to do their own laundry and her husband to cook breakfast. Talking about these ingrained expectations from our parents' families can help loosen their hold on men's feelings of deprivation and women's feelings of guilt. Shaping new roles requires much talking to exchange information and feelings.

Fathering Classes

Boys do not usually learn how to do child care in home economics classes, by babysitting, or from reading their mother's family magazines as girls do. Men need encouragement to nurture, just as women need encouragement to learn mechanical skills. Classes for fathers are one way to create a positive father identity and give men more confidence and skills. Only around 400 "fathering" classes and play groups exist: More classes just for fathers are essential as men stay more involved in fathering after taking a class.[26] (*Fatherhood U.S.A.*, the Fatherhood Project at the Bank Street College of Education in New York City, and "Nurturing Today" quarterly can be consulted for local classes.)

Hal Yoergler, who teaches classes "For Daddies Only" in Los Angeles, explained that in mixed-gender parenting groups, fathers invariably sit a little behind their wives as observers rather than full participants.[27] He finds that wives usually prod their husbands to take parenting classes, and divorced and older fathers are the most willing to take classes. Since men are less likely to seek help than women, their training in masculinity inhibits them from enrolling in classes for fathers. Like Robert Sayers, Yoergler starts his group off by asking men to talk about their own fathers. Usually they, too, feel angry and disappointed about the lack of closeness and want to be different. The implications of men's upbringing is analyzed; for example, they were praised for being big strong boys, and delicately handling a small infant fills them with anxiety, Yoergler observes.

To encourage continued interest in fathering, Yoergler appeals to men's intellectual curiosity, their interest in learning about their child's development, their project and goal orientation, their sense of importance to the child, the need to protect their investment of twenty-three chromosomes that shaped the infant, and the joy of establishing intimacy. If a father always hands his baby to his wife when it needs soothing, diaper changing, or feeding, he is teaching it that there are limits to his care, to how much the child can depend on him and trust him. Yoergler encourages fathers to include children in daily tasks, such as shaving, taking out the garbage, or repairing a faucet. He suggests the model of teacher rather than judge as the way men can relate better with their children.

Unfortunately, in her exhaustive survey of parenting classes for the resource book *Fatherhood U.S.A.*, Debra Klinman found that "men stay away in droves. The silence is deafening."[28] Their male coworkers would think men were "off the wall" to go to a father-toddler class. A class about auto mechanics, yes; on relating with a toddler, no. One is seen as masculine and goal oriented and the other as feminine and nebulous. In addition, men are not accustomed to talking with each other about their children, sticking to the more impersonal subjects of work and sports.

Debra Klinman observed that men who do take classes for new fathers walk in treating their babies like china dolls and walk out treating them more like rag dolls. In all-male classes there is no woman to hand the baby to when it cries or needs a diaper change, so men gain confidence in their ability to handle an infant. They also learn to talk to other men about children, although they start with sports, and it takes a while to begin comparing notes about children's behavior. Klinman notes that men learn to identify themselves as parents in these classes. They stay involved with their children by setting up a special daily ritual at bathtime or at bedtime such as doing infant exercises or singing. Classes should be extended to include parent support groups that continue through the teen years.

Popular classes that do involve men in parenting are prenatal classes, required so that men can participate in the delivery of their child. Participating in the birth of their infant has a major impact on men. Ira, a California father of four, was not present when his two older children were born in a hospital. His younger children were born at home, into his hands. It was a radical difference, he found: "I was profoundly impressed with their helplessness and vulnerability. They were issued forth into our hands. That created bonding and closeness to them." Michael, a New Jersey father, felt, "I was present at a miracle, and that stayed with me a long time. I just buzzed on that." An estimated 80 percent of fathers attend their infants' births, and 3.5 million babies are born each year, so this is a hopeful development.

University courses such as "American Men's Lives," taught at Amherst College, and educational films such as *New Relations: A Film About Fathers and Sons* (1983) by Ben Achtenberg and *Heroes and*

Strangers: A Film About Men, Emotions, and the Family (1984) by Community Media Productions also bring up issues about fathering. Videotapes I have produced, *Changing Families*, *Parenting*, *Dual-Earner Families*, and *Men's Changing Roles*, also discuss involved fathers.

Workshops at national and regional men's conferences are another arena for discussing fathering. The Eighth Annual Men and Masculinity Conference (also the first meeting of National Organization for Changing Men) was held at the University of Michigan in 1983. Workshops included The Birth Experience, Images of Fatherhood—From Teen-Fathers to Grand-Fathers, Teaching About the Male Role in the Public Schools, and My Father, My Self.

In these workshops I heard men express regrets that men do not talk to each other about being fathers, their work-oriented fathers did not provide examples of involvement, they did not have training such as girls get as babysitters, few books are available for fathers, their wives do not want to give up control of the children or trust their husbands to take care of them alone, and it is easier to let wives take charge of problems such as getting up in the night with a sick child. They also shared feelings about having sons or daughters; some felt it is easier to have a daughter because preconceived notions of how to behave with her are not as strong as stereotypes about how to relate to a son. I sensed on the part of many men an uncertainty and deep concern about what it means to be a father.

"Most of us came upon fatherhood *cold*," with no background or education, S. Adams Sullivan reports in his useful book for fathers.[29] A corrective model is the "Oh boy! Babies" program for sixth-grade boys at the private Collegiate School in New York, where the boys take care of infants once a week. The Fatherhood Project at the Bank Street College of Education offered a similar program. Debra Klinman noted how much the babies light up when the boys walk into the playroom. All elementary schools could offer child care courses for boys and girls in the older grades, providing fun for babies in the neighborhood and relief for their caretakers.

Babysitting is how many girls gain experience with small children. Some communities provide classes for babysitters, teaching simple first aid, emergency procedures, and basic communication skills. Boys should be encouraged to enroll in these classes and to earn money by babysitting, perhaps resulting in a higher fee for all. Children's books that show boys and men in nurturing roles provide useful role models. Examples of such books are *The Daddy Book, George the Babysitter,* and *My Daddy Is a Nurse.*

Boys need pets, dolls, and stuffed animals to cuddle, feed, and dress as practice for their adult parenting role. They need to be held and given affection, not limited to just shaking hands with their father or wrestling with him. Most of all, boys need to see their father and other males in nurturing roles.

Research on Fathering

We need social scientists to provide more information about father involvement, since parent-child studies meant mother-child until the last decade. The effect of father's absence has been studied more than his presence. The editors of *Father and Child*, published in 1982, observed that the fact that psychoanalytic literature has "not thus far systematically looked at fathers is astounding, betraying our own vulnerability to the unconscious forces of resistance."[30] The current interest in studying the effects of fathering on children is beginning to expand to look at the effects of fathering on the spouses.

A social science debate centers around the effect of biology on parenting practices. The sociologist Alice Rossi suggests that women have a physiological predisposition to care for infants. She explains, "There is some predisposition in the female to be responsive to people and sounds, an edge in receiving, interpreting and giving back communication."[31] Rossi believes that "men have tendencies more congenial to interaction with an older child, with whom rough-and-tumble physical play, physical coordination, teaching of object manipulation are easier and more congenial." She emphasizes that these are predispositions, not absolutes. If we understand the ways in which the sexes learn differently, we could provide "compensatory training for each sex," so that both sexes might move in an androgynous direction, she concludes. Research on the impact of active fathers is itself in its infancy. As it develops, more work will look at the effect of fathers on older children, not just on pre-school children.

Cross-cultural studies also help us see the influence of our national culture. A study of parenting practices with six-year-olds in ten nations revealed that traits Americans think of as feminine, such as being comforting, were reversed in other countries and varied by class.[32] Middle-class parents expect more sex-role differences in daughters than in sons, while the reverse is true of working-class parents. When we have more studies like these available, we will be better able to understand what fathers and mothers do because of their culture and their class, and then know how to provide parent education.

Research and writing about involved fathers is increasing. In 1979 David Giveans began a newsletter in San Francisco called *Nurturing News*, now coedited with Michael Robinson, full-time father of two young sons. The newsletter was expanded in 1987 to include an eight-page section entitled "The Fathers' Exchange" and the title was changed to *Nurturing Today: For Self and Family Growth*. James Levine wrote *Who Will Raise the Children? New Options for Fathers (and Mothers)* in 1976. His was the first popular book to look at men's involvement with their children. He gave examples of fathers who shared the care of their children or did most of the care. Levine, like Giveans an early-childhood educator, looked for grants to study fathering more extensively. He was turned down until the film *Kramer vs. Kramer* (1980) changed the climate of interest so that involved fathers became a viable topic. As a result, the Fatherhood Project, directed by Levine, was funded in 1981 at the Bank Street College of Education in New York City. The project's codirectors, Michael Lamb and Joseph Pleck, conduct scholarly research about fathers. The project is no longer funded, but it continues as an information exchange, and it has updated *Fatherhood, U.S.A*.

As women become more responsible for providing income for their families, we move in the direction of coparenting. Women are slowly gaining success at work and men are gaining more fulfillment from their family involvement. Since our mental health is better when we have more than one purpose in life, this change is helpful for parents as well as their children. Men rejecting a single-minded devotion to work can best learn parenting skills by taking full responsibility for their share of child rearing, by attending classes for fathers, and by reading and talking with other fathers. The outcome is expression of love, appreciated by both children and fathers.

Steps for Fathers

1. Begin spending equal time with the baby at its birth—get up with the baby at night and burp it and change its diapers.

2. Spend regular time alone with the child.
3. Remind your wife that she must give up the gratification of being *the* child-rearing expert—she should not impose her standards when you are "on" with the child.
4. To become more of an expert on child rearing, read books and magazines about parenting skills and take classes for fathers.
5. Develop men's support groups with acquaintances who have children of similar ages to discuss issues of concern and to compare experiences.
6. Take time to talk with the child, such as by alternating the bedtime routine with your spouse or by driving the child to activities. Reduce television viewing.
7. Plan weekly times for fun activities with the child.
8. Look critically at the amount of time taken up by work and decide if this matches your values and priorities. If not, take a stand and cut back.
9. Talk with your own father about his hindsight on parenting.
10. Press for social supports for involved fathers, such as parental leave and flexible work hours.

8

Coparenting after Divorce

> Sharing a child is a difficult situation for us as adults, but Delila deserves the best I can give her. I cannot give her an intact family, but I can give her the next best thing, which is her individual relationship with each of us.
>
> — *Joneen, remarried mother of one*

> Hasn't the obvious dawned on social workers, judges and politicians? If you don't allow a man to feel like a father he'll stop acting like one.
>
> — *Joe, divorced father of one*

THE divorce rate in the United States is one of the highest in the world. Twelve million children under eighteen have divorced parents, and about a million additional children join them each year.[1] Almost a quarter of these children will experience a second divorce. "A child's self-esteem and image are built on that of their parents," making cooperation between divorced parents vital, a divorced mother, Joneen, explained. Children raised only by their mothers do not do as well in school and in their social development as those with more than one caretaker and those who maintain close contact with both parents.[2] The financial struggles of single mothers are part of the difficulties their children face.

A strong argument for coparenting after divorce is that children do best when they are involved with both of their parents and when the parents have a courteous relationship. Children especially need contact with the parent of the same gender. Children who have high self-esteem and develop normally after their parents divorce often have good father-child relationships.[3]

Although 50 percent of recent marriages will end in divorce, this frequency does not mean that divorce is easy. For many of the coparenting couples I interviewed, the divorce process was the most wrenching event of their lives: Like a death, said one divorced man. A remarried professor observed, "It was the most painful thing I've ever done to myself—very, very painful. I don't want to do that ever again. I'm willing to pay a large price to avoid going through that kind of pain again." (However, he recently divorced again.) Another father, who has not remarried and is not sure that he will, said that he was devastated by all his dreams about family being blown apart. He grew up in a large happy family which he expected to duplicate. His wife left him to be with another man: He feels in hindsight that his wife was not confident that he loved her because she was the one who wanted the marriage, engaging in "gross deception at times to convince me to be with her." It is difficult to give up childhood dreams of getting married and having children with everything "hunky dory," a divorced mother concluded.

Reasons for Divorce

I noted two common causes of divorce among coparents. First, couples married young and grew apart: They were ripe to separate when an attractive third person arrived on the scene. Second, some marriages faced so many demands that the couple relationship lost out and withered. An example of the second pattern is a couple with one young son. The wife, Bobbi, studied long hours in pharmacy graduate school and the husband, Matt, supported the family as a contractor and did much of the child care. They were both so busy that they did not have energy to give to each other. Matt explained, "It just boiled down to neither one of us were getting our needs met. I can vividly remember her really needing more of me and I just couldn't give it. I couldn't do more than I was doing. I can remember needing more, too."

Without "strokes" the couple found themselves losing tolerance for each other; Matt was irritated by the arguing between his wife and son, for example. Matt feels that parenting was the biggest strain on their marriage because, "Before we were parents there was always room to take care of yourself, to get away. If I needed time with the boys, I could go out." Also, the differences in their parenting styles was an aggravation. In the face of their irritation with each other, they would go for months without making love, and then "we didn't like the way each other did it. With that came lots of self-doubt." The glue that originally held the relationship together dried up without attention and time for each of the two individuals to find renewal.

Parenting held other couples together. One couple stayed together longer than was satisfying because they were the mom and the dad with two kids—"that's just what you did," Karen explained. Married at nineteen and a full-time homemaker, Karen was also afraid that she could not support the family by herself. She did not want to give up the time she spent making crafts and observing her boys' sports activities. She wondered, "Will I ever be able to afford new carpeting again?" She was angry when her husband left her for another woman because "I was being forced to be independent."

A Maine couple found too much of their energy going into deciding how to divide up family work fairly. Then "the spirit of helping each other was gone," and with that went affection and passion, explained Gale. A Michigan man attributed his divorce to the fact that he focused his attention on his wife's career development and her growing recognition as a journalist. In contrast, he said, "I didn't pay that much attention to the directions that I wanted to go in." After the divorce, he gave up his job to go into a Ph.D. graduate program, something he never would have permitted himself to do as a husband. On her side, his wife felt unsupported and drained by shouldering the responsibility of organizing the family life, making child care arrangements, and encouraging her husband to be an involved father. Again, neither of them felt supported or fulfilled in the marriage.

Other studies of causes of divorce discovered that couples argue over spending money, relations with relatives, disciplining children, and division of family work.[4] Divorced couples shared few interests and activities, had difficulty expressing affection, and lacked a sense of companionship. Their needs were unacknowledged by their spouse.[5] Couples with low family income and less education are more likely to divorce than couples with high incomes and college degrees.[6] Couples with at least one son are more likely to remain married than couples with only daughters or no children.[7] Wives are more likely to be dissatisfied and to initiate divorce than husbands.

How Children React to Divorce

Divorce is hardest in the long run on the children. They cope better if they can understand the reasons for divorce, but even when they are given rational reasons few are relieved.[8] Unlike many divorcing parents, the couples I interviewed explained to their preschoolers that the parents had many disagreements, did not get along well, and could not live together anymore. The children usually did not ask for more details. Despite the explanations, most children still hoped that their parents would reunite. This hope remained even ten years after the divorce for over half the children interviewed by Judith Wallerstein, despite the fact that only a third saw their fathers at least once a month.[9] Wallerstein also found in ten-year follow-up interviews that the divorce continued to evoke deep sadness for 30 percent of the children, and about a quarter of the children still disapproved of the divorce. This is consistent with the findings of Linda Bird Francke, who reported that most of the 100 children she talked with were sad and angry about the divorce.[10]

Coparents reported that some children would attempt to reunite them, suggesting that since their parents were getting along better after the separation, they should live together again. Kendra, a five-year-old, suggested that her mother spend the night with Kendra's father since they are not arguing anymore. My son, Jed, has suggested that his father, his stepmother, and their two dogs move in with us.

Some parents observed that their children were happier after the divorce, not having to sit in their rooms and listen to their parents yell at each other. Before, "they'd cry sometimes because they'd think they were responsible for it," said a divorced father.

Other parents noticed negative reactions from the children after the divorce: anger, withdrawing emotionally or "going into a shell," retreating to their rooms, and having problems at school. Diana, the mother of two children, was concerned about her daughter, Becky, who lost her sparkle and was depressed for months. Becky was angry that her parents separated and that she was not able to get them back together. She coped by dumping her anger on her father, making him the "bad" parent and her mother the "good" parent, despite the fact that her mother was the one who left the marriage and moved in with another man. Diana thought that Becky did not want to risk being angry at both of her parents.

A study of divorces in Virginia families with preschool children found that the children's behavior problems improved with time. By the second year after the divorce, the children had fewer behavior problems than those in high-conflict intact families.[11] The children of divorced parents have more problems than tension-free intact families, but recent studies indicate that conflict between parents is worse for children than divorce.[12] As is typical, the boys in Virginia had more behavior problems than girls, and their fathers were spending less time with the children by the second year.

Children react to divorce according to their developmental stage. Preschoolers often blame the divorce on their own misbehavior and regress; children aged six to eight are particularly sad about the divorce; and children nine to twelve are angry.[13] A New York father of two daughters noticed that his youngest daughter, an infant when her parents divorced, "does not feel as wronged as her older sister does, and is able to show warmth more easily," similar to Wallerstein's findings that younger children forget the pain of divorce more easily than older children.

Divorce is more difficult for boys than girls, partly because girls are more able to talk with and gain support from their friends. Boys whose parents are divorced have more behavior problems at home and in school than do girls whose parents are divorced or boys from intact families.[14] "Boys are simply more vulnerable to stress of any kind than girls," reports Jerome Kagan, a Harvard psychologist.[15] Boys who live with their single fathers were better adjusted than boys who live with their single mothers, and girls who live with their single mothers are better adjusted than those who live with their single fathers, according to a Texas study.[16] Clearly, it is especially important for boys to be involved with their fathers after divorce, a crucial argument for coparenting.

Dorothy Huntington, a psychologist who specializes in the effect of divorce on children, explains that the impact of divorce depends on a child's temperament.[17] Some children have difficulty making transitions from one place to another, are less flexible than others, and do not do well going back and forth frequently between their parents' homes. Huntington also points out that it takes a minimum of eighteen to twenty-four months for family members to pick up the pieces after divorce. She advocates support groups to help parents and children through the postdivorce crisis year.

Some single parents have a tendency to use their child too much as a confidant, so that the child feels responsible for the parent's well-being. Counselors warn against robbing children of their childhood by allowing them to take care of their parent. Another effect of divorce on some children, especially adolescent girls, is that it makes them cautious about marriage.[18] This caution might be positive, considering the almost two-thirds divorce rate for teenage marriages when the bride is pregnant. Teenagers in general report becoming more grown up after their parents' divorce. My female students report that young men raised by single mothers do not expect to be waited on and understand what it takes to manage a household. Children may become more liberal in their sex-role attitudes: In a Michigan study of single mothers, 80 percent of their children believed that wives and husbands should share cooking and earning money.[19] Girls were more liberal than the boys, as other studies show.

Fathering after Divorce

The increased involvement of divorced fathers in child care is a striking phenomenon. My survey showed that divorced fathers spent a mean of thirty-one hours per week in child care compared to twenty-five hours spent by divorced mothers. (Their children's mean ages are 7.1 for fathers and 8.9 for mothers: This may account for some of the difference.) Some divorced fathers report that they got to know their children better after the separation.[20] Diana, a separated wife who reunited with her husband, reported that as a result of being a single parent her husband became a more self-assured and better parent. She also changed; she does not intrude as much in his interaction with the children. This is a lesson to married mothers to give fathers time alone with their children.

Many of the divorced fathers I interviewed had assumed a traditional role in their marriage. Mike, a social worker, explained, "I pretty much was the passive man. I didn't see it at the time, but my wife was raising the two boys alone in a lot of respects. I was there for moral support, but she was really the doer. I was like an observer but still felt a real bond to the family." When they separated he decided that he was not going to lose his children as well as his wife. He was determined to see the boys more often than just when it was convenient for him. He had to learn to cook and clean and this, coupled with being lonely after the separation, made the adjustment to being an active father difficult. But as a result, Mike said, "Before I didn't have the kind of relationship with my boys that I have now where we are working together and interacting."

Liz described her ex-husband's previous passivity in contrast to his present shared care of their daughter: "If I was there Kim would just sit glued to the chair and she could be wet or screaming. Even if I tried not to jump in, it took a long time. She has a lot more of him than she would have if we were still together." Debra's ex-husband was so passive that he would spend his time caring for their daughter by taking her to his mother's house and falling asleep in front of the television. After the separation, "it all changed. He realized that there were so many things that he hadn't done, he wanted to do everything right away. He was really into being the best dad. It frees them," Debra concluded.

Dan, a factory worker in Indiana, noted that the men who talk about their children at work are divorced, while the married men look at "the old lady and the rug rats as a burden they are carrying around." The "child-absence syndrome" and "the masculinization of loneliness" are new labels for the pain of divorced fathers who do not see their children frequently.[21] Unfortunately, over half of fathers do not see their children regularly a year after the divorce.[22]

Divorced fathers' competition for children's approval often is an undercurrent that can spur fathers on to spend time with them. Children try to use competition between divorced parents to their advantage, but if the contest has positive results, and parents are not critical of each other in front of the children, this can be an effective motivator for fathers. Competition is something men are trained to respond to with vigor.

Mary, whose ex-husband is actively involved with his two boys, appreciates sharing responsibility for the children [post-divorce]. She explained that, previously,

> *He learned to do diapers, but everything that he learned he felt was an imposition on him. It took a campaign on my part to get him to*

recognize what was involved and what it was he needed to do with the boys. He didn't recognize his resistance and how draining it was. He could pick and choose what activities he wanted to have with the kids because there is no obligation for men. If he didn't get it done, miraculously somebody would come in and do it. The man is never the bottom line.

Mary finds that their parenting is much more balanced now that they are divorced. As Hugh spends more time with the boys, his expectations for their behavior are more realistic: "After he spent whole days with them and found you have forty things to correct about a child's behavior, the way they drink their milk isn't so important."

A major advantage of shared parenting is easing the burdens of single parenting, making a better environment for children. A study by Wallerstein and Kelly of families five years after divorce discovered that "the chronic emotional and economic overload was frequently intolerable for the custodial parent, and the cumulative effect on the children was all too visible in their unhappiness and depression."[23] Over a third of the children were depressed and unhappy and only a quarter had two involved parents: However, these are families who felt they needed counseling and perhaps are not entirely representative.

Clark, who became the primary parent for his two children when his wife moved to another town, describes what it is like to be a parent without a partner. His work starts at 8:00 A.M., but his daughter's school starts at 8:30 and his son has to be driven to the babysitter. After work he picks up the children at the babysitter:

They're exhausted, hungry, worn out. I'm exhausted, hungry, worn out. We end up in the house at 5:30 when it is dark, cold, nothing going on. I rummage around for something quick to eat. Then I get the guilties. I can't just have frozen TV dinners and I fix a regular meal. By 7:00 or so people are feeling good and we get into doing things.

Then he gets each of the children bathed and ready for bed and tells them a story, giving them individual attention. When he has them in bed by nine he is "wiped out."

Being a single parent is especially difficult, Clark notes, when a child gets sick. Two parents can sleep in shifts, alternating getting up with the child during the night. During the day, the babysitter does not want a sick child around her other charges, so Clark has to stay home with the child. The ultimate hard time is when he is sick too. Single fathers observed that single parenting is often harder for women, because when men learn the routine of organizing a household they get a lot of praise and help. They are only about 10 percent of single parents, so they seem special.

Other problems mentioned by single parents are that they miss having a back-up person to say, "Listen to your dad; he's right." A child who has a particular interest cannot go off and do it with one parent while another child who does not share that interest stays home with the other parent. A Pennsylvania father told me he misses being able to talk about his children with their mother, who is hostile to him. He dislikes raising them in isolation. He feels out of place at school and PTA meetings when the other parents are in couples, and out of place with single friends who do not have children.

Advantages of Joint Custody

In a more advantageous coparenting situation, Mary notes that since her divorce she has not had to deal with resentment or depression about being a single parent because duties are so evenly shared. The family eats dinner together frequently and maintains clear communication. She also notes that both parents' anxiety about losing the children has been diminished by sharing child care. Coparents appreciate blocks of time to be alone, to socialize, to do uninterrupted work, and to "get the best of both worlds." The mother of a six-year-old found it wonderful during her four days alone not to be interrupted all day long and to be able to go on a bike ride or to a movie on a whim without guilt about leaving her daughter.

Parents find that time away from their children makes it easier to appreciate them, reduces quarrels, and lessens conflict and irritation. After a few days with his daughter, a carpenter notices that he gets "grumpy and short with her," but then looks forward to seeing her after a break. "Most parents would love to have a break," a divorced mother notes. She has an "intense little kid" and sighs in relief when she goes. Then she is very glad to see her child when she comes back from her father's home. A Rhode Island mother noted,

> *I really like being a mother, but I don't think I'd like it if I had to do it all the time. As a matter of fact, my son (age 12) and I have gotten along better since the divorce because we are both pretty intense personalities. After we've been together for a week we're ready to get away from each other.*

Both children and parents appreciate each other more after a brief separation, as is true for people in most relationships.

Children of divorced coparents receive concentrated attention from each parent since "we are willing to give up more of our own lives when the kids are here," explains a mother in Maine. A camaraderie develops between a single parent and child, "because neither of us has to share the other person with anybody," and they share tasks together. One mother worries about her child thinking the world revolves around the little girl because she receives so much attention from each parent. Usually, though, a new stepparent and siblings enter the scene, as happened in her family later.

Coparents also share financial costs of child rearing. Over half of divorced fathers nationwide pay no child support, although legislation was passed in 1984 to correct this problem. For mothers who receive it, the average monthly payment in California is $150 per child, not much considering the costs of day care and shoes. A widely quoted California study by Lenore Weitzman found that mothers' incomes drop by 73 percent, while fathers' incomes rise by 42 percent, after divorce.[24] Fathers who spend time with their children are much more likely to contribute to their financial needs. One study reported that none of the joint-custody parents returned to court over financial conflicts, while over half of the single-custody mothers had to face this continuing battle.[25] A divorced father explained, "Hasn't the obvious dawned on social workers, judges and politicians? If you don't allow a man to feel like a father he'll stop acting like one."

Another benefit of coparenting is that children learn from having two homes, having "two kinds of ways of looking at the world." Parents note that going back and forth between two families requires flexibility, tactfulness, problem-solving skills, responsibility, openness to possibilities, defining individual values, and getting to know other adults intimately. The mother of a fifteen-year-old son who has four parent figures and three stepsiblings said, "Sometimes he would get angry at the differences in the houses, but in general it has made him understand differences and have to make up his own mind about how he feels about issues." A newspaper reporter who was raised in a large, loving, intact family observed that with "so much love and security, that became our expectation. When my brothers and sisters went out in the real world and got hit over the head by somebody, they fell apart." His children's experience is very different; they cope with a single father and their remarried mother's household with two half-siblings.

Studies on the impact of joint custody on children began in the late 1970s but are scarce and based on small numbers. Comparisons of children in joint and sole custody situations do not yet seem to reveal major differences. However, most children in single-custody families are discontent with the amount of time spent with their fathers, while most joint-custody children are content.[26]

Children need both their parents, and shared parenting after divorce encourages this contact. A Wisconsin study showed that joint-custody fathers spend much more time with their children and assume more responsibility than noncustodial fathers.[27] Because of joint custody, a father reported, "I'm not cut off from my child. I'm not reduced to Uncle Daddy which has happened to millions of men. I like my child. I have things to offer him. His mother feels the same way."

Going back and forth between two homes may not be easy for children, but they usually prefer it to having to choose between one parent or the other. Bob, a reporter, says of his four-year-old son,

> *He likes both parts of his life. He likes being with me and he likes being with Maureen. She has her whole universe of friends and associates, places she goes and things she does and I have mine. It's like twice as much. Twice as good. You know, we're not proud of it, but it gives him pleasure to be able to say, "I have two homes."*

How to Coparent after Divorce

Coparenting means that both parents assume "a responsibility for meeting a share of all the physical needs, as well as the financial and emotional needs of their children."[28] These responsibilities include taking care of a sick child, packing school lunches, talking to teachers, driving the child to lessons and the dentist, and shopping for clothes. Miriam Galper suggests keeping track of the children's expenses and at the end of the month figuring out who owes whom, based on the amount spent and earned by each parent. She also suggests listening to, but not supporting, the child's complaints about the other parent.

Parents need not like each other to be good coparents after divorce. Joneen explained, "Sharing a child is a difficult situation for us as adults, but Delila deserves the best I can give her. I cannot give her an intact family, but I can give her the next best thing, which is her individual relationship with each of us." Counselor and author Isolina Ricci suggests that the model for divorced parents to use is that of a business relationship.[29] If one treats the ex-spouse as a business associate, appropriate behavior is clearly to be on time for appointments, to abide by agreements, to avoid last minute requests for schedule changes, to be polite, and not to use children as go-betweens. By changing expectations to fit reality, divorced parents can minimize disappointment and anger. This is an important operating guide for coparents.

To deal with conflict Ricci suggests that each parent bring a list of what he or she is ready to talk about and is not yet ready to talk about, set a time limit of thirty minutes a session, and begin with the easiest issues first. In a deadlock, use a mediator such as a therapist. Ricci suggests planning ahead for holidays, which are often difficult times for divorced parents, and writing out the specific agreements. Ricci maintains that our use of language is very important. The term *broken home* is not constructive. A parent does not *lose* a child after divorce, nor does a child merely *visit* one parent. The child gains two homes, *Mom's House, Dad's House*—the title of Ricci's book.

Parents report that establishing a consistent and specific schedule for transferring children from one house to the other is necessary. It is too much responsibility for young children to decide if they want to go to Mom's or Dad's. One couple who tried letting their five-year-old daughter decide found that she would make a choice, then change her mind. Another couple observed that their boys would expect to be at one place and felt disoriented when they ended up at the other parent's home. Their nine-year-old said, "It's sort of crazy going back and forth. We don't usually know which house we want to stay at." The parents also need a routine schedule so they can make plans.

Some parents find it easier to pick up their child at school or day care. These places are natural buffers and afford an easier transition than at home. A social worker found that it was very hard for his daughter to switch when he came to pick her up at her mother's house, because she was already home, and the same was true when her mother picked her up at his house. He and his ex-wife reduced the number of changeover times by each keeping her for a half a week.

One family became aware of a transition phenomenon they named the "GBBs"—the Good Bye Blues. Julio and Caryl realized that every Sunday evening "you could peel the kids off the ceiling, they were so obnoxious." One child is hers, two are his, and one is theirs. His children felt conflict between their love for their father's second family, including their half-brother, and their desire to be with their mother. They also disliked the fact that their father's family was ready for them to go. If they left feeling angry, it was easier to leave. Caryl and Julio's solution was to encourage the children to talk about the pull between wanting to see one parent and missing the other and to be aware of the tension, rather than acting out their anxiety and then feeling guilty.

Most parents maintain a room equipped with clothes in each home so that the child does not have to cart things back and forth. They often share the purchase of expensive items such as coats and shoes. Author Ciji Ware suggests making a checklist for transition time to prevent fights over "stupid things like lost socks."[30] Maureen, the mother of a four-year-old son, noted that she would buy clothes and they would end up at her ex-husband's house. He disagreed, "Oh, no. Now wait a minute. That's not true. I don't know what happens to your clothes." Parents with a toddler found that one of them would end up with 80 percent of the diapers and the other was left with only 20 percent, all dirty.

Schedules for child care range from alternating days to alternating years. Some parents split the week. Jim has his children on Monday and Tuesday, Diana has them on Wednesday and Thursday, and they alternate weekends. Every other week the children are at one home for five days. Diana worries that the children find it choppy going back and forth so often, but she feels that a week would be too long to go without seeing her elementary school–age children. She said that she finds it hard to establish a regular schedule of chores for her children when she only has them half a week.

Bruce, a father of two children, had to go through court-sponsored mediation to convince his wife to let their two children stay with him for extended periods. He has the children from Thursday after school through Monday, every other week, plus dinner together on the Mondays they are at their mother's home. She felt that the children needed one steady home and that it would "freak them out or confuse them or damage their brains or something" if they had two homes. After seeing the arrangement in action, she changed her view. Bruce did have to struggle for about two years before she would stop scheduling activities like birthday parties for the children during his time with them. He maintains that he is responsible for what happens during his time, although she still tries to tell him not to take the children over to the house of his woman friend and her children. Bruce reported that his two children felt "a little freaky" about the new arrangement at first, resisted it a bit, but then got used to it after a few weeks. He worries, though, about their mother moving away and taking the children. Other parents have pledged to each other not to move away.

Denise and Curtis found that switching Kerrie every three days created too much uncomfortable contact between the two of them and that it took a day or so to get her settled into her new routine. From Denise's view, Kerrie was difficult to discipline when she came back from her father's like a "little wild maniac." Her father let her stay up late, but Denise had to get her up early so Denise could go to work. Switching every week works better for them, although Denise says a week is a long time to be without her five-year-old daughter. Bob and Maureen also changed from alternating every three days. They felt that they did not get to work through a desired behavior change with their son in three days. They did not discipline him well; they were so glad to see him they did not make him go to bed on time, for example. They changed to alternating weeks, Monday night to Monday morning.

Margaret asked her twelve-year-old how it felt to change homes each week and was told he could not remember any other way. Margaret said when she and her son first started alternating weekly, it took time to get adjusted to each other. They were irritable until they got used to each other's rhythm. But for the last several years the adjustment seemed to happen almost instantly; partly, she feels, because he has gotten older and more sensitive. Margaret is slightly more lenient in her discipline than her ex-husband, but her son adapts and rarely complains at one house about the other. As long as each parent is consistent in their rules, children can adapt as they do to various teachers at school. They do thrive on order, routine, and consistency at each place they spend time.[31]

An Alabama couple alternate ten school days and a weekend because they feel they need two school weeks in a row to keep track of homework. California parents who live farther apart change the care of Jennifer each school semester. Telephone calls and a visit every three weeks kept their daughter in touch with her other parent, so it is not as hard for her to leave a parent as it was to leave her third-grade classroom.

Erica, an eleven-year-old, alternates every year between her parents, who live in the same town. She sleeps over at the other parent's home every Tuesday night and every other weekend. This schedule began when Erica was in kindergarten. Her mother, Maryann, remembers the day her ex-husband telephoned her and asked if he could keep Erica with him in another city where he was in law school for the next year. Her heart "made a big beat as if there wasn't enough room for it in my chest. Not having Erica never occurred to me. It was very hard." Erica's father moved his law practice to be in the same town as Maryann, which made the year-to-year plan easier for them. In Maine, coparents alternate every two years. Gale reports, "I think going back and forth is tough on the kids to some degree, but they have a lot of love in their various homes. That is the most important thing, because, in spite of all the confusion, both boys are pretty stable kids who like themselves."

In summary, the issues that may arise for divorced coparents are: (1) transporting the children and their possessions back and forth, (2) accepting two discipline styles and sets of parental expectations, (3) establishing a rhythm with the children after they return, and (4) adjusting to frequent contact with the ex-spouse. The issues that arise for children are: (1) feeling like ping-pong balls going back and forth between parents, (2) forgetting where they are supposed to be, (3) leaving desired objects at the other house, (4) losing things like socks, (5) wishing their parents were still together, and (6) having fantasies about "normal" families. An eight-year-old boy, Ryan, said that having two homes "is like seeing double; you're doing the same thing twice, like flunking a grade and having to do the same work twice. I have to water the garden twice and feed the animals twice." Ryan has only been in this arrangement for a year. Some children who have done it longer simply accept having Mom's house and Dad's house and are happy to have close contact with both their parents.

I talked with three couples who felt that, instead of their children going back and forth between two homes and two neighborhoods, the children should stay in the family home and the parents move back and forth. This is a difficult arrangement for the parents. A Michigan couple, Mary and Hugh, tried this arrangement but are not going to continue it. Mary finds that when she comes back to the house, she has to "unHugh" the place. She is annoyed because when she leaves the laundry is done and the refrigerator is stocked, but when Hugh leaves he forgets to do these chores for her. Hugh, however, maintains that the laundry is done, the kitchen cleaned, and the beds made when Mary comes back. "Each of us is committed to making the transition in a clean state," he said. Their different perceptions are an example of how men and women are trained differently about household standards. In some ways, sharing a house is like still being married, Mary concluded. Hugh said he finds it hard to pick up and move into the room he rents in a nearby house. The transition is disorienting, and he feels he loses a couple of days in the process of changing.

California ex-spouses, Elizabeth and Fred, agreed to share their family home to insure their three children's stability. Friday is the changing day, as one of their daughters calls it, when one parent moves out and the other moves in. They plan an hour overlap to exchange information about the children. It took them several years, including therapy, to learn how to work with each other after their separation. Fred feels that their good communication is unusual. They worked hard at understanding problems in their marriage and worked through a lot of their anger and upset feelings. They make the effort because they believe it is vital for their children's well-being. If they cannot resolve an issue, they use their therapist as a mediator. Each pays their share of the household bills, the percentage determined by their relative earnings.

Fred plans on getting his own house, however, because he said he wants his own "identity and space to control my own environment." Neatness and structure are more important to him than to Elizabeth. Like Mary, he gets irritated about coming home to dirty laundry and spoiling food left in the refrigerator, and said it feels like a quasi-marriage to be sharing the same house. Their friends also get confused about where they will be.

Another way to divide the care of children after a divorce is to split the custody of siblings. A New York couple agreed that their son would stay with his father, visiting his mother on the weekends and for most of the summers, although he visits less frequently as he has gotten older. The daughter is with her mother and visits her father: A satisfactory arrangement for all of them, the father reports. In another family, the son goes to his mother's home one weekend a month, and another weekend a month the daughter visits her father. The two children spend two weekends a month and the summers together.

Distance makes coparenting difficult. A California father, Ken, whose former wife lives an hour and a half away, uses the drive as his quiet time to think, although he does get frustrated with the distance. Ken telephones and writes to keep in frequent touch with his son.[32] He sends taped messages to be played on the child's tape recorder. Ken worries that as his son gets older and develops attachments to friends, school, and sports activities, it will be more difficult for him to go back and forth.

Getting Along as Coparents

Many divorced parents discussed having angry feelings about each other, but made a commitment to work through their anger since their children need cooperative parents. Nancy Weston, a counselor who works with divorcing parents in Los Angeles, advises parents to "minimize the conflict between themselves. The worst pain caused to children comes out of feeling torn between their two parents and sometimes having to choose one or the other."[33] The hostility is usually worse at first and then dissipates. Counselors and books teach specific techniques for how to fight fair, such as (1) stick to the present issue, (2) avoid sarcasm, (3) concentrate on specific solutions and compromises rather than blame, and (4) learn negotiation skills.[34] In the past therapists have discouraged ex-spouses from holding on to their relationship, but coparenting requires contact. Parents are able to develop a workable partnership by concentrating on the best interests of their children.

The first year after separation is the most difficult for parents and children. Mike and Joann found that it took them a year to be able to really hear what the other was saying. At first they were critical of each other, looking for "who was right and who was wrong." After a year they are more relaxed with each other, to the point that they were planning a family camping trip when I talked with them.

Liz, a therapist, related that she and her ex-husband, Kim, fought like cats and dogs over the sale of their house, although they were able to talk rationally about arrangements for their daughter. "We are able to keep issues separate, but it takes a lot of energy," Liz said. She added that sometimes she has wished that Kim did not exist, but she strongly believes that the best thing for her daughter is to have two involved parents. Kim's view is that many divorced spouses have ongoing animosity because, instead of examining their own behavior, they are "busy laying trips on the other person."

Kim found that the hardest adjustment for him after his separation was not learning to be a single father but the frequent association with Liz. He also would have liked to have taken a job in another state. Now he has to "consider another person who is not really involved in my life except that we're hooked together by this child who holds us both in great esteem and needs both of us."

As an example of how they handle conflict, Liz described how she wanted to get Valerie the bike for Christmas that the child requested. Kim thought Valerie was too little. They discussed the issue back and forth. Liz did not want to set a precedent of overriding him, hoping that in the future, if Valerie at age fourteen wanted to live with her boyfriend and Kim thought it was all right and Liz did not, he would not override her objections. "I tried to hear the things he was saying and tried to share my feelings about it. I told him I would take responsibility for watching her very closely and supervising her," Liz said. Kim finally agreed to the bike purchase.

Sheldon and Chris, a school psychologist and a nurse, share care of their three-year-old daughter, Orion. Sheldon explained that when they are feeling angry at each other and question whether their coparenting will work, they remind themselves that Orion is at the center of what they are doing and they need to focus on her best interests. They put effort into resolving their differences. When Chris yelled at Sheldon for being late to pick up Orion, instead of yelling back at her that she had been late dozens of times, he stopped and thought a minute and realized that something had probably gone wrong for Chris that day.

A potential conflict for parents is competition to be the most loved parent. This gives children a wedge to play off one parent against the other. One five-year-old's reaction to not getting her way is to manipulatively tell her mother, Lori, "That's not the way Daddy does it. I'm going to tell my Daddy. I want to be with my Daddy." When her children tell her about gifts their father gives them, Lori replies that they are lucky and refuses to play the competition game. She notes, though, that she spends a lot of money on her children and she feels constantly compared with her ex-husband. She observes that "divorced parents tend to indulge their children, having two sets of resources," and perhaps feeling guilty that their children go back and forth between two houses. However, when her daughter telephoned her from her father's home after a disagreement, asking Lori to pick her up, she did not comply or in any way undermine his authority. Her ex-husband also finds that the children tested him at first, making statements like, "At Mom's house we don't have to do so and so." He realized that children can be very skilled manipulators and that parents must stand together.

Parents can be hurt when a child expresses a preference for one parent over the other or does not want to go to one parent's home. A single mother, who has less money than her husband, finds that her boys like to be at their father's house because of his television and stereo and the fact that he has money to take them to movies and other entertainment. She feels anxious and hurt, on top of having to adjust to not being a full-time homemaker. A Massachusetts father, Sandy, observed that until his son was around two or three "he seemed to me more needy and clingy with his mother, but would also give her a harder time." As the boy got older, his attachments alternated between the two parents. Knowing the development stages of children and how that affects their attachments can help a parent in not feeling hurt by a child's current preference.

The most hostile feelings between former spouses are brought out in legal child custody disputes. Courts may grant various custody arrangements, depending on the state. One parent can be granted sole legal custody, or two can have joint legal custody. Joint legal custody mandates that the parents will share decisions about major areas of the child's life such as education, religion, and medical care. Where the child lives is granted as physical custody. One parent can have sole physical custody, or parents can share joint physical custody, with the child going back and forth between two homes. Courts often award joint legal custody with sole physical custody to the mother. Joint custody is now the preferred mode in some states including California, although the law there ambiguously adds "or to either parent."

Divorced parents I interviewed did not have positive words for lawyers or the court system, but found court-appointed mediators helpful.[35] Complaints were that lawyers tried to aggravate conflicts rather than working for a just compromise. Some couples who wanted to share custody found the courts unwilling to go along with the parents' agreement. A couple in Missouri agreed to give the father legal custody officially but to share the care of their children as they please. An Indiana couple did not wish to declare who had custody. Instead, they listed the responsibilities of each parent, which "drove the attorneys and the judge crazy." A Wisconsin mother, who is an attorney with joint legal custody, said that joint custody is not very well accepted in rural areas in her state. It is considered too much work for parents, is believed to tear the children apart, and is seen as only benefiting selfish parents. However, we have seen that when fathers have joint custody they are much more likely to stay involved and pay child support.

Once divorced parents have resolved legal issues and established a system for coparenting, they must learn to handle other personal issues, such as dating. It can be painful if one's former spouse begins dating first. Clark candidly remarked, "My ex having too good a time pissed me off to no end. I couldn't stand it." He realized that he was unrealistically looking through rose-colored glasses for a princess with whom to live happily ever after in the bliss he had not found in his first marriage. He had not dated for eleven years and wondered what he should say or do on a date. As a single parent, he had to arrange for a babysitter and cope with his guilt about leaving his children, so by the time he met his date at a bar, he would say, "Whew! Hi there. Do I look worn out?" He added, "When you're a single parent you are bound with the child a lot! It requires total planning all the time. If you want to have a romantic fling it's gotta be organized." Parents who share physical custody of their children have a much easier time dating because they have scheduled times when the children are away. Joint custody also alleviates fathers' sense that they are doing their ex-wives a favor to "babysit" for their children.

A further complication arises when two divorced parents date each other. Bob, the father of a six-year-old boy and a four-year-old girl, described going to a Hauf-Brau restaurant with his children and his companion's two girls, ages five and three. The five-year-old got her feelings hurt and would not get out of the car. Her mother spent a half hour outside with her, while Bob was trying to get the other three children through the food line. His son wanted to play video games and the two girls were quarreling. It was each child's worst night, he said. The two adults decided that a merger of the two families would not work and stopped going out with each other. Some parents worried about the jealousy and competition between their children and their romantic partner, as well as between two sets of children.

Once a parent does manage to become involved with another adult, he or she may worry about the child becoming attached to that new person and then going through yet another breakup. A mother in New York dates men she does not know well while her son is at his father's home. She explained, "I try very hard to keep my more frivolous male attachments out of his way when he is at his father's. My most important attachment I've brought home to him." The outcome is that "he has been able to view me as a woman who cares about and tries to have meaningful relationships with men." The mother of an eleven-year-old, Erica, in hindsight feels she has shared too much about her relationships: "It's like whenever I'm feeling sad, she feels it too."

Dating is more difficult for single mothers than fathers. Bob, a thirty-six-year-old man, commented that if he were wandering around by himself he would not have a chance with women, but being the primary parent for two young children has enhanced his appeal. "There are a bunch of women that think it's enormously cute," he said. Karen realized that she was beginning to blame and dislike her sons for preventing her from having a relationship with any man but their father. Her lover, Rick, and his son did move in with them, but it did not work because Rick was so critical and authoritarian with her sons. Also Rick's son had visions of sharing a bachelor apartment with his father and resisted Karen's discipline.

Support for Divorced Coparents

Time is the major healer of the pain of divorce. Court mediators were a preliminary help for some couples. One effective mediator spent the first three sessions with a couple encouraging them to express their anger at each other so they could move beyond animosity to making reasonable decisions for their family. Some community colleges offer helpful courses for divorced parents; some churches and synagogues offer support groups; and Parents without Partners, a national organization with local chapters, provides support groups and an informative magazine. Some schools organize groups for children of divorced parents.

Psychologist Dorothy Huntington recommends counselor-led discussion groups as a very effective aid for parents and for children as young as two and a half. Preschool children work with puppets to act out their feelings in their groups at The Center for the Family in Transition in Marin County, California. Several fathers mentioned participating in groups for the newly divorced where they learned the common stages that occur for a child and parent after a separation: (1) denial, (2) anger, (3) bargaining (that is, the child promises to be good), (4) depression, and (5) acceptance. These steps are similar to the grieving process after a death. Knowing that one will pass on to the next stage in time creates hope. Some couples go to a counselor together to make sure they are doing the work needed to establish effective coparenting and to learn how to deal with fears like the other parent's moving to another city. Some parents arrange for counselors for their children.

Grandparents or roommates are helpful sources of support for some. Two single fathers, Dan and Max, each with one child, moved in together. Dan explained that they had a "perfect marriage," because they split the housework and child care and gave each other emotional support. If one man was having a problem with his child, the other could step in and help. They celebrated holidays together as a family. Also, they did not have to ask each other's permission to have affairs. Max moved out eventually, though, because he wanted to have his own home and a separate bedroom for his son. Dan's daughter thought of the room the children shared as hers, because they were living in her dad's house.

Schools can support divorced parents by providing parent groups and information and referral services. School personnel can change their attitudes by not assuming that all a child's difficulties stem from a "broken home," coparents suggested. Schools can use textbooks that show a variety of family types, including single-parent families—the most rapidly growing family type. Most parents reported that schools do not recognize that children may have more than one home: They will not send out duplicate notices to both parents, for example. A Wisconsin mother specifically requested that her son's father be sent copies of notices and was ignored, despite the Family Educational Rights Act of 1974 that gives noncustodial parents access to pertinent records. Despite the large numbers of divorced parents, social institutions have not caught up with their needs.

Above all else, divorced parents need to act in the best interests of their children, seeking professional help in learning to negotiate conflict and not criticizing the child's other creator when the children are present. Doing what is fair is the goal and praising desirable behavior reinforces it for adults as well as children. Keeping fathers involved is imperative for children's well-being, a powerful incentive for coparenting after divorce. Needless suffering by children who feel abandoned by their fathers, mothers who need relief from the pressures of single parenting, and alienated fathers can be prevented by joint custody. Parents need not like each other to work together like business partners, keeping their children's interests foremost. Many ways of coparenting in two homes are possible.

Guidelines for Divorced Coparents

1. Put the best interests of your children above the temptation to punish your former spouse. Let fairness be your guide.
2. Refrain from criticizing your ex-spouse in front of your children—remember that half of their identity is shaped by that parent. Have realistic rather than idealistic expectations.

3. Relate to your ex-spouse as a business partner—be on time for meetings, follow through with agreements, and be polite. Give praise when it is due to encourage desirable behavior (behavior modification principles work on adults, too).
4. Make specific written agreements for financial arrangements and for difficult situations such as where the children will be on holidays and birthdays.
5. Keep your ex-spouse informed about the children's activities.
6. Have on hand the name of an effective family counselor who can serve as a mediator in case of a dispute between you and your ex-spouse.
7. Work with your ex-spouse and a counselor to cleanse the resentments and misunderstandings that accompanied your separation. Give your children the opportunity to participate in a group for children with divorced parents to help them overcome their negative feelings and understand the situation.
8. Consult with the other parent about important decisions such as religious upbringing, medical care, and schooling.
9. Have a specific schedule, known to all family members, about when the children are at their mother's home and when they are at their father's home.
10. Set up regular times to talk with the other parent about your children's progress and your parenting arrangement.
11. Listen to your children's concerns regularly, as in a weekly family meeting.

9

Stepparenting

If you view stepparenting as an adventure, it is going to be a lot different experience than a chore or a problem. Climbing a mountain can be a chore or a problem, but most people who are successful at it have an adventure.

— *Ken, stepfather of one*

Although I am not your mother, I made a choice to care about you.

— *Ann, mother of two and stepmother of four*

IN 1980 one in five families included a previously married spouse. Currently over 20 percent of children are part of a stepfamily.[1] Stepfamilies are one of the fastest growing family types; the divorce rate jumped 79 percent in the 1970s, leveled off in the 1980s, but remains high. Almost 40 percent of first marriages end in divorce, usually within seven years. Over a thousand new stepfamilies are formed every day due to the fact that 80 percent of divorced individuals remarry (83 percent of men, 75 percent of women), many within three years of their divorce. In trend-setting California, the number of first marriages and remarriages are about matched. Sixty percent of remarriages involve an adult with physical custody of a child.

How Stepfamilies Are Different from Intact Families

Despite stereotypes of wicked stepmothers, recent studies of stepchildren have not found major differences between children in stepfamilies or first-marriage families.[2] Relationships do not differ in terms of amount of family conflict in the various family types, for example. Most stepchildren reported liking their stepparents. In my survey at California State University, Chico, students were much more likely to state that having a stepparent added a new person to love and to learn from than that having a stepparent was a painful experience.[3]

Stepchildren who are not meshed in loyalty conflicts between their parents adapt best, as do spouses who do not feel pulled between children and mate. One survey of more than 100 teenagers in stepfamilies revealed that a major problem for children is one biological parent talking negatively about the other parent.[4] Children need frequent, tension-free contact with both parents.[5] In addition, having a stepfather is usually beneficial for boys, although girls may resent the attention that their mothers give to their new stepfathers.[6] Adolescents, especially boys, in single-mother families have more problems such as arrests and school discipline than boys who have another adult present in the home, according to a large national study.[7] However, the boys in stepfamilies were not better off than those in families with the mother as the only adult, an exception to the usual findings. A more recent in-depth study of 176 children concluded that stepchildren were "a little more stressed than children in traditional families . . . but, still pretty normal."[8] Despite the large numbers of stepfamilies, research about them is in its infancy and, as we have seen, sometimes contradictory.

Stepparents are of special interest in this book because they are more equal than couples in intact marriages in their division of family work, partly because stepfamily children are older. Eighty percent of the stepparents who filled out my written surveys performed equal amounts of family work, compared to 43 percent of first-marriage couples. Husbands in stepfamilies average 8.7 hours and wives 9.5 hours a week on housework; husbands average 13 hours and wives 24 hours a week on child care. Stepparents and their children were older than those in first marriages, resulting in less child care—a mean of 18 hours a week compared to 30 hours for all coparents surveyed.

The fact that both spouses were the single heads of households before their remarriage is an important influence on stepparents' family work. Barbara, a Wisconsin attorney, explained, "I was single for four years; the two boys and I shared and shared alike because we had to to survive. I was working, so my kids have been able to cook dinner and clean house since they were ten. I won't tolerate sexist roles." After divorce, most mothers—but only fathers who are custodial parents—become less traditional in their beliefs about gender equality.[9] A single father of two children explained, "I am not your classic male chauvinist pig, because I had to do it all by myself for a while."

Most parents including coparents seem to assume more responsibility for their own children in stepfamilies. A professor in Kansas finds that she does more of the work involving her daughter: "The kids want the original parent to do some of those things. My daughter's stepfather will drive her places or help her with something." In a Maryland family, Dave brought two boys into his second marriage, while his wife, Carol, had her first child with Dave. She ends up taking more responsibility for their daughter and he for the teenage boys because, she said, "She's my only biological child and Dave had already done it. He does more with our daughter than I probably do with the boys." The same thing is true for Randy, an attorney who married a woman with three children. He is very involved in his five-year-old son's care. He appreciates his closeness to his son, "as opposed to the mother being a parent and the father is just there," but does not feel very close to his stepchildren.

Some stepparents without their own children are more responsible for the care of their stepchildren than is the biological parent. Bob, a California biologist, spends more time taking care of his stepchildren than their mother does because he is home before she is and she often has to work in the evenings. The children's father feels that his daughter has Bob wrapped around her finger and that she manipulates him to get her way. Other stepfathers also mentioned doing more of the daily care because they were home more due to their work schedule or worked nearer to home. Practical considerations enter in the division of labor. Overall, however, it seems that parents do more with their own children.

Some parents try to blend their families and make no distinctions between his, hers, or ours. A San Francisco couple explain that they are "able to really care about the other person's kids. We didn't come into the situation looking out for one set above the others in anything. In the beginning we probably bent over backwards to reassure the other set that they're going to get fair treatment." A factor is that neither of the former spouses of this particular couple are around to interact with the children.

Couples often started out with an idealized vision of their second marriage. A South Dakota college administrator who had been a single parent since her son was nine months old had a "big fantasy" about a mother and a father in the same house. The reality of combining four children and dealing with new sets of grandparents and ex-spouses turned out to be much more complex than she or her husband imagined. Dave, in Maryland, wanted his second marriage to be "hunkey dory," fitting his "image about the way things were supposed to be that I was very possessive about and translated into controlling type of behavior," counterproductive to his marriage. He and Carol were at the point of divorce before he was able to let go of his image. Carol also had to let go of her ideas about the form that a happy family would take and be realistic about "the mode that worked with that particular family configuration." Clark, the father of two children who live with him and his partner, concluded that he has to "let go of the stuff I grew up with. These kids are turning out all right. It's just a different set-up."

Typically, the stepfamily is assumed to be like an intact family and its unique characteristics ignored. In television shows such as "The Brady Bunch" and "Eight Is Enough" conflicts are resolved easily. Greeting cards ignore stepfamily relationships, although one small company, called Stepfolk Cards, began business in New Jersey in 1983. Schools' disregard for stepfamilies often creates difficulties, such as when only two tickets per student are available for a graduation ceremony. A stepmother in South Dakota related an incident on Mother's Day when each school child planted a flower to give to his or her mother. Their daughter was unsure whether the one flower should go to the stepmother with whom the child lived or to the biological mother. Legal rights of stepparents are usually nil; California is an exception with a 1984 law giving stepparents and grandparents visitation rights after divorce.

Therapists who work with stepfamilies report that illusions of instant love and of being like intact families are major causes of difficulties. Emily Visher, a therapist and coauthor with psychiatrist John Visher of several books about stepfamilies, explained as an analogy that if you expect to get a horse and get a zebra, you will be disappointed, but if you expect a zebra, you can be pleased when you get one.[10] Parents who remarry should know in advance that a stepfamily is not like a biological family. Neal, in South Dakota, warns, "You are not going to recreate the nuclear family. Don't assume you are going to be one little happy family." Neal's parents created disharmony in his family by giving a dollar each to his stepchildren and ten dollars to their grandchildren. His wife's parents went overboard the other way, being so "gush, gush" to the stepgrandchildren that Carol's children felt ignored. Her mother did not know how to treat the new stepchildren and coped by feeding them quantities of food.

The complexity of merging ex-spouses, additional grandparents, other relatives, children, half-siblings, and parents at different stages creates a three-ring circus. The Vishers explain that stepfamilies do not have a family tree but rather a forest. Creating a new stepfamily has been likened to a corporate merger or an organ transplant. The stepfamily does not have a shared history, but instead has inherited different ideas and traditions about meals, holidays, discipline, religion and so forth. One California couple assumed, for example, that their attitudes toward their children's schoolwork were similar and did not require discussion before their marriage. They had a rough time dealing with the children when they discovered that he thought C grades were all right, but she "hit the wall" about them. When these minor but different habits are multiplied, much explanation, negotiation, and compromise is required.

In a first marriage it is difficult enough for two people to work out conflicting habits and expectations without interference from a prior spouse or sabotage from children who wish to reunite their parents. One stepfather immediately faced the resentment of his fourteen-year-old stepson: "I was coming in and replacing him as the man of the house. Since I was his second stepparent, I felt that I had a lot to overcome. I wasn't accepted very well." This example helps explain why the divorce rate is higher for stepparents then for first-marriage parents or second marriages without stepchildren. Somebody else always has a prior claim to your spouse or child, stepparents note. The Vishers point out that a stepfamily is based on loss, following a divorce or death of a spouse, with no honeymoon period without children. One mother explained that her four children experience normal problems between parents and teenagers, plus stepfamily problems, plus "a third layer to do with the fact that my husband's first wife had been ill for so long and she died relatively recently to the time we became official." Complexity increases when both stepparents are in joint custody situations. A mother explained, "Because of the joint custody, the previously married folks have regular contact with each other. Even in the best of second marriages, this may cause some competition between parents and stepparents to figure out who's in charge and how everybody feels about all that."

The role of a stepparent is at best unclear, and at worst tainted with images of wickedness and neglect. Lee, in Kansas, explained that he was raised in a very traditional farm family. He was not prepared for three stepchildren or for merging that family with the two new children he fathered. He noted that he lacks role models, training, and "anyone to talk to." Sybil, a Colorado mother, whose second husband, Gary, has no biological children of his own, feels, "It's too bad stepparents take such a bad rap. It's a negative term. You hear about abuse, but Gary has put so much thought into being a good parent."

An issue frequently raised by stepparents is being out of synchronization with children's development stages. A young woman living with a man with two "screaming maniacs" noted, "Now I know why God said you have nine months to get ready to have a kid—you need that time to build up patience." Another stepmother said that although she liked her stepsons, she was not at a stage in her career when she would have chosen to have children.

Stepparents find it easier to take on younger children, "so you can form them and work with them a little bit, rather than if they are already into their teens and semi-set," explained a stepfather of three children. Teenagers are notorious for their rebellion and pulling away from their parents, which is a major challenge for any parent, and more so for a stepparent. Sexuality can cause tension especially between stepfathers and adolescent stepdaughters and between teenage stepsiblings. Teenagers may also have a difficult time with the heightened sexual chemistry natural for newly married adults.

An Alabama stepmother's most important insight is to be aware of the characteristics of the stepchild's age group. Her natural reaction is to think that the little girl is behaving poorly because of the stepparent relationship, when in fact the behavior is characteristic of the child's particular age:

I'd think, "Oh, she's grumping and groaning because I'm her stepmother and she really resents me for telling her what to do." But then when I would talk to other people who had the same age children, they'd say, "Well, that's an eleven year old. My kids grump and groan, too," and I'd feel better.

She adds that it is easy to take the child's behavior as a personal rejection when you have not seen the child's personality develop.

A Wisconsin mother expected her sixteen-year-old stepson, David, to act like an adult because he was six years older than her oldest child. She did not remember what it was like to be sixteen, while she had seen her own children grow one year at a time and understood their capabilities. As a consequence she was harder on David than she was on her son when he became sixteen.

John, a father of grown children in Kansas, has been through child raising, and as a result is "a little tired of it and I don't have that much patience." Having raised older children, John relates, "Part of the friction between me and my stepdaughter is that I'm relying on old expectations that I remember from raising kids that don't apply now." His children were political activists and long-haired rebels, while his stepdaughter's generation is concerned with wearing fashionable clothes.

Therapists conclude that stepparents have an easier time if the families are younger, under thirteen for children and under forty for the stepmother.[11] Stepmothers have a more difficult time than stepfathers, especially with stepdaughters.[12] Stepmothers with no children of their own have an especially difficult time—they expect to be the family nurturer but feel left out of the established family. Stepfathers with no children have the greatest marital happiness, with no tug of allegiance or guilt about not spending enough time with their children.[13]

A different type of stepfamily, but one that experiences many of the same problems as the stepfamilies discussed thus far, is lesbian and gay couples with children. While the families I interviewed experienced many of the same issues as heterosexual stepfamilies, lesbian stepmothers were more accepting of their partners' giving children top priority. One woman said to her lover, "If your son needs your time, go give it to him. I may need it too, but don't feel I'm the first." Even lesbians who brought children into the world together, usually using artificial insemination, had to struggle against drifting into traditional parenting attitudes. The nonbiological mother tended to feel less responsible for the daily care, was a stricter disciplinarian, and viewed the biological mother as too permissive, similar to heterosexual stepparents. Overall, lesbians felt that they experienced more equality in homosexual than in previous heterosexual relationships. However, only 36 percent of the lesbian couples were within ten hours of each other on weekly housework and child care.

A problem for lesbians was a high separation rate, but studies have found that children of gays are not adversely affected in their development.[14] Children learn to be discriminating about how much information they reveal about their homosexual parent. Children of single mothers with no other adult in the family seem to have the most stress, compared to children in other family styles, indicating that shared parenting is desirable, no matter what the family style.

50-50 Stepmothers

Sandra, an Alabama stepmother, relates:

> *When you hear "stepmother," you think evil and wicked, because it's in the fairy tales, I guess. There's no such thing as a nice stepmother, so that was kind of hard. I felt I didn't have the right to tell my stepdaughter to make her bed and that kind of thing.*

What eventually made it easier was that her husband assured Sandra that she did have the right to discipline the child. Also, her stepdaughter is "a wonderful kid," although Sandra worries about her own future child not matching up. A Utah stepmother finds that she gets "written off as a wicked witch" when she tries to discipline her two stepsons. The image of the wicked stepmother is still very much alive. An eleven-year-old boy described his father's second wife to me as a "mean stepmother, who hasn't had kids in a long time." (The couple has since divorced.) A Kansas stepmother received a humorous note from her stepdaughter addressed to "Dear Wicked Stepmother."

The mother of four children observes that it is harder to be a stepmother than a stepfather and that she would not have married her husband if the four children were his rather than hers. When her husband's son came to live with them for several years, she became "the wicked stepmother" when she told him to wash his clothes and do dishes like the other children, or that he could not drink soda if there was not enough for all five children. "It's hard to swallow, like I failed," she says in retrospect.

One stepfather agrees that his wife had much more difficulty than he did because of her conflict with his oldest daughter, Sasha. Sasha had been the reigning woman of the household during her mother's long illness. She refused to talk seriously with her stepmother, who finally blew up, said she had had enough, and got results: "Sasha read the cards, changed as much as she had to and toned her actions down." Other stepmothers report competitiveness with the stepdaughter for the husband's attention. "You can't have my father," one stepdaughter stated, but got over most of her jealousy after about six months. Stepmothers and stepdaughters do not have a monopoly on conflict. The stepmother of Justin, a four-year-old boy, felt resentment from him too. Justin felt that she was an intruder and engaged in a tug of war with her for his father's attention.

Stepmothers may have more difficulty because their stepchildren are likely to come and go from their mother's home, while stepfathers usually have more consistent daily contact with their stepchildren and develop a routine. To cope with these adjustments and power struggles requires strength: "If you don't have a strong constitution, you can't do it," a stepmother concluded. Emily Visher asks, Who wants to be a replacement for somebody else? Stepmothers can emphasize their particular skills, abilities, and personalities without comparing themselves with the children's mother.

Stepmothers believe they are more objective with their stepchildren than biological parents are. A biological mother of two noted, "My frustrations run deeper because of the biological identity, they are an extension of myself. People judge them as if they are me." Stepmothers pointed out their husbands' ineffective behaviors, such as spoiling the children by giving them too much money, not giving them enough work around the house, or not insisting on better table manners. A father agreed that he tended to spoil his daughter, Lynn; "Mary gets more out of her," he noted. Another father reported that he gets his son "to do stuff by being gentle, sweet and kind while Claudia says that he should know what his responsibilities are and do them, period."

Barbara, the mother of four, explained, "The natural parent does tend to favor the natural child. It's there whether you like it or not, just like if you have four or five kids and there is one you like better than the others because he or she doesn't hassle you. It may not be nice, but it is honest." When stepparents bend over backwards to compensate for their favoritism, their own children feel resentful: "My kids felt their stepbrother could get away with more than they could because I was reticent about leaning on him since he wasn't mine," Barbara related. This is yet another lesson in the complexity of stepfamily interactions, although overall Barbara's children and stepson get along well together and adjusted quickly.

Other writers have mentioned that stepmothers feel martyred and resentful when they try to be supermothers to make up for the children's pain over a divorce or death of their mother.[15] Stepfathers do not generally feel this same responsibility to make everything all right for the child. However, none of the stepmothers I talked with expressed feelings of martyrdom, probably because their husbands do more of the family work than many husbands, and employment gives them successes to counterbalance frustrations with the stepchildren.

Stepmothers advised others to "go slowly" as relationships gain "a growing ease" with time. Emily and John Visher observe that it usually takes eighteen months to two years to settle in as a stepfamily, as children grow to like the stepparent and accept his or her authority. Conflict sometimes comes to a head between stepmothers and stepchildren and then the air clears. One stepmother told her stepson that she was not going to put up with his behavior anymore: "After that he was much nicer, I don't quite know why." Children's declarations such as "You're not my mother" and "You're not my boss" can be handled by having the biological parent affirm that the stepparent is to be obeyed, presenting a united front, and by affirming that the stepmother cares for the child. One stepmother said, "Although I am not your mother, I made a choice to care about you." She only had to repeat the statement twice before she got results. An Illinois stepmother coped by never trying to stand in for the mother, with whom her teenage stepchildren lived, but by trying to be their friend. She too has had "blowups, but they know where I stand. They respect me for it."

The stepmother's objectivity and conscious choice to love the child can create a special relationship. A Kansas stepmother finds that sometimes her stepdaughter will choose to talk to her about a problem first. Not having the same emotional involvement means that the stepmother can react with less egotism and without "feeling so much pain myself at times when my stepdaughter is feeling upset about something." Another stepmother loves to cook and knit and appreciates being able to do something for her young stepsons, who are "always receptive to what I cook."

A stepmother in California is overwhelmed by the noise and "static level" of having four teenagers around with their television and loud music and friends in and out. She feels that every time she starts something she is interrupted, while her husband thrives on the hubbub. She copes by insisting that she and her husband have time alone in their bedroom from 10:00 to 11:00 P.M. (a humorous sign on their door warns that only a bleeding child may knock). They also go out alone together once a week.

A stepmother must deal with networks of relationships composed of her stepchildren, their father, the stepchildren's mother, her own children, and their father. If the relationship between the father and his ex-wife is friendly that, too, can be a challenge for the new wife. For a Utah stepfamily, one problem is that the ex-spouse receives $650 a month in child support, plus medical insurance and money for piano lessons for the boys. The second wife resents that much outflow of their income. A Texas stepfamily where the two teenage boys live with their father, Rod, and his second wife, Margaret, report terrible relations with the boys' mother, Betty Sue. She tries to undermine the boys' choice to live with their father and to make them feel guilty and disloyal to her. The boys feel they are betraying their mother by liking Margaret and chose not to come to their father's wedding. Betty Sue blames Margaret for the breakup of her marriage, although Margaret did not even know Rod at that time. Another couple found out that the boys' mother had also told them that the divorce was their stepmother's fault. This was not true, but one of the sons believed his mother and rejected his stepmother for several years. Other couples mentioned boys' being very protective of their mothers: "Anything I can do she can do better," related a California stepmother.

Many families follow the rule of not criticizing the child's natural parent so as not to undermine the child's foundation. One couple discovered, however, that not discussing the biological mother's anger and temper tantrums made the boys "feel very much alone and kind of crazy, so now we don't pick on her, but encourage them to talk through what they're feeling."

Because of the struggles and challenge involved in being a stepparent, Emily Visher related that gestures such as an appreciative birthday card from a stepchild are a special thrill. She hears frequent reports that as stepchildren mature, their appreciation grows and so does personal satisfaction on the part of the stepparent who met the challenge of helping to raise a child through adolescence. Stepparents feel a deep sense of accomplishment more dramatic for having overcome the earlier tension.

50-50 Stepfathers

A stepfather, Ken, observed, "If you view it as an adventure, it is going to be a lot different experience than a chore or a problem. Climbing a mountain can be a chore and a problem, but most people who are successful at it have an adventure." He has also learned to give of himself rather than "just taking care of me," as he did before he became a stepparent.

One stepfather who is eighteen years older than his wife liked the idea of taking on young children because, he said, "Growing up with them, I would stay young and stay in contact and I wouldn't wither and wilt and mope. There is a challenge with children." A counselor who has no children of his own reports that he is enjoying his stepchildren much more than he thought he would. Stepfathers like being good friends with their stepchildren and enjoy activities such as teaching a sixth grader to be a cyclist and repair her own bike.

Warren describes his experiences living with an eleven-year-old girl and her mother:

> *Megan does not easily express feelings, so exploring the fragile balance between nurturance and discipline that would make that possible—and then dealing with the feelings we asked for . . . ah, so growthful!*

> *In turn, waking up in the morning to Megan playing "Silent Night" on the piano, hanging stockings over the fireplace, chasing each other with water pistols, watching her at bat at Bobby Sox, playing with "the parents" against Megan's soccer team, laughing over her imitations of me being affectionate with her mother—all these have contributed such joy (except, of course, when she took me by surprise with the water pistol!).*

Feeling close takes time; a man who recently moved in with his lover and her two children feels like an outsider. The children's mother explains that "from their point of view this is a family of three and he is an intruder." Her son will march into Jack's room and announce, "You are not my father," although Jack has more of a bond with the son than with the daughter, who is polite but distant. Other studies also report stepfathers feeling like outsiders in their own homes.[16] Studies have found stepfathers to be more pessimistic about the well-being of their families than either the mother or the stepchildren.[17] Perhaps this is because stepfathers are not usually living with their own children, or perhaps they find it harder to deal with complex emotional situations that are not easily resolved with rational thinking or authority. Lee, for example, feels frustrated "over things I had no control over," like the divisive effect of the children's natural father.

Being compared with the biological father is painful. In a Michigan family, the wife's children had a strict father, while her second husband, Roger, was much more lenient with his children. His stepson thought that Roger "wasn't doing his job because he wasn't coming down on them with harsh discipline." Counselors report that the greatest area of conflict for stepfathers is being viewed as either too remote or too dominant.[18] In comparison with biological fathers, however, some studies have found stepfathers to be more effective—in part because they are more self-critical about their parenting.[19] They are less threatened by misbehavior because their egos are not as involved, are more democratic in their treatment of sons, and are "more attentive to the needs of their children."

Some stepfathers find it difficult to be involved when the biological father is an excellent and frequent caretaker and is very involved in his children's lives. A Missouri physician says that he feels like a second-class father. His stepchildren are "very nice to me, but I don't fulfill the father's role because their own father is a super father. I'm sure I would get along a lot better with my stepchildren if their father was not so dominant in the picture." One stepfather whose stepchildren do not spend much time with their father, who lives in another state, believes that this makes it easier for him. Other stepparents find, however, that it is important for children to keep regular contact with the biological father to reduce the halo effect of absence. The stepfathers I talked with who were very close to stepchildren with involved fathers also frequently spend time with their children.

A teenage child can make life especially difficult for a stepfather. A Kansas father, Lee, faces a hostile fourteen-year-old stepdaughter. To make matters worse, her father is vengeful, ignores Lee, and tells his children "they do not have to mind me," Lee reported. Lee is tired of being put down by his stepdaughter, and said he feels like he has "been through a mine field, and had both my legs blown off" and is a failure as a stepparent. His wife is critical, telling him she wants him to be "a warmer, more giving parent." He feels blamed although his wife said she is not trying to blame him and feels frustrated by his perception. His only positive note is that his stepchildren take good care of their younger half-siblings, are close to them, and are available as babysitters. Lee's reaction is to concentrate on his own two children and be there when they need him. These kinds of loyalty struggles are frequent in stepfamilies.

Stepfathers may feel left out of the circle of mother and children. When his own children come to visit, a stepfather may be more lenient than he is with the stepchildren whom he sees daily, which sets up more difficulties. "I want them to feel they can come to me to be comforted," says a Utah father whose wife is upset about his failure to discipline his boys' unruly behavior. One way he compensates is taking his sons and stepdaughter off skiing or hiking to give his wife some peace. A Missouri father reports that he gets upset when his stepchildren's beds are not made or their clothes are scattered over their room, but when his son visited from another state he "would not jump on him." He also finds it difficult to spend money on his stepchildren while his own son is washing dishes to earn money.

In Washington, Geof, who had no children of his own when he met Nan, feels appreciative that she encouraged him when he felt uncomfortable, self-conscious, and like he was "butting in" on an established family. Nan comments, "I tried to leave it as open as possible for him to establish the relationship that he wanted. I don't think I expected anything in particular. That really worked." As a result, Geof feels like "the kids' father because I was given the freedom to choose that. We got rid of the expectation right away that I was going to *have* to be their father."

Like stepmothers, stepfathers find themselves being stricter disciplinarians than the original parent and less vulnerable to guilt manipulation by clever children. Stepfathers also mentioned children testing their authority. One five-year-old was "trying to find out whether she could push my button, poke me, move me around in a flat battle of wills. She would pick one subject and jump to the next when that didn't work," her stepfather, Ken, related. In one particular incident, he held firm and finally she gave up, cried, and wanted to be picked up and held by him. Since that contest of wills she will test him once in a while but has generally accepted his authority, and they have become good friends. He also changed his attitude from putting up with her to recognizing a lifelong bond with her. He felt very gratified when the "little pixie" (at other times called a tasmanian devil) climbed on his lap, said she wanted to look at him, kissed him on the nose, and said what a nice family they have. Without previous experience with children, Ken said, being a stepfather is "a hell of a learning experience."

An Iowa father finds that sometimes when he disciplines his stepdaughter his wife interferes to side with the girl. They are aware of the power struggles in their triangle and are working on them. Some recent stepfathers feel they are walking on eggshells with their new stepchildren and are afraid of being thought overbearing or an unfair ogre if they try to correct the children. The stepfather of three teenagers in Colorado said he "took it real easy," trying to let them set the pace of their relationship. Counselors advise that the stepparent establish a friendship bond with the stepchildren before trying to give them much direction. Discipline is not effective if the child has no desire to please, an important principle for stepfathers to remember. A frequent error is for a stepfather to try to shape up the family too quickly; he should limit himself to working on less than five changes at a time. Positive reinforcement of good behavior works better than criticism. A stepparent also needs to let the children know what disturbs him, using "I" rather than blaming "you" messages.

Since one California stepfather works close to home and his wife has a long drive to work, he has become "the mother-father figure." He was the parent called when his sixteen-year-old stepdaughter was raped. He handled the situation well and was with her during the trial that followed. His wife commented, "It cemented a bond between them and he has become her father." In a dispute with a twenty-three-year-old son who had gotten into debt, another stepfather "was much more understanding, kinder about the whole thing and much more rational than I was," observed his wife. Clearly, spending time with a child is required before trust and caring develop, as in any friendship.

Coparented Stepchildren

Stepchildren gain from the skills, knowledge, interests, and attention of another close adult. A Missouri mother told her second husband, "There are things that the children can learn from you that they will never learn from their father because he has a different personality. You are very open about hugging and kissing and sex, in contrast to our very reserved families."

What children like most and find the easiest adjustment is having other children as stepsiblings. In one family that joined four children, the two boys were already best friends at elementary school and were excited about living together. The children were more concerned about getting along with each other than about their new stepparent. They regarded their families as having joined in "our marriage," not just the adults' marriage. The children were like the Brady Bunch for about two months, until they started getting on each others' nerves. Sharing a room at home and being in the same class at school was too much for the boys, and a new room in the garage had to be built for one of them. The oldest girl, age twelve, tried to boss the younger children until her parents told her that it was not her job to take care of the others. As her stepmother explained, the girl was reacting territorially to an invasion by three new people.

In a Missouri home, two teenage stepsisters sometimes stay up "until three in the morning and giggle." The younger one, who cannot drive, appreciates going places with her older stepsister. Two elementary school–age brothers and a stepsister in Utah are referred to as the three musketeers: The worst punishment for them is to separate them. However, the boys are resentful that Tonia has more possessions than they do because her grandmother sends her money. Her mother worries about Tonia's feeling that she is responsible for the boys' behavior. Tonia sits between them in the car, intercepting their aggressive moves, and apologizes for them on Sunday night after a rambunctious weekend stay. She also defends her mother if the boys say something negative about her and tries to please her stepfather. "I worry about the stress it places on Tonia. I told her she didn't own that responsibility," her mother related.

Stepchildren may change each other's birth order in the blended family. Children who were the youngest appreciate having a toddler to look up to them, but also must adjust to becoming a middle child. One such child has had "some trouble finding where she's at," her stepmother reported. The younger of two brothers finds it difficult to have an older brother who is a star achiever and a younger half-sister who is doted on. As a consequence he retreated emotionally for some time. Logan, a five-year-old with three teenage half-siblings, at times feels that he is at the low end of the totem pole and has many people giving him directions. On the other hand, the older children are also willing to entertain and talk with him. His father observes that as a consequence Logan is ahead of his age in intellectual and social development and has skipped a grade in school.

A new baby can tie the stepfamily together because everyone is related to her or him and shares a common history. Logan was born at home, in Colorado, with his half-siblings attending the birth. His mother thinks that the older children have learned useful skills from babysitting and playing with Logan, have gained patience and responsibility, and have learned about a child's stages of development.

One of the most difficult issues for stepchildren is loyalty conflicts. Some feel guilty if they start to get close to their stepparent and then create a conflict to pull away. Children feel freer to like their stepparent and adjust to having two homes if their parents refrain from fighting with each other. One activity to bond stepchildren and stepparent is for stepchildren to make a history book to illustrate their years before they met their stepparent. A useful workbook for stepchildren is *What's Special About Our Stepfamily?* by Mala Schuster Burt and Roger B. Burt.

Holidays are another charged area for stepchildren. A Jewish family found that the children were very sensitive about whose menorah was going to be used in the Chanukah celebration, as well as about whose silverware was used at dinner. Their solution was simply to use both. Christmas is a nightmare for another family, since four sets of grandparents want to see them: They "run around like fools, two hours here and two hours there." Some families are able to join all grandparents by going to church on Christmas Eve, or celebrating children's birthdays, graduations, and family reunions together.

Children in stepfamilies can learn from other family traditions, creating an enriched extended family. They gain a caring adult to talk with about problems that may be too emotionally charged for a parent and siblings. They may see the dynamics of a more egalitarian and successful marriage than that of their biological parents. They can gain understanding of how relationships work because of the complexities that bring differences and misunderstandings to the surface where they must be explored. Growing up in a stepfamily is a course in diplomacy, reported Emily Visher. If the family seeks counseling, children learn communication skills, negotiating, and problem solving from a professional. Visher observed that even when stepchildren have a rocky relationship with their stepparent, they grow up to appreciate her or him.

Counselors Ed and Marilyn Winter-Tamkin offer the following suggestions for working with children in a stepfamily:[20]

1. Emphasize that it takes time to feel comfortable in a stepfamily.
2. Listen to children's concerns and make sure you understand them correctly. Hold family meetings.
3. Encourage a strong bond with the other biological parent.
4. Frequently use praise and rewards.
5. Demonstrate support for the spouse in front of the children.

The Coparent Relationship

Surveys of second marriages usually find that stepchildren are the number one source of difficulty (followed by the prior spouse, money, and power struggles).[21] Author Elizabeth Einstein reports that most of the stepchildren she interviewed were aware that they were the center of battles.[22] In her own stepfamily, she writes, "soon the kids were in control, manipulating us through guilt, jealousy, and triangles." A California couple relate, "There have been times when divorce has reared its ugly head because of the children," especially their irritating fourteen-year-old girl who will not follow rules. Some parents feel protective of their children when the stepparent disciplines them: One stepfather thinks to himself, "How dare you say my kid is lazy." This loyalty conflict puts a strain on his intimacy with his wife. In the face of such difficulties in their second marriage, spouses may blame themselves instead of acknowledging the built-in complexities. A large study of 360 remarried couples concluded that the presence of children did not have as significant an impact on the second marriage as how frequently couples felt they agreed on family issues.[23]

Children can take advantage of hostility between parents: Julio and Caryl realized that "the kids started to play off the two of us." Their junior high–age son's emotional well-being was at stake, so all three parents went to Diane's (the biological mother's) counselor. Eventually they were able to do activities together with the children, like go out for pizza to talk together, so that the children could not manipulate them through lack of information. They learned to say what was bothering them and to listen carefully to the other parent in return. It took several years of hard work, but they became "really good friends." The stepson finally accepted that Caryl was not trying to usurp his mother's place.

Some couples reported that their children tried to "do a job" on their marriage so as to get their original parents back together. Two Utah boys told their stepsister that her mother, Donna, was mean and that they hoped the adults would keep on fighting so that their father, Jerry, would remarry their mother. While Donna and Jerry were dating, one of the boys told the other, "Don't worry about her, she'll go too," like the last two women their father had dated. Couples who stay together must act firmly, not allowing children to manipulate them through guilt or fear of losing their love or getting sucked into competition over which parent is loved the most. Hope is offered by a study that reported a higher level of marital satisfaction among 369 remarried individuals than couples in first marriages.[24] Some children work to preserve the second marriage, "put effort into making things nice," because they do not want to go through another divorce. One child may take the lead in urging the others to accept the new stepparent.

Stepparents often find themselves in triangles with their stepchildren, competing for attention and feeling left out. The stepmother of Simon, age thirteen, feels out of place at baseball games when the boy is sitting between them discussing game statistics with his father. If they go someplace like the beach, Simon feels left out because, his stepmother said, "we are still in that newlywed stage of coupledom." Couples often report that their children plant themselves in the middle when they try to hug and kiss. A stepfather explains, "We triangulate on Aletha and each of us is making demands on her. We are more concerned about our relationship to Aletha than with each other." Many would agree with the assessment of the Utah couple that they do much better when the children are at their other parent's home. When the child is away for a week at a time, the couple may find they fall into a comfortable schedule and then "it's an effort to fit her into the routine."

Parents emphasize that it is imperative that "you love each other and back each other or they can tear you apart," as an Illinois couple, Don and Ann, explained. The married couple needs to define "where you're coming from and then the children know." New Mexico stepparents of five children made a commitment early in their marriage to give the couple relationship priority; otherwise, the children "could have destroyed us." They realized that their teenagers would leave home soon. "Few relationships can withstand the bombardment that adults in a stepfamily are subject to unless there is also constant nurturance," concluded Elizabeth Einstein.[25] Couples find that time eases much of the strain and that they forge a close relationship through handling difficult situations together.

Couples state that it is important to discuss child-rearing beliefs before marriage. Topics to discuss include discipline, religious upbringing, finances, manners, chores, acceptable grades, curfew, use of the telephone and car, television, teenage drinking, smoking, and sex. Ann explains, "If you haven't really looked at it, it can come as a real big blow, and you may suddenly find yourself with a family that's going every which way." The Stepfamily Foundation in New York City suggests that couples formulate written job descriptions and financial agreements before they marry.[26]

Suggestions for New Stepfamilies

One mother, Rosie, offers three crucial suggestions for blending families based on her experience. The first is, if possible, move into a different house so that one group does not feel invaded. If it is not possible to move, do major rearranging to suit the new group's tastes and needs. She suggests that if the children are over eight they need separate spaces, even if it means partitioning rooms into very small units. She also suggests getting rid of a rectangular dinner table and replacing it with a round one. This seems like a minor detail, she notes, but it makes a major difference in their family gatherings. She warns that the new family should not feel that all problems can be solved quickly and children should know that it will take time. She observes that there is unspoken understanding between biological families, and much more effort is required to talk about how the new family thinks. Many families use weekly meetings as their forum.

Some stepfamilies found that going to a counselor helped them understand each other. A Michigan stepmother learned from a counselor not to try to be a parent to an older teenager and to shut the door on the messy bedroom that bothered her. The stepmother has reservations about this tactic, though, feeling it put her husband in the middle of interactions with her stepson. A New Mexico couple was having trouble with their teenage son but found out that his counselor believed the boy's lies. It would have been better for the family as a whole to have gone to one counselor. They decided to establish clear ground rules that the teenager must abide by if he was to live with them. He did not and went to live with his mother.

A counselor helped another family "really level with each other." She would stop a person who was angrily condemning another, and ask that blaming "you" messages (as in "You are a slob") be replaced with "I feel" and specific requests for what the other person could do differently. An example is, "I feel terrible when our room looks like a hurricane hit. Can you help me clean it up before we go to bed each evening?" The counselor would ask, "What specifically do you want changed in your brother's behavior?" then ask the brother to respond and negotiate a contract about changes that could be made. Feelings cannot be changed quickly, but behavior can be changed. Some counselors who are not trained to work with stepfamilies try to push them to bond more quickly than is possible, but an experienced counselor can help a stepfamily objectively understand its complexities.[27]

The Vishers warn stepparents not to permit children to play one household off against the other or use children as messengers between households. If the adults cannot talk to each other, they need a counselor or mediator. Boundaries need to be established between households and former spouses, for example, by limiting contacts with former spouses, or picking up children at school rather than at the former spouse's home.

Stepparent organizations provide information about support groups for parents and teenagers, counseling, and bibliographies. The Stepfamily Association of America was formed in 1979 by Emily and John Visher, with sixty-three chapters in twenty-eight states by 1986. Local chapters have monthly meetings with guest speakers and organize support groups for couples and for teenagers. National conferences for stepfamilies are held each year. Their newsletter is called the *Stepfamily Bulletin*. (Their address is 602 East Joppa Road, Baltimore, Maryland, 21204.) The Stepfamily Foundation was organized in 1975, with Jeannette Lofas as director. It provides information, support groups for stepfamilies, training for professionals, and telephone counseling. (The address of the Stepfamily Foundation is 333 West End Avenue, New York, New York, 10023.) Another newsletter for stepfamilies is *Stepfamilies and Beyond* (8716 Pine Avenue, Gary, Indiana, 46403). It includes short articles, letters from readers, and resources.

Stepfamilies had the most difficulty of any of the six family types I interviewed. Many couples expressed pain over their conflicts about how to discipline the children without alienating each other. Solving problems can lead to growth and to appreciation for the companions who "climbed the mountain together." The key is to keep the couple bond strong and nourished and to seek help in understanding the stepfamily from counselors, stepparent groups, and books. The complexities are too overwhelming and too different from those of intact families to tackle without support and understanding. Stepparents need the techniques of 50-50 parenting—the structuring of tasks, the democratic procedures, and the equal involvement of both parents—to cope with the difficulties of combining two families.

Guidelines for Stepparents

1. Include children in planning and participating in the marriage ceremony.
2. Be informed about the ways a stepfamily is different from a first marriage, since unrealistic expectations cause disappointment and inflexibility. Read books and participate in stepfamily groups. Subscribe to a stepfamily newsletter.
3. As soon as possible, talk about division of labor and finances, how you will handle child discipline, and so on, so that you have a plan for coping with daily issues. Schedule regular times to revise your game plan to meet changing circumstances. Think of it like fighting a war, with an arsenal of offensive strategies for various possibilities rather than defensive reactions to each skirmish.
4. Inform each other about your previous family history and traditions, as if you were two foreign cultures learning to conduct diplomatic relations. For example, discuss holiday and birthday celebrations and work out in advance how various customs can be combined.
5. Encourage the children's biological parent to be regularly involved in child rearing.
6. Stepfamily relationships can be so complex that spending some time with a family therapist may be useful in learning how to relate to ex-spouses and many sets of grandparents, new birth orders for stepchildren, disciplining a stepchild, and sexual feelings between nonbiologically related family members.
7. Schedule weekly family meetings to talk about the previous week. Rotate leadership of the meeting among all family members.

8. Create an individual space for each family member, in your home, even if it is very small.
9. Talk with grandparents about how you would like them to treat step-grandchildren.
10. Encourage schools to acknowledge the role of stepparents, as in inviting them to graduations and similar events.

10

Communal Parenting

> The nuclear family is too isolated and the housework has to be split between two people. It's a terrific advantage to have [the] housework rotated among more adults and have the sociability of other adults around.
>
> — *Louise, mother of one living in an urban group house*

> I would be scared if I was going to become a father on the outside. The nuclear family is too much pressure; it's hard not to spank if you're with a kid all day with no support. Here, the children are not dependent on one or two people.
>
> — *Gene, prospective father and child care giver, living in a rural commune*

WORKING parents often feel that they have too many demands on their time. In many other societies, parents live in extended families with other caring adults who help rear the children. Gree, a member of a group house and a father, explains, "Shared parenting with people other than the parents is a return to our history of extended families and tribes when the boundaries of family were not so narrow." To recreate this old and widespread family form, some groups form an intentional extended family. Various families choose to live together in a large house, a small apartment complex, or several adjacent houses. This chapter describes groups ranging from two couples and their children living in one house to over sixty people living at the Twin Oaks Community in Virginia, where the Federation of Egalitarian Communities was founded. I interviewed parents who live in collective houses in Providence, Philadelphia, Baltimore, St. Paul, Boulder, Seattle, Spokane, Berkeley, San Francisco, and small towns in Virginia, Missouri, and California as well as each group in the Federation of Egalitarian Communities.

Parents mentioned the following advantages of collective living: (1) child care backup, (2) companions for only children, (3) less housework, (4) other adults to talk with and learn from, (5) a variety of parenting techniques nearby to observe, and (6) the fun of sharing meals, holidays, and other rituals. Parents mentioned as disadvantages conflicts over housekeeping—usually about kitchen neatness, children disrupting dinner conversations, and being different from others. Families can duplicate with their friends and neighbors some of the cooperative techniques described here without actually living in one space.

Collective Houses

The Providence group, mostly academics, has lived in a three-story, eighteen-room duplex since 1973. On each side of the house a couple and their child live on the second floor, and two single adults live on the third floor. The first floor is common space. The couples are the stable members of the group, while the single people are usually graduate students who eventually leave the area. The children are a boy, age four, and a girl, age three and a half. The adults sign up weekly to cook dinner and clean up afterwards. If more than four people are going to be gone on a certain day, that meal is not assigned and the people at home eat leftovers. No one cooks more than once a week, so each one can put his or her best efforts into the preparation.

The group divides house cleaning chores into four sets rotated among the adults: vacuuming the living room, cleaning the kitchen floor, cleaning the kitchen other than the floor, and cleaning the bathroom. Grocery shopping is also rotated. Sometimes people are late in doing their task, but generally all do their share.

Louise, one of the mothers, commented,

> *I don't like living in a nuclear family because it's too isolated and the housework has to be split between two people; you are always*

> *doing the vacuuming, or the dishes or having to do a meal. It is a terrific advantage to have that sort of housework rotated among more adults, and have the sociability of other adults around.*

Child care is mainly the responsibility of the parents, who hire a babysitter if they go out, but the other adults assist the babysitter and help out sometimes. Wally, a single man, has become the four-year-old boy's best friend, playing music with him and helping him with crafts. The parents sometimes take turns caring for the children on weekends, and either couple will take over when necessary. For example, while one couple was packing for a trip, the father next door took both children to the park. The children are also in the same day-care center three afternoons a week and their parents share those transportation duties. The children are very close, like brother and sister. The main impact of living in the collective house is having a close companion for each child and for adults too. Peter explained, "When I am there alone with my son, I am not in fact alone with him. There is some other adult around to talk to, and that makes a big difference. It also means there is usually somebody else cooking dinner."

One issue that arises about sharing space in the Providence group is that children disrupt mealtime: "You end up having a conversation focused on the kids, and everybody else gets sucked into it and you can't carry on a normal conversation over these shrieking kids," Louise observed. Having two children does mean that sometimes they will go off and play together; then "you get some calm and quiet so you can have a conversation." Some disagreements arise over discipline. One of the roommates feels that Peter and Louise are too lax with their son, as is common for group members who are not the child's parents. House meetings and "side meetings" are held monthly to discuss issues that arise from sharing child care and housework, the impact of guests on the common space, and so on.

In a Philadelphia group, six adults and two children have lived together since 1979. Their expenses are only $200 a month per adult. Living collectively permits Rosie to pursue her career as an opera singer, since she and Jonathan could not have afforded all the child care needed when she attends her frequent rehearsals. In terms of the effect of collective living on the couple relationship, Jonathan explained, "I used to be really cynical. They put pressure on me to open up emotionally. Opening is painful; I was raised to be a macho person. Only in the past six months or so have I really been making changes." Rosie agrees that the house is good for them. Before, Jonathan was more dependent on her since he did not have close friends. Also, if they need to talk together in their bedroom, other people will watch the children. (Similar advantages are described in *An Urban Commune* about an earlier Philadelphia commune.)[1]

In the Philadelphia house, personal dynamics are discussed in meetings that operate by consensus, following "feminist rules," so that a few people do not dominate conversations and each person takes a turn at facilitating a meeting. Ken explained that their goal is growth through sharing feelings and "bouncing off each other." The group has experimented with ways to express feelings other than by talking, such as by singing, role playing, and new games. House members gain perspective by living with more than one other adult.

A rural group that has lived together in two farmhouses in Virginia since 1972 is the most collective small group I talked with, in that the members pool their earnings. Three of the six adults work outside the home (two of those three are women) and the others do more of the house and farm work. The five children range in age from six to nineteen. One woman, Evelyn, explained that she lived collectively because she wanted to continue her work as a college teacher but did not want to put her children in day-care centers. She liked the fact that some of the adults were home most of the time. Her husband, Andy, used to work in the bureaucracy in Washington, D.C., but wanted to change to country living in a nonsexist environment, and to have more sharing and closeness with a group. The group eats all their meals together and conducted their own school for the children for seven years, so the closeness that Andy sought is realized.

To keep the community wheels greased, the group holds meetings twice a week to deal with emotional issues as well as housekeeping. They also plan a weekend each year to bring in an outside therapist to work with them in an encounter group format. Initially, power issues were important in the group's dynamics. "There were a lot of males fighting for power," Andy explained. "I had a really hard time giving up having things my own way—I still do sometimes. It was just easier ultimately, to let other people make the decisions in some areas as long as I could contribute in areas where I felt competent."

Evelyn and Andy appreciate being able to go out and leave the children with trusted friends and having help with chores and transporting the children. The adult with kitchen duty in the morning or afternoon also takes care of the children. Experienced parents are available with suggestions when others have problems with the children. Evelyn states, "I've often gone to one or the other woman who has older children and they have been very helpful, letting me know this too will pass." Being in a fishbowl with other adults observing your child rearing can be uncomfortable, but it keeps you from child abuse, Evelyn and Andy reported.

Merry, a twelve-year-old girl, has lived in the Virginia community since she was two. Recently she began going to school in the city, living with her father. Merry is not sure if she would want to bring up her children in a commune, but overall has high praise for the group. She likes having many people around, recalling that there was always someone to put her in bed at night when she was young. She had more freedom because "it's not like if your parents are out you can't go anywhere because you have to ask your parents. You just have to notify someone." A group of kids around is fun, she reports—for having squirt gun fights, going camping, or putting on plays for the grownups. "We all learned to share a whole lot. We all loved each other," she said.

For Merry, the difficult part about the group was getting attached to someone and then having them leave: "You want something that will always be there, that you can trust." Merry reports that the other girl near her age in the commune is ashamed to tell her friends about the unusual place where she lives and is embarrassed to invite her friends over, which is one of the reasons her family is leaving the farm.

Jeannie, fourteen, grew up in a group in Boulder, Colorado. I was impressed with her self-confidence, ease of expression, and brightness. Her parents, her older brother, and a single man share her house. Her uncle and his wife and their son, age twelve, live next door. Each adult in the group has assigned child care hours, including transportation. Each cooks once a week and has a permanent task such as food shopping or keeping the books.

Jeannie likes the attention she gets from the various adults, but feels outnumbered by them sometimes. An extended family is "a different experience because you are around so many people." She is not at all bothered by living in a different situation than her friends, saying that she learns about sharing and leadership. She also likes having a friend close to her age, "somebody to take on and get in fights with." She feels that the children are listened to seriously if they attend the Monday night meetings when an important decision is being made, such as accepting a new member or deciding how they are going to celebrate holidays. However, the children do not usually attend meetings. It would depend on the situation whether she would want to live collectively as an adult, she concluded.

In a Berkeley group sharing an apartment complex, parents are responsible for their own children. One father, Duby, sees "an unwillingness to share parenting," except for an exchange between the parents of each of the two boys. His partner, Ruth, feels that the difficulty centers around people not staying long enough in the community to really get to know the children:

> *If they don't genuinely love and understand the child, shared parenting doesn't work. Children are creatures from outer space, different from adults. It's very hard for adults to remember what it was like when they were that age. It takes a long time for you to really understand the way they function and think.*

Ruth points out that the other adults do occasionally take care of the children. For example, while I interviewed her, one of the men was going to take the boys to the movies. The result, Ruth feels, is that her son has matured more quickly, his vocabulary is much larger, his communication is better, and he expresses his emotions very easily compared to children raised in nuclear families. Sometimes David wishes they were not different from his friends' families, but Ruth thinks that in a nuclear family he would miss the stimulation of the other child and adults. David agrees that it is fun: "It is not like being alone with just your mother and father. You have kids to play with and a big space to jump around in." He likes the fact that he can participate in house meetings, such as when he complained that the children were being left out of activities. The outcome was that he selected the job of dumping the garbage. He would like to start a community of his own when he grows up.

In a Washington group, two married couples in their thirties, Carol and Steve, and Gail and Dan, share a house. They explained that collective houses are common in Seattle because there are more houses than apartments there. "We're good friends and we've enjoyed each other and we've shared a lot, but we don't feel married to each other," Carol observed. One couple has a fifteen-month-old boy and the other has an eleven-month-old girl. The adults are social workers and therapists.

Conflicts in this house tend to be worked out in the couples rather than among the group. Steve explains, "If I was irritated with anybody in the house, I would take it out on Carol. I think we've gotten somewhat better at that. I think we need to be better at resolving conflicts cross-couple. That does seem like the toughest thing." The couple relationship can be helped, though, when someone points out "a foolish dopey argument." These parents mainly care for their own children, but they spell each other briefly to take showers or run errands. Carol is surprised at how little they have used each other for "major breaks; we say we ought to make a regular deal of it and we don't." The main advantage of sharing the house is that "nobody felt that kind of terrible isolation that others talk about" after having a baby. Parents also like the close relationship forming between the two children, especially the balance between a boy and a girl so close in age. The children are comfortable and outgoing with different people.

"I think some of the rigid family patterns that produce some of the more negative aspects of parent-child relationships can be tempered by having more options available," Steve notes. Other people in the house act as safety valves to tone down the intensity of an angry parent. They also serve as safety valves for the children. After a conflict, the little boy goes to the other couple for a while and then comes back: "That contact seems to be really valuable," Carol said.

Most members of collective houses stressed the joys of having other adults around to talk with and provide short-term child care. However, stress can occur when families join together, as illustrated by a group in a small rural northern California town, where two couples are buying a four-bedroom house together. Margaret and Pete have a baby girl, and Joan and Dave have a son, Hank, age five. The complication is Joan's daughter from her first marriage. Joan explained that Carla had made up her mind not to like their living situation before they moved in with the other family in 1979. Carla was twelve when she left the group in 1983 to live with her father and brother in the more urban university town nearby. Pete stated frankly, "Carla left because of me and Meg. She created a lot of tension. I was ready to kill her or leave. She wouldn't take discipline from anybody but her mother." Margaret said she never felt at ease when Carla was living there, since Carla treated them as trespassers. The teenager likes them much better now that she is not living with them. They have found it much easier to adjust to Hank's presence. They were present at his birth, and Hank thinks of them as part of his family and calls their baby his sister.

Pete likes learning from his roommates, saying that they "are very good at dealing with stuff in a way that's not oppressive. It's rubbed off." In turn, they appreciate his and Margaret's verbal skills. All agree that it is good for the children to have access to different personality styles. The families have fun together; for example, Dave cooks a ritual Sunday morning breakfast to which their friends have an open invitation. At Christmas all the children and Dave and Joan's ex-spouses help light candles and open gifts. Margaret and Pete organize another major celebration at Passover. (They have recently moved out to have more physical space.)

Collective groups across the country face very similar issues. Biological parents do most of the child care, without much exchange between couples. The weight of tradition is so strong that it is difficult to expand the mother/father/child unit. The exceptions are characterized by what Ruth in Berkeley pointed out—a sense of permanent attachment to the child. Including child care as part of house duties helps involve nonparents.

A perspective common to coparents living in groups is that the nuclear family is lonely and isolated, without resources for understanding child rearing or gaining insight from more experienced parents. The extended family gives those resources to its members. Parents put the emotional contact with other adults on the top of the list of advantages of communal living, along with the practical benefits of less housework and saving money.

A San Francisco group called the Kerista Commune have found out some interesting factors about child rearing in conditions not duplicated elsewhere. In this group, seventeen adults and two children live in two flats and an apartment and use a store front for meetings and public events. No one has his or her own particular room. The group was founded in 1971 by Jud and Eve. Most of the members I met seemed to be in their twenties or thirties, with the exception of Jud, who is older. Jud's age causes some issues of "agism," "founderism," and "what is truly shared leadership?" to emerge.

The group's goal is to "create a model of culture" that can be replicated. Members believe that their intentional tribal life of best friends is a futuristic utopian experiment. The model includes "polyfidelity," which can be called group marriage but which they refer to as a B-FIC—Best Friend Identity Cluster. One B-FIC is called the Purple Submarine and is composed of nine women and five men who are faithful to each other, including a structured, heterosexual sleeping schedule based on the order in which people came into the group. Tye, a young woman I interviewed, understood that "it might be hard for you to imagine being in love with more than one person." Members of Purple Submarine believe that "intelligence is the ultimate aphrodisiac." The other B-FIC, called the Crystal Vision, is composed of two men and one woman who brought her two children into the group with her. These groups may change at will; Purple Submarine was joined by Sanity Mix and Hearthside as of 1986.

Keristans share their incomes: Earnings over $600 a month go to the group, which votes on expenditures. Some of the members work on group publishing efforts, including periodicals, *The Utopian Classroom*[2] and *The Node*. Others work in their house-cleaning and gardening collectives. Keristans share clothes—two rooms, for example, have women's clothes for members to choose from. Cooking is taken on by whomever is inspired. If no one feels like it, everyone cooks for themselves. Chores are frequently done in "bees" (like quilting bees) to clean the houses.

Psychological work is done continually through a process called "Gestalt-O-Rama," where emotions arising from past "inegalitarian conditioning" are confronted: "We have found that if you talk about your frustrations and concerns as soon as they come up, then they don't blow up," Tye explained. In addition to their formulation of emotional processes, group members have designed their own religious iconography. Their deities, such as Sister Kerista, who is black, represent different ethnic groups and qualities. The deities are not only symbolic but are consulted for their opinions on an alphabet board similar to a Ouija board that spells out responses to questions.

The Keristans have two little girls who were born into the community and are raised by multiple parents, referred to as playmates. The adults initially attempted to raise the children in a completely egalitarian nonsexist environment, thinking that the transfer of neurosis from parent to child could be prevented and that their children could grow up neurosis-free. The girls did not watch television, except for edited portions of "Sesame Street" spliced with pictures of the Islanders added for fun, or go to preschool or child care, but had classes at home. When a single mother, Isa, joined the group, her two children (ages seven and nine) from "the other culture" were not permitted to associate closely with the Keristan girls (ages two and three).

The Keristans discovered that they were naive and unrealistic in their notions of childhood innocence. Despite their carefully shaped rational environment, the girls behaved much like other children, fighting with each other, crying and having "fits," and exhibiting other "creepy" behavior. Now the girls attend nursery school, watch unedited television, and share the apartment with the two older children.

The group has identified unconscious "voices of perversity," or subpersonalities, in all people that can be irrational and cause NEMs—non-violent episodic malfunctions. A NEM is identified as having a beginning, a middle, and an end, so discussion should be delayed until the NEM is over and rationality returns. The children are able to identify with these concepts. They remark, "Oh, my NEM wasn't as long as it was last week." Revery calls her negative subpersonality Creepy Jeanne and talks about how she makes deals with her not to get out of the cage and disrupt things. The girls also confront each other and the adults about negative behavior. The girls are described by Tye as very verbal, outgoing, confident, and able to do abstract thinking beyond most children their age. I agreed with this assessment, based on my brief meeting with them. (It did take me aback that they did not pay special attention to their biological mothers.)

I asked Isa, who brought her two children into the group from "the other culture," how her child-rearing practices were modified in the group. Different adults take turns with three-and-a-half-hour shifts with the children in their apartment, called Sparrow Village. Isa explained:

I'm sure you've had the experience of trying to fold the laundry or read a letter and the child is asking questions that you just don't have the mental energy to engage. But Liberty and Revery, because there is always a fresh adult coming on shift with them, have had countless numbers of very deep intellectual dialogues with all kinds of different people about why things work the way they do. I feel like I could be a missionary for multiple parenting.

Isa reported that after joining the Kerista Commune she began to look at her parenting situation more rationally. She discovered that she was dealing

with this neurosis called momism or popism where you see your children as an extension of yourself. You get emotionally involved so that when they do something creepy, you react more strongly seeing it as a reflection on you. I believe this is an irrational attitude and that it undermines the mental health of the parent and thwarts the child's development toward independence.

Isa has since left the group.

Egalitarian Communities

Earlier communities have shared child care, housework, and money making. One of the most interesting is the Oneida Community, founded in 1848 in upstate New York by John Humphrey Noyes. Noyes believed that true Christianity is communistic and nonpossessive. Exclusive attachments—"special love" or "partiality"—including bonds between husband and wife or parent and child are not Christian. Noyes instituted "complex marriage," a kind of group marriage in some ways similar to that of the Keristans. Members were urged to "keep in circulation" to avoid "sticky" attachments to just one person.

Noyes' son, Pierrepont, wrote intriguing accounts of growing up with 16 other children and 300 adults at Oneida.[3] He explained that members who wanted to become parents made an application to the community, to insure rational breeding. After a year with their mothers, children moved to the South Wing of the mansion, where they were cared for by the children's department, which had a male head and female care givers. The aim of the children's department was to increase parental/child love by avoiding "smother-mother" love and not burdening mothers. Pierrepont visited his mother in her room several times a week. He felt that the rule against being "sticky" to one's parents was harder on the mothers than on their children.

In the Oneida Community both women and men made steel traps, tableware, and silk thread and canned their crops for sale. Work was rotated to prevent boredom and to teach new skills. The women wore short dresses, pantalettes, and short hair as a practical aid in their work as well as to discourage vanity. Group members danced Virginia reels and quadrilles, listened to their band, performed pantomimes and plays, sang, skated, played croquet and cards, and went on picnics. They also practiced "mutual criticism," mixing praise with fault finding to hasten spiritual growth. Pierrepont dreaded the criticism sessions and loved the entertainment and outdoor play. He noted that plans that the children of the community would be different from conventional children were dispelled when they turned out to be "selfish little animals," just as the Keristans discovered.

Most of the groups I have described do not know each other and their shared ideologies are coincidental. In contrast, the Federation of Egalitarian Communities is composed of groups that work together to create nonsexist, nonracist, nonviolent, nonconsumerist, noncompetitive, cooperative, and ecologically sound places to live and rear children. The mother community, founded in 1967, is Twin Oaks in Louisa, Virginia, where the federation magazine, *Communities*, originated.[4] The other member communities, in order of their founding, are East Wind in Missouri (1974), Sandhill in Missouri (1974), Dandelion in Ontario (1975), Appletree in Oregon (1982), and Chrysalis in Indiana (1983). The two largest are Twin Oaks, which has around sixty-five adults and seventeen children, and Eastwind, which has over fifty adults and six children. Other communities are much smaller: Sandhill has five adults and one child; Appletree has six adults and one child. The federation meets every six months in a conference. I interviewed nine members of Twin Oaks and one or two members from each of the other communities.

The organization of Twin Oaks was based on the idealized community described in B. F. Skinner's novel *Walden Two* (1948). Skinner envisioned widespread groups of independent communities instead of a split between cities and rural dwellings. He believed that environment is crucial in shaping behavior. Adults in *Walden Two* live in small, individual, dormitory-style rooms, with shared facilities for cooking, dining, listening to music, and reading, and extensive grounds for recreation and farming. Adults are obligated to work a certain number of hours a week at various jobs of their choice. Children are cared for kibbutz style, in a children's house with skilled child care workers who use behavior modification techniques. Managers are in charge of various projects, like the dairy or community outreach. A small board of planners oversees the long-range development of the community. Differences in sex roles are minimal since housekeeping, child rearing, and breadwinning are assumed by the community; women do not depend on their husbands for financial support nor do husbands depend on their wives for domestic support. These policies are all put into practice at Twin Oaks.

Twin Oaks was founded after a 1967 conference at the University of Michigan. A founder, Kathleen Kinkade, described the struggles of the fledgling community with a $1,200 per person gross income in her book, *A Walden Two Experiment*.[5] She went on to help found Eastwind and is currently back at Twin Oaks. About half of the members of Twin Oaks are college educated, most are middle class and white, about a third are Jewish, and only two are black. Most are from the East Coast. The average age has risen over the years and is now the early thirties. The ratio of males to females is about 60 to 40. Homosexuals and other underrepresented groups are recruited. The recent turnover rate is about 25 percent, since some get impatient with group decision making and some do not "plug in socially or find fulfilling work." Others leave to have access to more earning power and ownership.

Each person at Twin Oaks is required to work around forty-five hours a week. Taking care of the children or nursing a baby counts as much as doing auto mechanics or making rope hammocks and chairs, the group's major source of income. People turn in preference cards for their weekly jobs, which are assigned by computer. Everyone, including infants, receives an allowance of $11 a month and can earn a yearly four-week vacation.

The nonpossessive ideal of the community at first discouraged monogamous relationships. However, this has changed over the years, and now Twin Oak members generally practice serial monogamy. Marriage is the exception rather than the rule, and most spouses were married before they came to Twin Oaks. At Dandelion, "if two people are always off by themselves, that's something we get involved with. We want everyone to be a part of the group; caring for everyone else is important," a thirty-four-year-old mother of four children said. On the other hand, she appreciates having her own room for the first time in her life. At Appletree, with two couples and a single man and woman, "All of us are very active with each other, not just with one person," said Cat, a mother of one daughter at Appletree.

The communities share holidays, especially the four equinoxes and solstices. The summer celebration is combined with the anniversary of the founding of Twin Oaks. Almost everyone takes time off from work to dance, eat special food, and enjoy an art show. Some participate in a surprise activity, such as being blindfolded to play in a pit of cooking oil, or squirting whipped cream at each other, or eating with no hands from a food trough. East Wind's tenth anniversary celebration included a treasure hunt with two teams—the Easties and the Windies. They had a huge dinner, sang "We gather together, the meaties and the veggies together," told old stories, and had a hilarious talent show. Mystery "elves" are active at East Wind from December 23 to 31, secretly giving small gifts, poems, and clues to their partners. The elves reveal their identity at the New Year's Eve party. Valentine's Day is renamed validation day, when each person receives cards describing his or her valued qualities and behavior.

Twin Oaks established a child program in 1973 to circumvent nuclear family child rearing; before then the group did not feel prepared to take on children, especially ones brought to the group from the outside. The fourteen girls and three boys, all under eleven, have their own house, the Degania. Most were born at Twin Oaks. They are cared for by "metas," who have four-hour shifts credited toward their weekly work requirement. (The term is a derivative of the Israeli term for kibbutz child care workers, called metapellets.) Because the shifts are short, the metas have "juicy" energy to give to their charges and are not frazzled by them. Metas are responsible for cleaning the children's house and preparing the children's breakfast (children often eat dinner with adults in the courtyard). Children see both men and women doing domestic tasks and mechanical tasks such as driving tractors. Children might also see women wearing overalls and men wearing skirts. (A man explained to me that it is fun to search among the community clothes and to "flame out" and put on a skirt. Skirts are comfortable, he said; he thinks he looks good in one; and he feels he is making a liberated gesture, although he would certainly not wear a skirt elsewhere.)

Saturday meetings are held for at least two hours to discuss the children with metas, parents, and primaries (like aunts and uncles). Each child has around three or four primaries in addition to the parents who spend regular time with the child. Selected by the parents and child when she is old enough, a primary spends 6:00 P.M. to 9:00 P.M. with a child and gets some work credit for doing so. Parents may spend three evenings with a child and each of the three or four primaries takes the other evenings during a week. They eat dinner with the children, play with them, and get them to bed. A primary says about his charge, "I feel a strong contact with her, and she can rely on me."

Parents are warned that they need to "give up exclusive decision making" about their children and become part of a team. When the children's program was begun at Twin Oaks, children were viewed as the community's children, not the exclusive responsibility of their parents. As soon as babies were sleeping through the night they were brought to the Degania to be cared for by the metas. However, just as on the kibbutzim, there has been a move toward more time spent with the nuclear family. The most recent Twin Oaks babies have spent most of their time with their parents. The parents, instead of the metas, set up medical appointments and assume other responsibilities. Policy has not changed but practice has.

One mother, Minet, at East Wind explained that they are "trying to come up with the perfect child care system. We haven't quite made it, but it's quite good." Her son has access to three other "primaries" and eight metas. A less-pleased mother, Jay, left Twin Oaks partly because she wanted to spend more time with her son and have more control over his rearing, without having to consult the metas or the Child Board. She did not want to go along with their decision about where the children should go to school (currently a nearby private cooperative school, taught by a Twin Oaks member). "I'd go and take him away from the people so I could be with him by myself and some people would be angry with me for that," Jay said. Jay does feel her son gained a lot from Twin Oaks in terms of being less "macho" and violent than other boys his age.

Skinner's behavior modification technique of "juicing" or praising children for desirable behavior, and ignoring negative behavior, is still used at Twin Oaks.[5] An observer, Ingrid Komar, believes that the philosophy of "ignore it and it will go away" does not give children enough room to express their negative feelings.[6] Violence is considered the most serious offense. Time outs are given: Children are put on their bed for a set amount of time, depending on the child's age. Or they may lose a privilege, such as eating in the courtyard. Metas ask children to "take space" if they are arguing over a toy; that is, to leave the location of the negative behavior. Then the meta helps the children solve problems, saying "offer a trade, grabbing is not okay," or asking, "What could you have done besides bite Julio? You could have put it in words that you were angry. You could have hit a pillow or beaten on a tree." "We help them to find other ways to deal with their anger and not just punish them," a meta said. A nine-year-old girl, Seren, agreed, "If I have a quarrel with another kid, a meta helps us talk about it." Metas record comments about the children during their shift, to be read by the next metas.

I asked a meta about his perceptions of having a child in the community. Gene, who recently applied to have a child, said, "I would be scared if I was going to become a father on the outside. The nuclear family is too much pressure; it's hard not to spank if you're with a kid all day with no support. Here, the children are not dependent on one or two people." Ace, a father, confirmed, "Having a baby at Twin Oaks was very easy. There is a lot of support, like making sure there was a vehicle ready to go when we needed one and having someone to drive us to the hospital. The bills went to someone else, too." Wonderful meals, clean laundry, and education are provided. If parents gets sick or want to go out, they can put up a card requesting evening care for a child. Work flexibility means that Ace can take an hour off in the middle of the day to visit his daughter since he is only ten minutes from Degania. He works as a meta as another way to spend time with his daughter and the other children. However, he feels there is not enough support for fathers, with the labor credits provided only for nursing mothers.

Ace wanted to raise a child in a nonsexist community that did not watch television. Shows like "The Dukes of Hazzard" teach "instant violence instead of thinking about putting feelings into words," Ann Marie, his partner, said. Even at Twin Oaks, Ace notices that the girls play more with dolls and boys with trucks in the sandbox.

Seren says, though, "I don't like dolls so much. I like to swim and play tag. I like walking in the woods." To counter the Barbie dolls provided by grandparents and the macho behavior of friends raised outside the community, the adults discuss "the sexist mystique around Barbie dolls" and other toys and provide a wide range of experience. Both girls and boys get lessons in woodworking and auto mechanics. The children's books are edited to say "co" instead of "his," sometimes refer to a doctor as "she," and include female characters.

Pine, another father, compared Twin Oaks to his experiences on an Israeli kibbutz and in a nuclear family in the United States. On the kibbutz, with a forty-eight-hour work week, he had only a brief time after a meal during the day to say hello to his two children. In the United States, "When I lived on the outside, I didn't have much space for family when I came home from a full time job. It took until around 7:00 P.M. to recoup my mental space," he said. At Twin Oaks, he can take a walk with his children during the day. He works at his own schedule buying food, cooking, making cheese, and doing meta shifts and office work.

Pine also appreciates the two evenings when other primaries are with his two children, so that he and his wife can have time together. He finds it easier to have a good relationship with her because of fewer resentments and stress, the kind that build up when a woman stays home with a baby all day. He likes having his own room to express his own taste, a place to retreat to read or listen to music. He adds, "If you're angry with the other person, you don't have to stomp out to a bar or to mother's house, because you have your own room."

Pine believes that it is impossible for the nuclear family to provide all a child's needs. The extended family used to include Grandma's story telling and Uncle Joe's carpentry abilities. At Twin Oaks, the children have sixty adults to answer their questions. If they want to know why the sky is blue, they can talk to McGregor, who knows about physics. A fourteen-year-old girl who recently joined her mother at Dandelion notes that her mother "loves me more since she has more freedom; she didn't have much freedom before" in her nuclear family.

Josie, who came to Twin Oaks as a teenager, is now a mother there. The community is a teenager's nirvana, she said, recalling how she stayed out late talking with members and visitors, weaseled out of her work, and learned to milk cows and to manage a kitchen. She dropped out of tenth grade, but later went to college and is now in medical school. Twin Oaks will pay her university expenses if she stays in the community.

When Josie had a daughter eleven years ago, at age twenty, the ideology was that parents would not be more responsible for the child than the metas. The plan was to use behaviorist techniques to raise neurosis-free children. Josie fell in love with her, baby, Robin, but unless she wanted to be a meta, which she did not, she could not have much influence with the child, nor could she take her out of the Degania to sleep with her. She felt responsibility for her child, but "she'd push me away in favor of the metas who spent more time with her." Yet when some of Robin's close caretakers left, Josie was expected to be responsible for her. She took over as a single mother when Robin was three and a half.

The community still believes that it should provide for its children. For example, Robin requires physical therapy. A crew of six people work with her each day, and her clinic is amazed at the progress she makes. The community provides encompassing care for an individual the way a tribe or extended family does in other cultures. However, Twin Oaks may have to reexamine its lack of demands on children to exert their talents, and the goal of "trying to create a society without heroes." The fear of competition and noncooperation may ignore healthy individual striving.

Jay, whose son was born at Twin Oaks, returned for a visit in 1984. She observed that the commune children were not high achievers because of permissive child-rearing practices. They are not encouraged to excel or compete and are given almost automatic acceptance. A private psychological testing service brought in to examine the children remarked that the children did not exert themselves. Jay feels that the metas need more extensive training and consistency and that the children who have developed best have the most consistent and loving parents.

Permissive child rearing, egalitarian values, and expectations that children be self-reliant tend to characterize other communes.[7] In Bernice Eiduson's study comparing child rearing in different family types, communal children had less stress than other children during their first six years, while highest stress scores were for children of single mothers.[8] Eiduson's overall conclusion is that middle-class parents raise their children with similar emotional interaction no matter what their current family style. My interviews lead me to the same view. It is as if we are imprinted with a particular parental style growing up and, despite experiments with alternatives on the kibbutzim or at Twin Oaks, the parent-child bond remains strong.

All the parents I interviewed for this chapter agree that being isolated in a nuclear family is burdensome. The intentional extended family gives adults companionship, fun, a reduced workload, advice, a chance to learn by observation, and counseling for their couple relationship. Children gain companions, adult experts in various areas, a chance to observe various adult personality styles, mediators for conflicts with their parents, and more adult attention. Neighbors and other groups of parents can adopt some of the sharing described in this chapter, by taking turns cooking, doing work "bees," sharing backyard space for children's playgrounds, forming babysitting cooperatives and neighborhood "summer camps," and meeting together to exchange thoughts about coparenting. Coparenting is less stressful than parenting alone. This principle extends from two parents in a household to group parenting.

11

Help for Employed Parents

Government and corporations have to show more flexibility; I think people are going to have to push a lot harder. A fairly significant number of people hold these values, but something prevents them from putting them into practice.

— *Bill, father of four*

Our prevailing system of values stands in the way of further movement.

— *Dana E. Friedman, Conference Board*

THE work place must be changed to accommodate parents who are sharing both work and family responsibility. A Utah mother of three explains, "Shared parenting is joyful with the right partner, but maintaining the logistics and organization necessary is often overwhelming—we live at the limits of our energies." Most working wives will give birth to a child while they are employed, and by 1990 around 80 percent of couples will be dual earners.[1] Most dual-earner couples face at least ten hours a day when one or both of them are at work or commuting. A General Mills study of working parents found that only 36 percent of the working mothers felt they had enough time for themselves; this was the same number who reported that they shared child care with their husbands.[2] In contrast, 60 percent of the fathers reported that they had enough time for themselves. Working parents of both genders, especially parents of preschool children, complain of strain, fatigue, and irritability; but 70 percent of mothers compared to 49 percent of fathers reported being under stress in a *Fortune* survey.[3] Fairness requires coparenting. Gail Schaper found in her study of 255 working mothers that those who coped best took time out for themselves, as well as set priorities and then gave the top priority undivided attention.[4]

The majority of the parents surveyed for General Mills judged that the effects of both parents working outside the home were generally negative, yet most would continue to work if they had the choice. Parents want to work outside the home and also want time for themselves and for their children. Advertisers tell us that a woman who wears the right perfume can come home from work, put down her briefcase, whip up a gourmet meal, slip into a glamourous outfit, and as Gloria Steinem put it, have orgasms until dawn. Most of us do not have that kind of stamina. We need institutional changes to make combining work and child rearing less stressful.

My survey results indicate that being a worker is the most demanding but least satisfying role for both genders. In a survey filled out by 380 dual-career individuals, spouse and children were rated as a higher priority than work by both men and women.[5] Men gave a little more emphasis to the spouse role as number one, and women gave a little more emphasis to their parent role. Of the 107 dual-career individuals interviewed over the phone, 55 percent of the respondents ranked their satisfaction with their work as high, compared to 80 percent who ranked satisfaction with their spouse as high. Stress at work is mainly caused by the environment, other people, and time pressures. The fact that men and women had similar values indicates the need for widespread work place changes to accommodate families.

Employers who are committed to meeting the actual needs of their employees do exist. In 1987 I visited the corporate headquarters of Levi Strauss in San Francisco. I found a physical environment that is inspiringly pleasant, with art on the walls, airy spaces, and comfortable lounges on each floor. A library is stocked with books and audiovisual materials about health and family. A fitness center staffed by two instructors offers aerobics classes and equipment. Noontime seminars are offered on various topics such as parenting, and child care referral, counseling, and other employee services are provided by employee assistance counselors. Parental leave, flexible work hours, and permanent part-time jobs are available; the highest ranking woman vice president took extensive maternity leave with each of her two children, and a female attorney works half time. A new program deducts child care costs from employees' salaries so that it is tax exempt.

Ellen Galinsky directs the Corporate Work and Family Life Project at the Bank Street College of Education in New York City, which looks at how people balance their work and family life and how helpful changes can be made in the work place. Begun in 1983, her study is affiliated with similar ones in England, Sweden, and West Germany. Galinsky reports that time is the main problem for the working parents she has interviewed, especially for women.[6] She confirms that even in the face of numerous demands men seem to find time for themselves, while women do not.

Galinsky notes that another major concern of parents is what to do about caring for a sick child. Scheduling appointments with doctors and dentists can be difficult too. Most child care centers will not take sick children, although over fifty centers for ill children, such as Berkeley's Wheezles and Sneezles Day Care Center, are in operation around the country.[7] Around 80 employers offer sick-child care at home, contracting with a local hospital service. Realizing that sick children are a major cause of costly absenteeism, 3M Company in St. Paul began a pilot program in 1984 to provide health care for employees and their dependents at home at a reduced cost. In Sweden, cities provide this service routinely.

Another major problem Galinsky observed is parents bringing home work-related stress. The transition from the work mode to dealing with children is often disjointed. Responding to "Mommy, watch me, Daddy watch me, watch me draw," is different from getting a task done without interruption at work. In an odd way, you are less in control at home, Galinsky notes. Some of the workers she interviewed found ways to make the transition less hectic. Some listen to music or books using headphones on the way from work. Others spend the last minutes at work clearing their minds, sitting quietly. One mother has her babysitter stay on for fifteen minutes after she returns from work. A single mother has carrot sticks and other finger food prepared for her children to eat as soon as they get home, while she rests for a while. A father sits on the floor and lets his children climb all over him and be with him as much as they want to when he first gets home, then he goes off by himself for a while to recharge his batteries. A couple I interviewed drink coffee together for half an hour after work; their three boys know not to disturb their parents during this time.

These suggestions about smoother transitions from work to home involve individual solutions. Institutions surrounding the family, including businesses, unions, churches and synagogues, family service associations, schools, and government, must also be part of the solution. Galinsky points out that government or employers cannot be the sole solution, but that all the institutions surrounding the family must move forward. Nancy Walker, the president of the San Francisco Board of Supervisors, succeeded in getting legislation passed in 1985 requiring large new buildings to include space for child care or to donate to a city child care fund. She envisions partnership or a consortium between the private sector, unions, schools, and city government to provide child care support. She advocates that society put children first and make it a plus to be a parent. When child care is provided through the critical junior high period, employers gain from the reduced stress level of their employees, she explained in a telephone interview (April, 1987). "We all fare better if children are given tender loving care," Supervisor Walker noted. She proposes parental leave, child care on site for young children, after school care, special centers for sick children, personal leave to take care of children or aging parents, and sex education in schools to reduce unplanned pregnancies. Private and public organizations must join hands to begin to implement her goal of shared responsibility.

"Our prevailing system of values stands in the way of further movement" in changes at work, states Dana E. Friedman, senior researcher for the Conference Board, the research arm of the Fortune 500 Companies, in New York City.[8] Many Americans believe that mothers of young children should be at home with them all day or that mothers choose to work and employers have no obligation to accommodate them. As former San Francisco Mayor Diane Feinstein, the mother of a grown daughter, stated, "I don't think the work market has to accommodate itself to women having children. I believe that women have the choice. If they make the choice for career and children, there is no question there are problems. Certainly there were for me."[9] But the parents of the seven million latchkey children under age thirteen do not feel that they have a choice. Mayor Feinstein's statement illustrates the erroneous but common belief that work and family are separate spheres. In fact, work dictates much of how we organize family life, where we live, how often we move, and how much time we spend with our children.

Involved parenting requires less time at work, with a "cost for work involvement," Michael Lamb notes.[10] For most of the fathers he has studied in the United States and Sweden, "work still came first. I think as long as men continue to see breadwinning as their primary role and their primary source of fulfillment, this is going to be a really important barrier." Backing up his observation is the fact that many of the involved fathers studied by Russell, Radin, and Sapp changed to making work a priority.[11] As more women assume careers, too, the work place must change or children will not receive optimal care.

Employers can provide child care assistance, permanent part-time work, flexible work hours, parental leave, and counseling for families. Rosabeth Moss Kanter, an expert on corporate structure, found in comparing progressive and traditional company policies that the innovative firms are more successful in sales and profits.[12] As women are becoming the majority of new entrants into the work force and the labor pool diminishes due to the aging of the American population, employers will need to accommodate the needs of working parents. Coparenting will become more common.

Parental Leave

Eighty-five percent of working women will have children. Interviews with new fathers in dual-career marriages reveal that they would like to have time at home with their babies, but are reluctant to ask for personal leave for fear of jeopardizing their career advancement.[13] In a 1984 Catalyst study of large corporations, 37 percent offered unpaid parental leave, but only 9 of 114 companies reported that men had taken advantage of the policy.[14] Almost two-thirds of the companies believed paternity leave was unreasonable, although 96 percent offered short-term maternity benefits. Meg Franklin, personnel manager at Levi Strauss in San Francisco, related that only five fathers of newborns have taken advantage of the five-month unpaid paternity leave available to them at Levi Strauss.[15] Franklin believes that men are worried about the effect that such a leave would have on their bosses' opinions of them. Older male bosses never considered taking time off for their babies, so younger fathers are afraid their bosses would doubt their commitment to work if they took paternity leave. Even at firms like Levi Strauss, traditional pressures inhibit men from coparenting.

The Ford Foundation was probably the first employer to provide eight weeks of paid leave to both mothers and fathers, including those who adopt children. Few other employers have followed Ford's lead. Some do permit fathers to take a few days off with pay at the time of the birth. Even in Sweden, where the government has an official policy and media campaigns to encourage fathers to take paid paternity leave (sports figures are shown tending babies), most men do not take advantage of the six-month opportunity. About 22 percent of Swedish fathers take a leave, averaging 47 days or 5 percent of the leave days utilized, double the number that did so in earlier years.[16] Most Swedish men do take off a week or so at the time of the birth and take paid leave to stay home with sick children. Men's role, cross-culturally, still is heavily weighted toward their earning capacity and job position, while women's role is child rearing. As Swedes frequently told me when I visited there in 1980, attitudes lag behind legislative change.

A survey of more than 5,000 working women who had recently given birth found that two-thirds of them were back at work within three months—a third of them within six weeks.[17] Only 15 percent of the mothers felt ready to go back to work when they did, and almost a third said they felt guilty about leaving their babies so soon. The burden was lightened for only 42 percent of the mothers whose husbands got up at night to care for the baby. More than half of the mothers could not afford to stay away from work any longer; 39 percent received no paid maternity leave. Only 20 percent of the jobs in the United States pay enough to support a family of four above the poverty line, so mothers must continue working. Going back to work so early after the birth causes fatigue, perhaps impairs bonding with the infant, can reduce productivity and increase errors, and can be so stressful as to cause valuable employees to resign.

Except for the United States, almost all the advanced industrial societies (and around 100 countries) have paid maternity-leave policies with job protection. Fewer than 40 percent of American working women are entitled to maternity leaves.[18] The minimal legislation that comes closest to a maternity policy is the Pregnancy Disability

Act of 1978, which requires employers to treat pregnancy as a disability, providing the same leave benefits received by any person out of work with an injury. If a company does not provide disability benefits, then it is not required to provide maternity leave. An important 1987 Supreme Court ruling upheld California's law requiring up to four months unpaid leave for pregnancy; similar laws exist in five other states. The California law had been challenged as being discriminatory to men! Many large firms consider six to eight weeks appropriate paid maternity leave. Sick leave to care for ill dependents is almost nonexistent.

In 1985 Congresswoman Patricia Schroeder proposed the Parental and Disability Leave Act, which would guarantee jobs to parents who take leaves of 18 weeks or less, and would establish a commission to design a national paid parental and disability leave policy. When provision for care of elderly parents was added, the title was changed to the Family and Medical Leave Act. The act exempts employers of under 15 employees. During hearings Congressman Austin Murphy commented, "I say be careful. You know some of us guys really don't want this protection. We might have to stay home and take care of the kids. [Laughter]."[19] His attitude reveals much about why the United States lags behind other countries and why equal parenting is rare.

Child Care and Other Assistance Programs

Over half of American children have a working mother: Only about a quarter of young children were cared for in their own homes for the entire day in 1982.[20] Day-care costs for two preschool children can consume 30 percent of a family's income, and this cost is usually viewed by the family as the mother's expense.[21] Although almost half of the mothers of infants are employed, infant care is even more expensive and hard to find. According to Sheila Kamerman, in survey after survey working parents state that the most important problem they face is child care, and Ellen Galinsky reports that child care is the major cause of "unproductive time at work."[22] Over eight million children under six have working mothers, while there are only around a million child care center slots.

Employers of working parents can help find or provide care for children. Day care at the work place is receiving much attention, although only around 150 companies provide it. An additional 3,000 companies—the number has doubled in two years—offered some other form of assistance in 1986, usually information referral and flexible child care benefits.[23] Procter & Gamble in Cincinnati offers flexible benefits and a day-care referral service, helps fund two community day-care centers that give priority to its employees, and provides two months' paid leave for new mothers and six months' unpaid leave for new parents. Employers benefit from increased productivity if parents do not have to worry about their children's well-being or be late or absent from work. In a study of 5,000 companies, 48 percent of the women and 25 percent of the men employed stated that they had spent unproductive time at work due to child care problems.[24]

Nyloncraft, a plastics company in Indiana, found through an employee survey that child care problems were causing high absenteeism and turnover rates.[25] To solve the problem the company opened a twenty-four-hour day-care center on site. Absenteeism dropped to less than 3 percent and the turnover rate diminished greatly. Costs saved in training new employees make up for the $20,000 yearly operating loss. The company pays about half of the $50-a-week child care fee, provides free care during overtime work, and picks up children after school to bring them to the site.

The Reagan administration made employer-provided day care its central technique to help working families. Its strategy was to invite corporate officers to lunch forums in various parts of the country. It encouraged employer support of child care by making costs tax-deductible for employers and a tax-free benefit to workers. Most parents, however, say they do not want child care at work. The logistics of daily commuting with young children can be nerve wracking, industrial areas may have more air pollution, and being dependent on the employer is undesirable for some workers. Working parents asked about the helpfulness of child care at the work place are not enthusiastic. In one survey, 62 percent said it would help little if any at all, while only 20 percent said it would help a great deal. In a more recent survey 54 percent of women desired this benefit, compared to 38 percent of fathers.[26]

Employers help with child care in ways other than providing it on site. The service easiest to provide and the most in vogue is I&R—information and referral. Companies either have their own computerized list of available slots in neighborhood day care centers or they contract with agencies who provide that information to employees. Other benefits for working parents that some companies provide are: child care subsidies for off-site care, sick-child care, help with starting up day-care centers as needed, a library with parenting resources, lunch hour seminars on family themes, classes in yoga and stress reduction, and an after-school call-in program for employees' children. Another service suggested by Ellen Galinsky and others is a computer bank of in-house employee resources so parents can locate a math tutor, for example. To coordinate these programs, employers like 3M and Harvard Medical School employ a resource coordinator for parents.

Boston's Zayre Corporation offers employees with preschool children a $20 weekly subsidy. The Ford Foundation and Polaroid subsidize child care costs for employees with family incomes below $25,000. Some companies provide initial start-up and operating funds for local nonprofit child care centers. In Los Angeles, a consortium of businesses is working with United Way in a nonprofit plan to convert unused buildings into child care centers. A group of California corporate foundations led by the Bank of America Foundation raised money to recruit and train day-care providers and convert existing buildings to centers. The program began with $700,000 in six pilot regions around the state. The incentive was a 1984 report that 54,714 California children would not find day-care slots.

Around 1,000 companies offer "cafeteria benefits" that allow an employee to select an individualized benefit package, which can include child care. American Can is a leader in flexible benefit plans, with essentially a different plan for each employee. It began offering employee benefit choices in 1978 and became the first firm to include a child care option in 1982. The GMDCA Employee Assistance Fund in Minneapolis helps employers establish a child care benefit, shows them how to use tax credits and tax deductions for child care, pays the child care provider and bills the employer monthly, places employees' children in the type of care selected by the parent, and sets up a sliding-scale fee tailored to the employees' resources.

Some businesses would only consider child care benefits if they were proposed by the union. Unions, however, have done very little for working parents, perhaps because few women occupy union leadership positions. Also, unions mainly represent long-established industries with a preponderance of male workers. Unions are in a time of retrenchment rather than expansion of their power. The exception is the activism of garment makers' unions (ACTWU and ILGW), which sponsor day-care centers for their mainly female members.

Companies that do not provide child care maintain that it is not their responsibility, it is too expensive, it involves legal liability problems and complicated regulations, no space is available, the labor force is too changeable, companies will seem paternalistic and interfering, or workers do not want or need child care assistance. These companies point out that less than one-fifth of U.S. workers have children under six. However, in a 1983 survey of 282 companies providing child care, 75 percent concluded that the benefits in recruiting and retaining employees far outweighed the problems associated with child care.[27]

Employer supports for families is becoming a popular research topic, as brought to public attention by the film *Nine to Five.* In that film women employees played by Lily Tomlin, Jane Fonda, and Dolly Parton instituted a day-care center, flexible working hours, job sharing, and a more appealing work environment. Increasing numbers of organizations are providing conferences, seminars, and reports about innovations in employer services.[28]

Some progressive firms provide fitness centers and exercise classes. Having an opportunity to exercise and blow off some steam during the work day helps parents be on a more even keel when they return home to their children. Rockwell in Los Angeles has provided employees with extensive recreational facilities since the 1950s, in order to attract new workers. Their San Fernando Valley Park has swimming pools, tennis courts, a gymnasium, a ceramics shop, classes ranging from aerobics to scuba diving to art, and numerous clubs such as a ski club that arranges trips for members. Rockwell also provides summer camps for employees' children ages six to twelve, including a weekly excursion.

An estimated one in five American families relocates each year because of job transfers.[29] As the number of dual-earner couples increases, more companies are offering assistance in finding a new job to "trailing" spouses. Nineteen percent routinely offer spouse job assistance as company policy, according to a Catalyst survey of corporate relocation practices.[30] The fact that so few U.S. companies are involved with child care and other needs of employed parents means that the burdens fall on parents, usually on the mother, who feels guilty that she cannot do even more. She may cut back her work hours while her husband works longer, making family roles lopsided and depriving children of time with their fathers.

Flexible Working Hours

Flexible working hours are often mentioned as an effective and inexpensive way that the work place can accommodate working parents, yet around 20 percent of workers have this option.[31] Companies that offer flextime were usually motivated initially by nonfamily issues such as alleviating traffic congestion or fully using equipment. Job flexibility is an important factor in shared parenting. A study of Nebraska parents who shared child rearing found that 67 percent described their work as flexible, yet one of their main difficulties was matching the spouses' work schedules and child care.[32] Another study of role sharers found that husbands' flexible hours made a positive difference.[33] A more representative study of federal employees with flexible working hours found that they had more time with their families, but that working mothers still felt strained and carried the primary responsibility for children.[34]

A Gallup Poll found that employees consider flexible working hours to be the most useful work place change (54 percent), followed by sick leave to care for family members (37 percent) and provision of child care facilities (28 percent).[35] Flexible working hours can mean flextime, where workers have a band of mandatory time at work (usually 10:00 A.M. to 2:00 P.M.) with variable starting and departure times, allowing one parent to get the children off to school and the other to be home to greet them after school, a major step toward shared parenting. Another variation on flexible working hours is maxiflex, which requires core hours only Tuesday through Thursday, allowing workers to take three- or four-day weekends. Flexiplace, in which employees work at home, may provide the most flexibility in work schedules. Honeywell and Control Data, in Minneapolis, permit employees to work at home computer terminals. Perhaps 15,000 telecommuters currently work at home.

In a flexiyear, employees contract to work an arranged pattern for a year, for example, following the children's school year. Some employees at the Connecticut Savings Bank in New Haven work 9:30 A.M. to 2:30 P.M. during the school year and take summers off without pay. They receive all but two benefits, but these are major ones—health and life insurance. Beck's department store introduced the flexiyear to its New York City employees in 1984. A computer account keeps track of overdrawn or extra hours at work. Some employees use their credit hours to take a three-month vacation while some mothers work only a few hours a day.

Permanent part-time employees work 35 hours a week or less. A 63 percent increase in professionals' use of part-time arrangements, mainly by women, occurred from 1976 to 1981. When family members were asked in a General Mills survey if part-time work with full benefits would be helpful, 42 percent thought it would help a great deal.[36] In the same survey, 51 percent of professional women and 41 percent of all working women indicated that they would prefer part-time work, compared to 28 percent of the men. General Motors now has "flexible service employees" working usually four-fifth to three-fifth time, with job security and benefits matching the percent of time worked.

I interviewed two reporters who share parenting and a job covering the Washington, D.C., bureau. Margaret and Bill have four young children and appreciate not having to use babysitters to care for their children. Before their third child was born they decided they did not want to be both working full time, so they proposed sharing a job. Initial reservations by their managers were about how they could pay into their pension fund, how others would know if the person they needed would be at work, and "underlying it all was doubt as to whether we would be serious about the job if we were only doing it half time," Margaret explained. Once they started sharing the job, however, their managing editor quickly saw that he would "get more for his money." Margaret usually works in the morning and Bill works in the afternoon. Often they end up writing stories at night when the children are in bed, giving the paper extra hours—as do many job sharers. Flexible working hours and permanent part-time jobs are supports for working parents that employers can provide with only minor additional costs for utilities and record keeping.

Other Organizational Supports

When the Fatherhood Project searched for religious support programs for parents as a part of a study conducted for *Fatherhood*

U.S.A., Dr. Debra Klinman was surprised to find how little help these organizations provided. Support groups for involved fathers and mothers could be part of church and synagogue activity. Religious institutions could provide more preschool and after-school care in their Sunday school facilities.

Family service organizations are multiplying and need to reach out to fathers. For example, in Boston the Child Care Resource Center, founded in 1971, helps parents locate a child care program, playgroups, and babysitting and provides referrals to other family service agencies free of charge. The center provides workshops and support groups for child care providers, and publishes a monthly newsletter. Employers can subscribe to information and referral for their employees.

At the Children's Health Council in Palo Alto, California, Jane Bryan-Jones taught parent education classes, duplicating sessions at night so that working mothers and fathers could attend (more mothers take the classes).[37] One of the egalitarian couples I interviewed for this book felt that the class helped shore up their marriage after the shock of adjusting to their first baby.

Bryan-Jones finds that the new baby causes the intensity of the couple relationship to diffuse, so her class is designed to refocus their bond. Couples are greeted by soft music, flowers, and candlelight as they enter the classroom, and are asked to write down the qualities they most appreciate in their mate. The beginning sessions reestablish rapport between the spouses. Couples are asked to explain to their spouse what makes them feel cared for. One wife does not like to bake, but she made cookies for her husband when he let her know it was an important gesture to him. A wife's fantasy was for her husband to take her out for an evening, including finding a babysitter and making reservations. Bryan-Jones points out that it is important not to assume that if one's spouse really cared he or she would know what is desired. Another class exercise is to write thirty things the couple most enjoy doing together and identify how many they are still doing together and which ones they can do they with their baby.

In the last sessions couples move toward intimacy by doing a "withholding" exercise. They take turns sharing feelings they have held back. The partner simply responds, "Thank you for sharing that with me." Examples of withheld feelings are "I can't stand it that you talk about the baby so much," or "When you get home late I feel hurt and angry." Another intimacy exercise is for one partner to physically curl up in a tight, tense ball. The goal is to relax and uncurl the partner, nonverbally, by touching. Bryan-Jones tells parents to make time for themselves, to be willing to leave their child and go away for a weekend or have lunch together on a regular basis. Courting behavior needs to be reestablished, she teaches. Family service organizations, religious groups, and adult education programs can offer these types of courses for parents, being mindful of the needs of fathers.

Hospitals can help families by encouraging father-coached births, permitting fathers to room in with the mother and baby, and providing classes for parents. Men's role as coach requires that they attend prenatal classes such as Lamaze, which can also introduce techniques of caring for a newborn. Men who teach fathering classes warn about the secondary or support role that coaching the birth implies for men and stress that classes should emphasize the importance of both parents. Classes "For Father and His Baby" are needed to teach skills and give fathers an opportunity to share their experiences. St. Joseph's Hospital in St. Paul offers such classes, which should continue for parents of children in the various developmental stages, with special outreach for fathers.

Schools can be a major support for working parents because they are located in every neighborhood and have facilities geared for children. The school year could be longer, as it is in most other industrial nations. Summer programs could be offered for every grade. Schools could provide extended kindergarten classes, preschool programs for four-year-olds, and after-school care.[38] Only around 125 school districts provided before- or after-school care in 1984. In Burbank, California, the school district turned an unused school over to a consortium of employers who help pay for child care, provided by school district employers. Parents pay $50 a week for a toddler's care.

Schools can also accommodate working parents by scheduling meetings and programs in the evening. They can teach children useful domestic skills, as Sweden does, in home economics courses required for all boys and girls, and prepare the children to function in egalitarian families of their own. Some schools are teaching child care through hands-on contact with infants and toddlers. A child care class at Westhill High School in Stamford, Connecticut, provides free child care for parents of three- to four-year-olds twice a week. The teacher of the class hopes her program will draw in some of the male students who consider child-development theory for girls only. It is imperative that high schools and universities provide courses about the realities of career and family life. Students need a realistic view of the work required by marriage and child rearing and useful skills like clear communication. They need to examine gender roles rationally to create more democratic families. Catalyst has developed materials to be used in such courses, including classroom exercises and a bibliography.

Perhaps the bottom line of inequality in the home is the fact that women earn 64 percent of what men earn: Women with college degrees still earn less than male high school dropouts. Schools can help equalize the earnings of men and women if they encourage students to consider nontraditional jobs—highly paid technical areas for women and social service jobs for men. In education, as in other ways, the Swedes are a model for equality programs. They take students on field trips to nonstereotyped jobs and discuss biases in job choices. Students also spend three weeks working on job sites. So far the Swedes have not been very successful in equalizing the distribution of the sexes in scientific and service areas but they are looking for ways to make more impact on students. Paying social service professionals more is one solution.

In France, a "Careers Have No Sex" program is designed to raise awareness about job opportunities. A media campaign is directed at young people; schools are encouraged by the Ministry of Women's Rights to remove sexist passages in textbooks. An Anti-Sexism Law prohibits public degradation of women and incitements to violence against them, applying mainly to advertisements. These laws and campaigns are necessary to combat stereotypes that restrict career choices. Schools in the United States also need to pay careful attention to gender stereotypes in textbooks, in career counseling, and in the gender of administrators and teachers. Attitudes about sex roles are crucial, as indicated by the fact that even when mothers and fathers work the same number of hours, mothers still do more child care.[39] Teacher education curriculum is sorely lacking in instruction about gender stereotyping, so new teachers continue the old biases.

Government Programs

The federal government is beginning to recognize the "growing mutual dependence between business and the family."[40] This is useful since about a third of U.S. workers are employed by governments or nonprofit organizations. Since 1981 the federal government's main expenditure has been on child care tax deductions benefiting middle- and upper-income parents. Working parents can deduct a percentage of child care costs for children under fifteen and for disabled dependents. Families that do not earn enough to owe income tax do not benefit from child care deductions, so proposals have been made to refund child care expenses to them. Overall, as Labor Secretary William Brock observed, it is incredible that the increase in working women has been met with so little change.[41] Brock suggests, "It is a problem of sufficient magnitude that everybody is going to have to play a role: families, individuals, businesses, local government, state government." He left out the federal government.

The federal government has been very reluctant to support child care except as a social welfare program for low-income families.[42] This program is inadequate for the one in five children who lives below the poverty line.[43] Congressional proposals to extend successful Head Start–type programs to all preschool children were defeated by President Nixon in 1971. Only during World War II was middle-income families' need for child care acknowledged. Then industry and government joined forces to provide child care for the more than three million married women who entered the work force. Recently the United States has gone backward rather than forward: 75 percent of the nation's day-care centers have had to cut back programs due to the Reagan administration's cuts.[44] The number of children provided with child care has decreased rather than increased in the 1980s. A positive note in an otherwise bleak picture is that legislation to compel divorced parents to pay child support has had an indirect effect on child care by providing mothers with additional funds for adequate care.

Some state and local governments are becoming aware of family and work place interaction. The Massachusetts Department of Social Services funds programs to involve employers in child care, mostly for low-income families. In San Francisco the mayor's office sponsored a conference on Parents at Work, with follow-up seminars. In New York City garment manufacturers, their employees, and city government joined to finance the Garment District Day Care Center of Chinatown, begun in 1983. Cities also need to provide special outreach to teen fathers to include them in their children's upbringing.

Compared to other developed nations the United States does almost nothing for middle-income parents. The French government provides widely used preschool care because the French believe children's development requires it whether their parents are both employed or not. City governments subsidize day care for children over three months of age. Parents pay on a sliding scale ranging from the equivalent of $1 to $10 dollars a day, tax deductible. City and federal government pay the rest of the $20-a-day cost, providing a staff ratio of one adult to five children. The local director is free to build an individual program as long as government standards are met. In Paris, every district has from one to fifteen crèches, open from 7:00 A.M. to 7:00 P.M. Parents who work unusual hours can find care for their children in day homes with two to three other children, carefully supervised by the neighboring crèche and supplied with clothing and food. The crèches will also care for children for a few hours a day to relieve a homemaker. Over 10,000 children are served in Paris, with a waiting list of 5,000.

Centers provide clothes for the children to change into, to save laundry work by parents. They also provide monthly checkups by a doctor and vaccinations. The father of a child cared for in a French crèche remarked, "Seeing how amiable and adaptable our children are, we've realized what a healthy way this is for young children to grow up."[45] In addition, 150 French regional women's centers provide information about women's rights, contraception and abortion, the eligibility of wives of independent workers for social benefits, and equal opportunity in employment.

Sweden has offered paid parental leave since 1974. Parents can divide twelve months of leave between them. For nine months the parent receives 90 percent of his or her income, limited by a ceiling. The next three months are at minimal pay. Parents can work a six-hour day until the child is eight: Many mothers—but few fathers—choose this option of a reduced work day (45 percent of women and 5 percent of men work part time). Fathers also receive two weeks' paid leave at childbirth. Parents are provided with sixty paid days a year to stay home with each child age twelve or younger, or they can opt for a visiting nurse. Parents can take paid leave to help a child adjust to a new day-care center. Since only a quarter of the fathers take advantage of the extensive parental leave, officials have proposed that part of the leave should be reserved for fathers only. The governing Social Democratic Party would also like to provide all parents of young children with a six-hour work day, but Sweden cannot afford to do so. Flexible work hours, and enough day-care centers for each preschool child by 1991, are other goals.

Since most mothers are employed, excellent child care is provided to Swedes on a sliding scale; 65 percent is subsidized by city and national government. Since there are not enough centers, home child care providers are paid and supervised by local authorities as well. After-school care is provided for 12 percent of the children aged seven to ten. Local maternal and child health centers provide education and counseling for young parents and are used by almost all parents. Families also receive allowances for children and for housing. Single parents are guaranteed a minimum income, yet welfare consumes only 1 percent of total government spending. Sweden is dedicated to full employment rather than welfare, so that workers who lose jobs are retrained and/or relocated. Each adult is encouraged to be self-supporting: Spouses are taxed as individuals, with no financial loss to dual-career couples. There is no reason that a country as wealthy as the United States cannot provide similar programs guaranteeing maternal and child health care, parental leave, excellent child care including after-school care, and allowances so that families with children have a standard of living similar to families without children.

The programs described in this chapter occur in the United States on a very small scale, but they are expanding. Most U.S. policies have been designed to keep mothers at home with young children, as in the closing of government-sponsored day care after World War II and President Nixon's veto of a child care bill because it would jeopardize the traditional family structure. Having children alone at home after school is what jeopardizes the family: Children who are alone for more than two hours a day have less self-esteem than other children.[46] Although resistance to mothers' of young children working outside the home continues, the reality is that women are combining motherhood with employment, but they are not superwomen. As fathers are taking on more family work, they too are feeling anxious.[47] Families suffer from stress because institutions that interface with families are slow to change. Realistic planning by employers, schools, and government is required to support the contemporary family. Coparenting will be more common when employed parents have parental leave, flexible work hours, part-time jobs, and child care assistance. As dual-career individuals enter upper management, these changes will occur more commonly.

Checklist of Employer-Sponsored Benefits for Working Parents

1. Flexible work hours.
2. Permanent part-time jobs.
3. Cafeteria benefits.
4. Personal leave to take care of a family member.
5. Child care information and referral services.
6. Option to have employee costs for child care deducted from one's salary to avoid taxation.
7. Child care on or near the work site provided by a consortium of companies.
8. Noontime seminars providing information useful to parents.
9. A library of print and nonprint resources useful to parents, such as communication or efficiency techniques.
10. Counseling services, including stress management courses.
11. A fitness center on the premises.
12. Parental leave with pay, and more extensive time off work without pay, including the option to return to work part time during the child's infancy.
13. Access to a telephone to make calls to children during work hours.
14. Yearly activities that introduce children to their parents' work place.
15. Job placement assistance for the "trailing spouse" in a job transfer.

12

The Future of Parenting

I believe that if men were involved in the day-to-day caring for their children, this would be a much more just and peaceful place.

— *Marty, mother of two*

The future of our society demands that we raise our children with equal access to all opportunities. Feminine input to issues such as militarism may help in avoiding nuclear war.

— *Ron, father of one*

WE live in "a time of parenthesis, the time between eras."[1] We are caught between the ebb of a centralized, hierarchical, standardized industrial society and the flow of a decentralized, democratic, individualized society based on the production of information. Less than a third of our workers manufacture goods, only 4 percent are farmers, and more than two-thirds are service and information workers.[2] Most professionals, managers, clerks, bankers, data processors, and salespeople provide information. The legacy of hierarchical industrial organization is still pervasive, manifest in the patriarchal nuclear family. But the standard of the mother at home with two or three children, the father at work, and an intact marriage belongs to the past. The family is taking many forms, and this trend toward diversity will continue in the "multiple option" society of the future.[3]

We have seen that employment patterns have a major impact on family styles. The change from an industrial economy to one that provides information and services, relying on brains rather than brawn, encourages women's entry into the work force. So does inflation, which requires two earners per family to pay for housing and children's expenses. It now costs over $200,000 to raise two children from birth until graduation from a public college. By the year 2000 at least three-fourths of married couples will be dual earners. This large increase in working mothers means that child rearing must be shared with other adults, including fathers and day-care workers.

The increase in numbers of working wives may be linked with higher divorce rates, which doubled in the 1960s as women gained more economic independence. Although the divorce rate has leveled off in the 1980s, about half of recent marriages will end in divorce, often after seven to nine years. The United States has one of the highest divorce rates in the world, but most divorced Americans will remarry. Social scientists predict that by 2000 the most common family pattern will be to marry and have a child, divorce to form a single-parent family, and then remarry to form a blended family.[4]

Other possible family forms of the future are serial marriages—the first without children, the second with children, and the third in old age (perhaps polygamous because of the shortage of elderly men), renewable contract marriages, communal groups of adults with or without children, group marriages based on common interests such as sports or religion, extended families formed by personal choice rather than kinship, homosexual marriages with or without children, single men with adopted children or children borne by surrogate mothers, and househusbands. As we have seen, families are already experimenting with some of these forms. Parenting issues of the future will revolve around single parents, joint custody after divorce, stepparenting, male/female role sharing, and social supports for employed parents.

The rapid increase in numbers of employed mothers contributes to the growing number of one-child families and first children born to parents in their thirties. Americans, especially those with college educations, are delaying marriage and childbirth. In the future more children will be born to mature parents and most children will be planned and wanted. Many couples are deciding not to have any children at all: About a quarter of the women currently in childbearing years will not give birth.[5] The modern child, then, will have slightly older working parents, not more than one sister or brother, and about a 50 percent chance of living in a single-parent family.

A historical perspective indicates that the family patterns of the late 1940s and the 1950s, which seemed the norm to many of us, were exceptions to a longer trend. Overall the birth rate has declined since the 1820s and the divorce rate has climbed since the Civil War. Family life is "likely to become even more complex, diverse, and unpredictable in the next two decades," population experts conclude.[6]

Impact of Computer Technology

The way we work is archaic, designed for industrial culture and its nuclear family. The computer has the potential to radically change the organization of work and family life. Alvin Toffler named the centuries of agricultural society the First Wave, our immediate past the Second Wave, and our computer-dominated present and future the Third Wave. He believes that "the computer will smash the pyramid: We created the hierarchical, pyramidal, managerial system because we needed it to keep track of people and things people did. With the computer to keep track, we can restructure our institutions horizontally."[7] The electronic cottage, futurists suggest, will be prominent in Third Wave society. That is, in the information age people will work at home, linked to their central office and to other workers around the country by a computer, telephone, closed-circuit television, and teleconference facilities using communication satellites. Variously called "flexiplace," "telecommuting," "remote work," or "home work," this will enable workers to choose where they work and to improve child care arrangements. Many will want to spend some time each week at a central office to have personal contact with their colleagues and a change from the home environment. At home families may work together on jobs, using teenagers as paid participants and thus changing their role in the family.

Futurists believe that computer work will give the home importance and centrality in the new society. As husband and wife spend more time at home and less time getting ready for and traveling to work, they will have more time for family. If the father works at home and the mother does not, obvious changes in family patterns will result. Families may not need to uproot geographically as often for job transfers: Computers and teleconferencing will link them to distant central offices.

Parents may work fewer hours with the advent of the two-earner family and the growing use of robots and computers. Workers will have more time to make goods at home and grow vegetable gardens. Western Europeans are already cutting back on work hours to cope with unemployment. If working hours are shorter—thirty-hour work weeks and less are predicted—people will spend more time in their neighborhoods. A new emphasis on the local community will develop. People will join together in neighborhood projects, activities, and self-help groups. This trend may be an antidote to frequent alienation and loneliness: "Decentralization is the great facilitator of social change," maintains John Naisbitt.[8]

A major community activity will be providing programs for children, with more local involvement in shaping education. As people spend less time commuting to work and place more emphasis on their neighborhoods, we will see the proliferation of tutoring programs by senior citizens, parent education classes, parent discussion groups, supervision for latchkey kids, public preschool and after-school education, Big Brother and Big Sister programs, lending libraries of toys and educational games, children's used clothing exchanges, parent-run babysitting cooperatives, crisis telephone counseling, visiting nurse programs for families with infants or sick or handicapped children, and telephone lines and drop-in centers staffed by teachers, nurses, and therapists to answer children's and parents' questions.

Currently workers are gaining more decision-making power with their employers, and the number of small firms, where workers are likely to be heard, is mushrooming. Small corporations, not the Fortune 1000 companies, have created most of the new jobs in the last decade. The growing emphasis on family, father involvement, and the dynamics of human relationships and the recognition of the harmful physical effects of high-stress jobs will lead workers to shape policies that suit the needs of coparents.

In response to this chapter, Joseph Pleck commented:

> What seems missing or underemphasized among all those quite optimistic projections are the more negative long-term economic trends: The underclass is increasing, the rate of productivity increase is declining, real standard of living is declining, the proportion of children living in poverty is increasing, etc. Also, the decline in childbearing and the aging of the population do not have

positive implications for parenting; this reduces the pressure to provide more resources and accommodations to working families.[9]

Others see additional problems looming in our changing society. Some fear that flexiplace will lead to sweat shop exploitation of clerical workers, especially low-paid women workers who, in the isolation of their homes, will lose out on opportunities for advancement. Health hazards of working daily with video display terminals are an issue especially for pregnant women. The division between the information-rich white-collar workers and information-poor blue-collar workers may widen, since high schools in wealthy districts are much more likely to offer computer courses than schools in poorer districts. Computers have the potential either to lessen or to heighten traditional class and sex roles.

To rationally plan our future, we must make our governments and industries respond to the needs of egalitarian families. Our political system reacts to pressure groups. Those who care about relieving the strains on families need to formulate clear goals and push for them. Lobbying for flexible work hours is a place to begin.

Science Fiction View of the Future

What would a society be like if gender equality existed? A number of science fiction authors have described truly egalitarian societies. Feminist writers, male and female, portray a future in which the basic unit of society is the individual, surrounded by a small, closely knit tribal community with a decentralized government. In this future the nuclear family is no longer expected to provide members' economic and social needs. Child care is never the primary responsibility of just the mother.

One such utopia, described by Edward Bellamy in *Looking Backward* (1888), is a collective and service-oriented society. People need few possessions here: there are public dining halls, laundries, clubhouses, and gardens. Men and women serve in the industrial army, which is segregated in two branches that provide services for all citizens. Bellamy's female characters are frank and unconstrained, he explains, because they do not depend on a man for economic support.

In another utopian society, Aldous Huxley's *Island* (1962), families join Mutual Adoption Clubs (MAC), composed of fifteen to twenty-five families. Children are free to go back and forth between the homes in their MAC. They are not treated like guests but are expected to assume duties in whatever home they chose. Work, school, and child care are integrated.

Ernest Callenback's *Ecotopia* (1975) describes a revolution in which northern California, Oregon, and Washington break away from the United States to form their own utopian country, led by a woman. Ecotopia's primary concerns are living ecologically and humanely and decentralizing power. Schools, hospitals, and businesses are run by their workers/owners. Picture telephones enable citizens to watch government deliberations and call in their opinions, the move toward participatory government described by Naisbitt. Ecotopians bulldoze down row houses and do away with cars, build homes in the first floors of city buildings, and play volleyball and ping-pong in the streets. They have time for recreation because their work week is twenty hours. Many people live in communal groups centering on vocational or other common interests. The main character lives in a press commune, where he cooks and gardens collectively and shares a library, a gymnasium, and a press room. As in *Island*, women have access to frozen sperm associated with specific talents of the donors.

Marge Piercy's *Woman on the Edge of Time* (1976) describes a rationally conceived egalitarian society that in some ways resembles Twin Oaks and the Federation of Egalitarian Communities. Set in the year 2036, this utopian community gives each adult his or her own room; children live in a children's house where twenty-four-hour-a-day child care is provided by community workers. Children are the responsibility of the group, not just of their parents. Ecologically sound living is stressed. As at Twin Oaks, people live in small communities whose size encourages democratic participation in government.

Other feminist utopias share Piercy's view of parenting as the community's responsibility. Society becomes "home-like," Carol Pearson explains.[10] People live simply, ecologically, without class distinctions or much difference in wealth, and cooperate with each other. In *The Dispossessed* (Ursula LeGuin, 1974), children are cared for in a kibbutz-like children's house, eating with their parents in the communal dining hall. The nuclear family is usually replaced by group caretaking; in *The Female Man* (Joanna Russ, 1975) families often consist of around thirty persons. In the tribal society described in *The Kin of Ata Are Waiting for You* (Dorothy Bryant, 1976) the intruder-hero cannot tell who the natural parents are since all the adults care for the children. A character in *Herland* (Charlotte Perkins Gilman, 1915), an all-female society, explains to the males who discover them that the mother "is not the only one to care for them [the children]. There are others whom she knows to be wiser." Children select five share-mothers when they reach puberty in *Motherlines* (Suzy McKee Charnas, 1979). In *The Wanderground* (Sally Gearhart, 1979) small groups of women live simply in rural areas and rear their children together.

The biological role of the mother does not lead to an exclusive responsibility for twenty-four-hour child care by the mother, and some novels separate reproduction and mothering altogether. For example, in *The Legend of Biel* (Mary Staton, 1975) mentors guide the children through their initiation into adulthood, and a talking machine called a Gladdin monitors infant care. The father's role is eliminated altogether in the exclusively female societies described in *Herland*, *The Female Man*, *Motherlines*, and *The Wanderground*. However, the hero of *The Dispossessed* was cared for mainly by his father because his mother was not very interested in parenting. In *Woman on the Edge of Time* men co-mother. In *The Left Hand of Darkness* (1987) LeGuin describes a one-gender society, in which adults come into periodic estrus when any individual can become male or female. A child has multiple fathers in *The Marriages Between Zones Three, Four and Five* (Doris Lessing, 1980), a gene-father and mind-fathers who nurture the child. Children learn by being included in adult activities rather than being isolated in age-segregated schools, and are free to experiment sexually with other children.

These novels all look for alternatives to the isolated family alienated in an uncaring urban environment. Some of the ideas projected by science fiction have already become real, such as frozen sperm donated by talented men, current efforts by groups such as Unitarian churches to organize intentional extended families, and Twin Oaks's twenty-four-hour-a-day community child care.

The science fiction authors are unanimous in envisioning the opening out of the family to include nonrelated neighbors who share child rearing. Science fiction is useful in suggesting future relationships between the sexes and between adults and children. The unanimity with which egalitarian writers of both sexes leave behind sex-role divisions and the isolated nuclear family perhaps indicates future developments.

Impact of Reproductive Technology

Much social change arises from technological change, as portrayed in *Woman on the Edge of Time*. Technology is now changing human reproduction through genetic engineering, reproduction separated from intercourse, fertilization outside of the uterus, surrogate motherhood, gender selection, more effective male and female contraception, and elective sex changes by transsexuals.

The most far-reaching impact could arise from technology determining the sex of a child. Cross-culturally, spouses want a firstborn son to carry on the husband's family name, to prove his virility, and to provide a financial backup for the couple in old age. This preference for a firstborn male holds true for young couples in the United States.[11] Katherine Pope and I surveyed 178 college students in California and Texas about their preference for a firstborn: 52 percent of men preferred a boy, while only 11 percent preferred a girl. Similarly, half of the women preferred a boy, and 15 percent preferred a girl. The others did not have a preference. It is clear that boys would predominate among firstborns if parents could select their baby's gender.

Artificial insemination with selected sperm, either XX or XY, is currently being used to determine a baby's gender. A recent development with the potential for sex selection is the CVB test, performed during pregnancy eight to eleven weeks after the last menstrual period. Cells from the villi, projections from the outer sac surrounding the fetus, are withdrawn through the cervix in a procedure called a chorionic villi biopsy. The chromosomes indicate the sex of the fetus. Results are available in two to three weeks, so that if an abortion is desired it can be performed early in the pregnancy. A couple who recently had the test performed in San Francisco reported that it cost $850 and was paid for by their health insurance. This test is performed earlier and the results are quicker than for amniocentesis, the more common test for birth defects, which is performed seventeen to twenty weeks after conception. Early detection of a fetus's gender and early term abortion of the undesired sex could be used as a means of controlling the sex of an infant, as it was in China until stopped by the government.

The implications of gender selection need to be closely examined. Firstborn and only children have many advantages in terms of time alone with their parents and expectations for achievement. Studies of achieving women often find them to be firstborns: When I surveyed twenty-five Chico professional women, mainly professors, doctors, and psychologists, 65 percent were firstborn or only children. (The majority were also androgynous or masculine scoring on the Bem Sex-Role Inventory.) If people were able to select the sex of their children, we would see a proliferation of firstborn and only male children, as parents are more likely to have more children if they have a girl first.

If families of the future are composed of more boys, we could see an increase in male homosexuality, an increase in crime and war, cloistering of women, girls born more often to upper-middle-class families since they are less likely to believe in sex-role differentiation, a decrease in population, more pressure on women to become surrogate mothers, an increase in polyandry, and the loss of achievement motivation given to firstborn girls.

Another technological change in reproduction is out-of-uterus conception, or fertilization of eggs in a laboratory container. This technique is of benefit to over one-sixth of all couples who are infertile. The expensive process first led to Louise Brown's birth in England in 1978 and has led to more than 1,000 births since, currently a birth a day. One attempt can cost $5,000; usually at least three tries are required before a woman gets pregnant. Another reproductive technique, successfully performed at UCLA in 1984, is lavage, in which fertilized eggs are flushed from the uterus of a woman who conceived by artificial insemination. The eggs are implanted in the uterus of the sperm donor's wife, whose fallopian tubes are blocked. This procedure costs from $4,000 to $7,000. A baby now can have multiple parents: a sperm donor, an egg donor, and a surrogate mother who carries the implanted embryo to term for an infertile couple. Embryos are now being frozen and later implanted, as evidenced in England by the birth of a twin eighteen months later than her sister. Young couples could keep their embryos frozen until their careers were well established to avoid worries about aging parental chromosomes.

Does the high cost of ovum transfer and the cost of surrogate mothers, who are often paid over $10,000 plus medical expenses, mean that only the wealthy will be able to overcome infertility difficulties? Will the wealthy hire women to carry their embryos to term? Will embryos be available for purchase and by whom? Will genetic engineers tamper with the genes of a developing embryo before implantation? Aldous Huxley raised these issues in 1932 in his novel *Brave New World.* He portrayed four genetic types, recognized by their different colored uniforms, bred to perform specific functions in society. We now have the technological capabilities to breed humans selectively, since eggs and sperm are combined in laboratories by technicians.

The implications of out-of-uterus conception and artificial insemination are far-reaching. Since 1960 over 250,000 Americans have been born as a consequence of artificial insemination.[12] Artificial insemination babies are likely to be boys. A sperm bank of Nobel prize winners, established by Robert K. Graham in 1979 in California and titled the Repository for Germinal Choice, is an example of current genetic engineering with intent to produce a desired trait—intelligence, in this case. I talked with the second woman inseminated by this Palo Alto sperm bank. She is a psychologist who became interested in the program when she was investigating it for a client. She picked her donor from a catalogue of written descriptions of men identified by a number. She was attracted to Number 28's mathematical genius coupled with his musical talent. She now is the mother of a one-and-a-half-year-old son, born when she was single and 39. The children of this unusual experiment in genetic engineering are not yet old enough to show special brilliance or talent.

Science fiction writers describe even more radical genetic manipulation, such as extending our life spans indefinitely, producing people with special abilities such as telepathy, altering people so they can live in the ocean or on other planets, changing gender at will or producing hermaphrodites, cloning a child just like oneself, having more than two parents, and altering men so that they can give birth.[13] The latter is already being discussed by Australian scientists. Women with hysterectomies have carried fetuses to term with the embryo implanted on the intestine: Men could probably do this, too, as a male baboon carried a fetus for four months before the experiment was terminated. These alterations sound bizarre, but so did Jules Verne's description of a submarine in *20,000 Leagues Under the Sea* when it was published in 1870. Technological changes in human conception are occurring whether we approve or not. We need to ponder the ethical and social implications. The notion of parenthood and motherhood is altered by these artificial techniques of reproduction, which will have an impact on families in the future.

Housing of the Future

Technological change is also altering housework. Just as power looms and factory food processing took over much of women's work in the nineteenth century, so robots and computers may take over much of the housework of the twentieth century. Baking may be replaced by a programmed refrigerator/microwave that defrosts and cooks dinner. A house called Future Home, currently owned by a Dallas couple, is maintained by six computers, commanded by touching a light pen to a screen or pressing keys on the telephone. The electronic system to Future Home costs $500,000 and controls heating, security, audiovisuals, pool, and telephones.

The Citicorp Center in San Francisco is an example of a "smart" building. Its electronic "brain" can turn on lights, adjust building temperature, and transmit data. Computer systems like WALDO currently can turn on appliances and lights and set a thermostat. Smart appliances, such as dishwashers, toasters, and microwaves currently on the market, are programmed by silicone chips that can calculate time or temperature and process information from sensor pads. The Phone Slave, invented by Nicholas Negroponte at MIT, can recognize voices of frequent callers, take and deliver messages, and remind its owner of appointments. The phone can learn from the freezer when it is out of ice and pass the message on to its owner.

As home maintenance becomes more technological, stereotypes of domestic work will be altered and men may become more domestic.

To accommodate the family of the future, however, it will not be enough to place a house management computer, a robot, and a smart telephone into the existing suburban house. Dolores Hayden, a professor of architecture at UCLA, explains, "To recognize the desire of women and men to be both paid workers and parents is to search for a way to overcome the physical separation of paid jobs and parenting inherent in many urban settings."[14] The suburban home represents an "architecture of gender," perpetuating traditional sex roles by separating work and family life. A long commute to work from a suburban neighborhood is difficult for involved parents, who do not want to leave their child with a babysitter from 7:00 A.M. to 6:00 P.M. They want to be near their children in case of an accident or illness, to participate in school activities, and take them to their lessons or appointments. Presently, men are more likely to commute to high-paying jobs and women to work at low-paying jobs nearer home. Women are less likely to drive cars and more likely to use mass transit than men,[15] although mass transit is not readily available in suburbs. The segregation of homes away from work and stores has "affected women more than men, because our lives have never been so neatly partitioned between the different areas of work, leisure and home in the way that men's have," according to the authors of one study.[16] Public places need to reflect the needs of parents, including short-term child care in stores, play areas in banks and airports (as in Boston's Logan International), and spaces to change diapers in men's and women's restrooms.

Although the suburban home is portrayed by advertisers as fulfilling for women, these homes require considerable housework.[17] Studies indicate that many women prefer condominium-type high-density homes that require little work and are close to jobs. "Women don't want to be relegated to the fringes of life," concluded a study of 800 women in San Jose, California.[18] The post–World War II home perpetuates traditional sex roles through its kitchen designed for one cook with many appliances to service, elaborate bathrooms, many rooms with polished floors, and a large yard touted as a woman's dream come true. Until the mid-1960s women spent as much time doing housework as their grandmothers did. As they have entered the paid work force, however, women have cut back on the time they spend on housework, by using methods such as buying convenience foods. As anthropologist Margaret Mead pointed out

> Our present residential style—the single house with its expensive use of energy and space, and its isolation from others—is designed for the single family with several children. We now need entirely new designs, ones that make new provision for privacy for parents away from children, for care of children in groups, for houses that do not demand the continuous attention of a woman, and for services that can be obtained centrally.[19]

Suburbs tend to segregate people by race and age. Mead suggested that an effective community includes three generations living nearby.[20] Grandparents can spend time with children and provide family continuity while parents are at work. An integrated community would provide footpaths for older people to walk to shopping centers, to visit each other, and to be with children at day-care centers. This kind of cluster housing near community services currently exists in planned towns such as Reston, Virginia, the nascent Cerro Gordo community near Cottage Grove, Oregon, and the Stelle community in Illinois.

The Stelle community is an example of a progressive "intentional" community. The group, begun in 1963 by Richard Kieninger, is committed to a vision of the future described in Kieninger's book *The Ultimate Frontier.*[21] The vision is of a New Age city, the center of a new renaissance,[22] and it includes the creation of an extended family to prevent the isolation of the nuclear family. The Stelle community was formed in 1974 on 200 acres among Illinois cornfields. Its 45 privately owned homes shelter 125 residents; several homes are cooperatively rented by single persons. The community supports families in the following ways.

Stelle has built two schools, a community center, and a factory for work. Residents are experimenting with the production of alternative power sources, including solar greenhouses, alcohol fuel, and an "envelope" home with a double wall containing a layer of insulating air. They have formed a credit union, a car co-op, and a video center. Meetings are held monthly to shape Stelle's growth, with decisions made by majority vote. Mediation is offered to settle disputes among neighbors. Socials, including potluck dinners and formal dances, are held at least once a month. To encourage the growth of its residents, the community offers skill-training programs and frequent workshops and seminars about emotional, spiritual, and physical health.

Stelle provides parents with abundant support systems, although in a way that perpetuates traditional role division of child rearing. Classes in birthing, child development, and education are usually for women. Mothers are expected to spend three to four hours a day educating preschool children. I would change this approach to include fathers equally, but the idea of community parenting classes is worth duplicating elsewhere. Linda Guinn, the Montessori teacher at Stelle, reported that the majority of her six-year-olds read at the third-grade level or above.[23] Mother School, including "circle sessions" to share feelings about parenting, is held in the mornings. Mothers are expected to devote themselves full time to the education of their children until the children are in school. Education of children is considered a profession: "You don't have a child unless you're really prepared to go into mothering as a career," Guinn stated. Stelle children are raised to be "much more than anything that we have been aware of in our society before." Teaching a child is viewed as expression of parents' love: "A child feels like they are somebody. It increases their self-esteem to teach children skills. They just glow," Guinn observed.

A staff resource teacher visits parents every week to discuss the education of the child, discipline techniques, and feelings about parenting. The home visits are part of the attempt to overcome the isolation of the nuclear family and to create an extended family. Potlucks are held every two months or so to enable families to share their experiences as new parents. A Parents' Resources Center is stocked with books for parents and children, learning toys, and films. A newsletter for parents, "Parenting for Excellence," is published by the Stelle Group. A mother of two children at Stelle told me that she appreciates living in a community where everyone knows and likes her family, although sometimes she has "a little trouble with a community so small, so active, with meetings and parties, and being expected to teach the kids."

Many communities established collective services before the Stelle community. Nineteenth-century society experimented with collective services until U.S. business interests, coining slogans such as "good homes make contented workers," pressured twentieth-century Americans into choosing isolated, single-family dwellings with individually owned appliances. If the momentum of collective services had continued, we would be living in a far more egalitarian society.

The Swedes picked up the concept of collective services where the Americans left off, building "family hotels" in the 1930s. Evening meals, child care, and recreational facilities are provided in these Swedish apartment complexes. I stayed in one of the original family hotels in Stockholm in 1980. Preschool children eat their lunch on picnic tables in the central courtyard adjacent to the day-care center, and dinner at nearby Hässlby collective house is like a dinner party with residents who take turns preparing dinner just once every two weeks. Another Swedish collective apartment house, built in Linköping in 1980, has a ground floor containing a library, kitchen, dining room, coffee room, playroom, and workshops for ceramics, weaving, and carpentry. It is designed to combine the needs of the elderly, the handicapped, and the children and to enable people to spend time together in the common areas. Renting an apartment in this collective house costs about the same as renting any other new apartment.

Dolores Hayden terms the ideological push for more practical housing "material feminism." Hayden maintains that we need "a clear spatial ideology" to transform suburban homes.[24] She advocates that every forty suburban homes should have facilities for day care and after-school care, laundromats, take-out food, a food co-op, and a garage with dial-a-ride services.[25] Large houses could be converted to duplexes and triplexes and garages turned into offices, food co-ops, and other service areas. These ideas are being put into practice by Anne Howell's nonprofit corporation Innovative Housing in Fairfax, California.

A first step in creating more practical housing is to change zoning laws and building codes. Homeowners (64 percent of Americans own their own homes) should be able to have businesses in their homes and add on apartments for elderly parents, a college student who helps with child care and housework, an extended family of friends, or a renter who supplements the family income. Apartments could be constructed as they are in Sweden, with an additional kitchenette and a separate but adjoining space for adolescents or grandparents. These kinds of accommodations, plus community swimming pools, sports fields, child care facilities, and access to public transportation, should be required as part of all new housing developments.

Families do not have to wait for planned housing in order to have the benefits of sharing space. Three houses in San Francisco made collective space and services by taking down the fences dividing their adjacent back yards, for example. Together they constructed a garden, tool shed, and hot tub. They watched with delight as one family's eight-year-old developed a special bond with another family's baby. They started bartering labor, such as trading fresh baked bread for babysitting, and sharing a Saturday morning brunch under the trees or a birthday barbeque for one of the children. In Berkeley, the residents of a whole city block on Derby Street transformed their yards into a park and play area for children, and started a day-care center in one of the homes.

Changes in Psychology

Modifying our housing design and acquiring "smart" appliances will not do much to change rigid sex-role division if our attitudes and psychology do not change. One illustration of current uncertainty and anxiety about changes in sex roles is the popular interest in "gender benders," rock music stars who act out fantasies of dressing like the opposite sex. Popular films also explore what it is like to behave like the other sex—for example, Dustin Hoffman as Tootsie, Julie Andrews as *Victor/Victoria*, and Barbra Streisand as Yentl.[26]

Psychologists as well as the media are reexamining their definitions of what is normal, healthy, male and female behavior. They used to define the sexes very differently, considering women to be emotionally expressive, nurturant, passive, and dependent, and men to be goal-oriented, independent, and assertive. When therapists counseled families, they discouraged "inappropriate" behavior, such as a mother wanting to have a career, or a father giving more priority to child raising than to climbing a career ladder.

Sandra Bem, a psychology professor, realized that "we need a new standard of psychological health for the sexes."[27] She established the standard of *androgyny*, although she warns about glorifying this as another absolute, preferring to transcend masculine and feminine labels altogether. Encouraging androgynous behavior is now a goal for progressive psychologists and counselors. Androgyny is the integration of instrumental/masculine and expressive/feminine traits in one personality. An androgynous person can flexibly shift from one set of traits to the other as appropriate for different situations and as imperative for role sharing. She or he can take care of a baby or repair an object, comfort a friend or ask for a pay raise. This does not exclude being attractive to the other sex, but allows for fully mature behavior, ultimately more appealing and interesting.

In 1974 Bem designed the Bem Sex-Role Inventory, used in numerous studies to test for psychological androgyny. Janet Spence and Robert Helmreich have since designed another scale for androgyny.[28] Bem found that androgynous persons have higher self-esteem and are more likely to be flexible, creative, and well-adjusted than highly sex-typed persons (men scoring masculine and women scoring feminine).[29] Other researchers emphasize that the high masculinity score is what is crucial for self-esteem.[30] It only makes sense that repressing half of our human qualities would diminish creativity and increase anxiety.

Spence and Helmreich believe that androgynous parents are the most effective of all parent types.[31] A contradictory finding by Diana Baumrind is that androgynous parents are too child-centered and permissive, and their children are less competent than those with more traditional, sex-typed parents.[32] Of the coparents I interviewed for this book, only around a quarter are sex-typed, similar to those in another study of role-sharing parents.[33] The couples I interviewed for *The 50-50 Marriage* most frequently scored androgynous and masculine, compared to the traditional couples who most frequently scored sex-typed. The children of the former have higher self-esteem than the children of traditional sex-typed parents.

Sex type is not a fixed personality trait. Groups of feminine-scoring women became more androgynous through assertiveness training and consciousness-raising techniques.[34] People change their Bem score over their lifetime, especially after major changes such as getting married or having a baby.[35] Role-sharing behavior is probably both a result and a cause of personality sex type. Despite the lack of clarity about what androgyny scores really mean, or if scores can predict behavior, we can say that there is a movement away from the old psychological norm of classifying healthy female behavior as only expressive and healthy male behavior as only instrumental. The new thrust is integration of both modes. As parents adopt a wider range of behaviors, so will their children.

The Men's Liberation Movement

Major social change requires two conditions. Warren Farrell explains that large numbers of people must be economically hurt and feel personal rejection.[36] For example, the American Revolution was fueled by the British imposing taxes on the colonists and rejecting them as citizens with equal representation in the commonwealth. Information about the problem must also be widely available. Then a crisis situation will ignite protest.[37] Farrell explains that divorced fathers are the first group of men in American history to suffer economic hurt from our traditional sex roles, as they are forced to pay child and spouse support. Their lack of shared custody creates a sense of personal rejection. Divorced fathers' rights groups are in fact the largest branch of the current men's movement.

Men are not going to change because of women, many men's liberation leaders say; men must change because of other men. Men's esteem has a powerful influence on sex roles. Men involved in domestic tasks may receive negative comments from their friends, such as, "You're getting us in trouble with our wives!" Cross-culturally, one task least likely to be done by men is hanging out the laundry where neighbors can see them. This is true even in Cuba where, after much public discussion, the government passed a Family Code in 1976 legislating shared family responsibilities and duties. (Cuban children discuss equality in the home at school, changing these old attitudes among young people).[38] To see widespread changes in men's roles, we need legislation for equality and a men's movement as compelling as the women's liberation movement in showing the hazards of restrictive sex roles.

Unknown to many, the men's movement is growing. It consists of consciousness-raising groups, local centers, newsletters and magazines, books, and national organizations. Its members can be labeled feminists, masculinists, fathers' rights advocates, or nurturing men. One of the first activist men's groups was the Berkeley Men's Center, which published its manifesto in 1973. However, most men have not yet articulated the restrictions caused by their traditional role. While Betty Friedan provided a vocabulary of liberation for women when she "named the problem that had no name" in *The Feminine Mystique* (1963), men still lack the words of liberation. Herb Goldberg's *The Hazards of Being Male* was an important step forward for men, but it has not struck the same chord in many men.

The men's movement has been influenced by the technique of discussion groups used by feminists. Men's consciousness-raising or support groups began in 1969 in cities like Boston and New York, according to Warren Farrell. Small groups of men meet in each other's homes to learn to be emotionally expressive and nurturant and to lessen their dependence on women for emotional support and validation. They struggle with fears about homosexuality, hugging each other during group meetings. They discuss ways the male role turns them into "success objects," judged by their job status and bank accounts rather than their character. They agree about being tired of always having to take the initiative with women. They talk about the ways that they feel unable or unwilling to live up to media images of masculinity and discuss their longing for contact with their fathers and how they will be different from their fathers. They struggle with new definitions of male power. Most of all they try to express their feelings, after so many years of hearing big boys don't cry, don't be a sissy, take it like a man, keep a stiff upper lip, be in charge, and be cool. The rejection of James Bond, John Wayne, and Superman—men who are without a family, unexpressive, always cool, and in charge—is of great value to husbands and fathers.

A recent branch of the men's movement tells men that they have gone too far and gotten too "soft" in trying to please feminist women, that they need to make contact with the "wildman" masculine energy in their psyche. The terminology comes from a widely discussed interview with the poet Robert Bly, published in *New Age* magazine in 1982. Bly observed a deep sadness in young men:

> Part of the grief was a remoteness from their fathers, which they felt keenly, but part, too, came from trouble in their marriages or relationships. They had learned to be receptive, and it wasn't enough to carry their marriages. The man of the 1970s was nurturing . . . but he could not say what he wanted, and stick by it; that was a different matter. . . . What males need now is an energy that can face this [new] energy in women, and meet it.[39]

Other branches of the men's movement are masculinists and profeminists, who have some conflicts. Masculinists emphasize the ways that men are hurt by the traditional male role. Profeminists agree with this emphasis, but add commitment to ending violence against women and subordination of women. In a 1983 issue of *Transitions*, the newsletter of the masculinist organization Free Men, Herb Goldberg wrote, "The militant, feminist men are strong on moral abstractions (content) but actually very macho and destructive in their process. They attack, criticize, judge, moralize and presume superiority and righteousness toward those who are in disagreement with them."[40] Robert Brannon had previously written in the profeminist magazine *M.*, "Goldberg's mixture of aggressive male self-interest, pop psychology, and barely disguised hostility to women struck exactly the right note," for Free Men masculinists.[41]

As chairperson of the National Organization of Changing Men (NOCM), Brannon defined the goals of the organization in its magazine, *Brother*, when NOCM was launched in 1983.[42] Masculinists agree with his first goal of "working to unlearn our life-long indoctrination in the male sex role, and to discover new ways of living and relating to others which will make us freer, happier, and . . . healthier in every sense of the word." Implementation of this shared goal is necessary for role sharing.

Brannon's second goal is to join the fight for full equality for woman; to eradicate rape, battering, pornography, child abuse, and incest; and to fight for ERA and reproductive choice. Free Men calls this concern with violence against women flagellation, self-blame, and guilt, neglecting the ways men are victimized by violence in their roles as soldiers, protectors, athletes, and over-stressed family breadwinners. Masculinists favor feminism when it advocates sharing responsibilities: Herb Goldberg said that feminism is the best thing that ever happened to men, if it means shared breadwinning and reduction of women's unassertiveness, passivity, sexual and emotional manipulation, and blaming of men.[43]

Brannon's third goal is to eradicate homophobia. He believes that fear of homosexuality is "probably the single most powerful source of opposition among men to changing the traditional masculine behaviors," and so it is an important issue for all changing men. Free Men is not vocal about homosexuality, and appears to have few gay members, but gay men are an active and playful presence at NOCM conferences.

Activists for divorced fathers' rights, the third branch of the men's movement, has the most groups and is the most vocal and well organized. These men are concerned mainly with shared custody of children, and also demand fair spousal and child support payments. Fathers Demanding Equal Justice, Equal Rights for Fathers, and Fathers for Equal Rights are examples of the over two hundred father's rights groups existing today. Their umbrella group is The National Congress for Men. Its director, Jack Kammer, wrote to me that

> women's changes to date have been women's gains. It is incumbent on women that they now accept a few losses to accommodate the gains men must make in order to re-balance the male-female relationship. The obvious male gain women must accept is our parental equality. You are no doubt familiar with women who say they *want* men to be more involved as fathers. We on the other hand, are familiar with women who tend to say things like, "But I'm the mother."[44]

The movement of nurturing men, described in chapter 7, is helping to create acceptance of men's involvement in child rearing both as fathers and as child care providers.

The California Anti-Sexist Men's Political Caucus distributes a flyer listing specific actions men can take to speed change: Spend more time with children because "they have much to teach and because their natural sense of emotional freedom needs support," learn to listen better, spend a period of time as a househusband, work to end sexism in school curriculum and career planning, and "keep your spirits up: The patriarchy is slowly crumbling." Men are changing and the men's movement can provide them with impetus and support for equality. "We believe that traditional masculine values of aggression, competition and internalization of feelings are destructive to ourselves and those around us," stated the Chicago Men's Gathering in a flyer advertising their newsletter. Most of all, men need words and concepts to realize and name the painful limitations of the John Wayne role to their emotional and physical well-being. Men's oppression is not as obvious as women's oppression because of men's privilege and status and the expectation that they will be indulged by women. Nevertheless, the pressures and restrictions on men are real barriers to family intimacy and to men's mental and emotional health.

Women's Liberation Movement

A feminist focus of the 1980s is on democratic family life, with shared responsibility between wives and husbands and social supports for employed parents. Recent criticism has been directed at groups like the National Organization for Women (NOW) and the National Women's Political Caucus (NWPC) for not putting more effort in this direction.[45] Gloria Steinem lists the four main goals of the women's movement of the 1980s as: democratic families, reproductive freedom, redefining the work place, and depoliticizing culture.[46] (An example of the last goal is equal representation of women and minorities on television.) Betty Friedan's *The Second Stage* calls for the next phase in the women's movement to bring about a revolution in values, where work and family are restructured to allow for equal participation of men at home and women at work.[47] In the second stage, "men's and women's needs converge," as we have seen in this book. Key issues of the second stage include child care, flexible work hours, and parental leave, as described in chapter 11.

Letty Cottin Pogrebin states in *Family Politics* that "what civil rights and Vietnam were to the Sixties, and women's rights and the environment were to the Seventies, family issues have become to the Eighties."[48] Until the late 1970s feminists shied away from intellectual examination of marriage and motherhood. In 1974 a pioneer, Jessie Bernard, wrote *The Future of Motherhood;* two years later Adrienne Rich published *Of Woman Born;* then Dorothy Dinnerstein came out with *The Mermaid and the Minotaur.* These writers looked critically at the impact of woman's function as the primary parent on her children, on herself, and on male-female relationships. Nancy Chodorow's *The Reproduction of Mothering* in 1978 signaled a proliferation of thinking about the family. However, the main focus of the feminist organizations NOW and NWPC is on changing laws as the ERA would do, electing women to political office, and allowing reproductive choice. Second-stage issues of child care and flexible work hours must be more central; a step forward is NOW's lobbying for the parental leave act.

"We have made the revolutionary discovery that children have two parents," remarked Gloria Steinem, noting the new attitude that men can be as loving and nurturing as women.[49] This belief makes shared parenthood seem feasible. When I asked Steinem how frequently she hears discussions of shared parenting as she travels around the country giving lectures, she said, "The country is staggering around some place between the 17th century and the 23rd century, so you can find anything. We're lurching toward change." But after years of speaking at college campuses, she has yet to hear a male student stand up and ask how he can combine a family and a career.

The women's movement has changed our expectations about the range of activities and expression open to the sexes. Alvin Toffler observes, "When I see role structures cracking and reforming then I know I am in the presence of a real, historical revolution."[50] As evidence, magazines spawned in the 1970s included *Ms.*, *Working Mother*, *Working Woman*, and *Savvy*. The traditional women's magazines now include feminist and dual-career family issues. However, we will know shared parenting is prevalent when we have a *Working Father* magazine with a larger circulation than David Giveans' *Nurturing Today*.[51]

To live in the midst of a revolution of expanded possibilities is both confusing and exhilarating. The men's and women's liberation movements are challenging our familiar ideas about how we live our daily lives. Change causes insecurity. It is not surprising that a powerful backlash exists, led by conservative politicians and religious fundamentalists who would like women to stay at home. The liberation movements provide support groups and literature to redefine rigid gender roles. The Third Wave is advancing; we can either hide our heads in the sand or stand on a surfboard and ride the crest of the wave where the view is clear.

Conclusion

We are in the midst of turbulent change, moving from the Second Wave society of uniformity to the Third Wave society of many options. Family forms are changing as both parents enter the paid work force, yet the important social institutions of industry, schools, and government act as if we were in the nineteenth century. Equal parenting is valued but not usually practiced. That the work structure and value system keeps men from equal participation in family life is a tragedy. Women who share in earning a living for their families while continuing to provide most of their unpaid domestic services bear a heavy burden. Dual-earner families are stressed by having too many demands made on their time, while the media adds insult to injury by making juggling career and family look glamorous. Justice requires social institutions to provide services for working parents. Flexible working hours, employer help with child care, after-school programs, and legislation mandating parental leave policies are examples of necessary reforms.[52]

People who draw their identity from various roles flourish better than those who depend on one main role as homemaker or breadwinner. Involved fathers feel closer to their children than fathers who give most of their time and energy to work. Involved fathers are proud of their bonds with their children and their influence on their children's development. Children thrive with the attention of two parents. The future of our planet may rest on men's increasing closeness to their children. Men who have opened their hearts will oppose the nuclear arms race and the pollution of the work place and the environment. Since wives are often gatekeepers to their husbands' involvement in child rearing, women and men share the power to create equal parenting. We can learn from the pioneers who are struggling to create equality at home to forge a new coparenting style, and raise a new generation of children with a full range of choices.

Appendix 1
General Description of the Study

I INTERVIEWED 291 coparents in 30 states: 83 couples in the West, 25 in the Northeast, 24 in the Midwest, and 13 in the South. The interviews were held between 1982 and 1986. My assumption was that the people most likely to be doing sustained equal parenting would be those who believe in equality between women and men. I requested interviews with mothers who did no more than 50% of the child care and fathers who did their equal share. These parents are not a representative sample of Americans, as the usual division of family work is mothers 70% and fathers 30%.

I interviewed at least 25 couples for each of six family styles: married parents, divorced parents, stepparents, lesbian and gay parents, fathers the primary parent, and communal parents. The distribution of interviews was:

Married: 23 couples, 1 individual = 47 total

Divorced: 13 coparents, 17 individuals, and 3 sets of couples living together of which one member was the divorced parent = 49 total

Stepparents: 31 couples = 62 total

Lesbian and gay: 20 lesbian couples, 2 lesbian individuals, 3 gay fathers = 45 total

Father primary: 17 married couples, 7 divorced men, 2 of their ex-wives, and 2 couples living together = 45 total

Communal: 10 single-house groups and 6 larger groups = 43 total

I found the parents by contacting the following groups, listed in order of greatest numerical response:

1. University coordinators of women's studies.
2. Regional chapters of the National Organization for Women.
3. Parents in California referred by my friends and each other, using a snowball technique.
4. Requests for interviews in newsletters and in *The 50-50 Marriage*.
5. Attendees of the eighth National Conference on Men and Masculinity in Ann Arbor, Michigan.
6. Requests for coparents to contact me made while I was speaking on television and radio shows.

As is usual for pacesetters, coparents are generally highly educated. Many have graduate degrees and professional jobs. Their attitudes toward sex roles and politics are liberal. The majority are in their thirties and have one or two children. Unfortunately, I had difficulty finding an ethnic diversity: all were white except for two black couples.

I interviewed the parents together, usually over the telephone, for at least one hour. I usually interviewed divorced parents separately; over half of the divorced parent interviews included only one of the coparents. The interviews were taped and transcribed, with names changed in the book. The information I asked of parents was:

1. A brief biographical sketch of each parent: age, highest degree, job, how long married, age and gender of children.
2. A personality profile of your child(ren).
3. How do you divide care of your children, on weekdays and on weekends?
4. What are the sources of conflict that require discipline and what are your discipline techniques?
5. What are your children's responsibilities around the house? How do you make sure their work gets done?
6. What do you do for fun with your children?
7. Do you find yourself treating sons and daughters differently? If so, how? Why or why not? How do you deal with media messages about girls growing up to be nurses and boys becoming doctors, girls playing with Barbie dolls and boys with vehicles?

8. Are schools doing their job?
9. What are your long-range goals for your children?
10. Is there anything you'd like to add about sharing parenting or raising nonsexist children?

In addition, I asked the following questions of specific family types:

For Single Parents: How has being a single parent influenced your social life? How does your child adjust to the transition from your ex-spouse's house to yours?

For Stepparents: Discuss the issues involved in stepparenting and dealing with former spouses. How do you get time alone for the two of you?

For Lesbians and Gays: How do you provide role models of the opposite sex? What kind of support network have you developed? Are there other issues of specific interest to lesbian and gay parents?

For Primary Fathers: What are the rewards and difficulties involved? What factors in your background enabled you to take on a nontraditional role for a man?

Over a period of three years, I also sent parents six written questionnaires to complete individually at home. One was Sandra Bem's Sex-Role Inventory (BSRI), a personality scale measuring psychological androgyny. Four results are possible: feminine, masculine, androgynous (high on both masculine and feminine), or undifferentiated (low on both masculine and feminine). A second questionnaire asked parents about their biography and attitudes toward politics and sex roles. A third "pie" asked parents to describe the amount of time they spend on their various roles. Married couples (84 individuals from this study and those interviewed previously for *The 50-50 Marriage*) also filled out the Locke-Wallace marital-satisfaction scale and a personality scale called the Gough-Heilbrun Adjective Checklist. The purpose of the questionnaires was to see if patterns exist in the backgrounds, attitudes, roles, and personality types of the coparents. I asked interviewees from *The 50-50 Marriage* study to write updated comments about coparenting: 21 couples responded with very thoughtful suggestions included in this book in chapters 2, 3, and 4. Couples who divorced since the publication of *The 50-50 Marriage* were also interviewed.

I also surveyed 264 more typical, randomly selected individuals (68%

female) in dual-career families in northern California, to have a context in which to compare the role-sharing couples. I contacted these dual-career couples, with and without children, by (1) sending surveys to professional women listed in the yellow pages of the telephone books for Sacramento and San Francisco, (2) approaching dual-career couples known to me or my students, and (3) asking through local schools and hospitals, mostly in Chico and neighboring communities. I asked each dual-earner to complete a survey describing how he or she juggles various roles and causes of strain. These results are reported in the booklet *Life After College: Combining Career and Family.* Eighty-four role-sharing couples including couples interviewed for this book and for *The 50-50 Marriage*, also took the same dual-career survey. Telephone interviews asking slightly different questions were conducted with 107 additional dual-career individuals. I also surveyed 755 students at California State University, Chico, about their goals and expectations for combining career and family, to understand the next generation of parents.

Further, I interviewed experts and authors including Diane Ehrensaft, Warren Farrell, Ellen Galinsky, David Giveans, Herb Goldberg, Arlie Russell Hochschild, Debra Klinman, Michael Lamb, Letty Cottin Pogrebin, Norma Radin, Robert Sayers, Gloria Steinem, Emily Visher, and John Visher. Joseph Pleck commented on several chapters of this book.

I compared children raised in traditional families, with the father as the main breadwinner and the mother as the main nurturer, with children of role sharers, matching traditional and egalitarian families that had fathers of similar occupational and educational backgrounds. Both sets of families were participants in *The 50-50 Marriage* study. In addition to those, Margaret Ferrin Cieslikowski, a graduate student in psychology (now a school psychologist) interviewed 9 children of egalitarian families whose parents were interviewed for this book and 18 traditional children from Chico. In total, Cieslikowski interviewed 41 children of traditional families and 42 children of egalitarian families (ages 8 to 18, about half male and half female). I interviewed 16 egalitarian children as a pretest. The various interviews and surveys were done between 1982 and 1987.

Coparents' Characteristics

A summary of the findings of the written questionnaire asking the 291 coparents about their backgrounds and attitudes follows in question and answer format.

Q: What are the characteristics of the 197 coparents (115 female, 82 male) who returned written surveys?

A: Characteristics are as follows:

> Respondents are well educated: 80% have a college degree and over half have graduate degrees (56% of men and 48% of women). Almost half (49%) are in professional careers.
>
> Religious backgrounds for the respondents are in this order: Protestant (53%), Catholic (21%), Jewish (14%), other (12%).
>
> Politically, respondents labeled themselves: liberal (60%), radical (23%), moderate (15%), or conservative (2%). Women are more to the left politically than men. Nearly a third (28%) of the divorced parents consider themselves radical.
>
> In their attitudes toward traditional sex roles, couples are mainly disapproving (78% con, 2% pro, 20% neutral). Divorced parents are a little more likely to be neutral (33%) than are stepparents (27%). Women are slightly more disapproving than men (83% compared to 72%). Respondents favor feminism (83% approving, 6% disapproving, and 10% neutral).

Q: What is striking about the survey results?

A: Even among married couples who were recommended as coparents and agreed to be interviewed on that topic, women still spend more hours on child care than men. Even wives of fathers who are the primary parent spend only ten hours less a week on child care than their husbands. However, 73% of married couples are within ten hours of each other on housework and child care or the father does more child care.

Q: Which family type spends the most/least hours on weekly housework?

A: Most—intact marrieds (12 hours). Least—divorced men (6 hours).

Q: How much weekly time did the different family types spend on housework?

A: The mean was 16 hours. The breakdown is:

Family Type	*Hours*		*Total Number of Individuals*
	Females	*Males*	
Intact marriages	12	12	42
Divorced	10	6	30
Stepparents	9	9	37
Lesbian and gay	8	11	27
Fathers primary	9	12	28
Communal parents	9	10	24

Q: Which family type spends the most/least hours on weekly child care?

A: Most—father the primary parent (40 hours). The mean age of the youngest child in this family type is 2.9 years. Least—stepparents (18 hours). The mean age of the youngest child in this family type is 11 years.

Q: How much weekly time did the different family types spend on child care?

A: The mean was 30 hours. The breakdown is:

Family Type	*Hours*		*Total Number of Individuals*
	Females	*Males*	
Intact marriages	41	29	42
Divorced	25	31	28
Stepparents	24	13	32
Lesbian and gay	29	20	25
Fathers primary	35	45	28
Communal parents	36	30	23

Q: What family types had the most equal division of family work?

A: Family types in order of most equal division of family work (based on the percentage of couples who report being within 10 hours of each other on child care and housework) are:

1. Step and divorced (many were not formerly married to each other), 86%
2. Fathers primary, 80%
3. Communal parents, 80%
4. Intact marriages, 52%
5. Lesbian and gay, 36%

Q: Were there family types where men did more family work?

A: Yes, fathers who are the primary parent and divorced fathers did more child care:

Fathers primary:
Child care: fathers 45 hours, wives 35 hours
Housework: fathers 12 hours, wives 9 hours

Divorced fathers:
Child care: fathers 31 hours, wives 25 hours
Housework: fathers 6 hours, wives 10 hours

Q: What are the characteristics of the married egalitarian (E) couples (within 10 hours of each other on both housework and child care) (52 individuals) compared to more traditional (T) couples (48 individuals)?

A: General characteristics are:

The age of children is crucial: Men do a greater percentage of work with older children. The mean age of stepparents' youngest child is 11, compared to 6.5 for parents as a whole. The mean age of the youngest child of divorced fathers is 7.1, compared to 8.9 for divorced mothers, who spend less time on child care. The more egalitarian couples in *The 50/50 Marriage* also had older children. Thus, the fewer total hours spent in child care, the greater percentage fathers do. The mean weekly hours spent by E parents on child care is 24, compared to 39 mean hours spent by T parents, a statistically significant difference. Hours spent on housework were not very different between E and T couples—10 hours compared to 12 hours.

Significant differences between E and T parents were not found in birth order, father's or mother's occupation, or political and sex-role attitudes.

E parents are more likely to be professionals than T parents (63% compared to 42%).

E parents are slightly more educated than T parents (35% of E parents have Ph.D.s compared to 15% of T parents).

More E parents score masculine on the BSRI than T parents do (a statistically significant difference, 38% compared to 14%).

Q: Looking at sex-role type, list groups in order of the most egalitarian in their family work.

A:

1. Masculine E individuals 71%, N = 34
2. Undifferentiated E individuals 43%, N = 34
3. Androgynous E individuals 36%, N = 33
4. Feminine E individuals 32%, N = 31

Q: What is the impact of sex type on egalitarian behavior?

A: Masculine scorers are more likely to be egalitarian (66%), followed by undifferentiateds (57%), feminine (41%), and androgynous (35%) (looking only at married couples, N = 92). Masculine scorers are also more likely to be in a profession (61%), followed by androgynous (52%), feminine (42%), and undifferentiated (39%), of married couples. A high femininity score is associated with traditional behavior (egalitarians have a mean of 94 on femininity and 104 on masculinity, while more traditional couples have a mean of 98 on femininity and 102 on masculinity).

Q: Did men and women differ on their BSRI sex type?

A: Yes, but not much:

Androgynous—22% women, 30% men

Undifferentiated—29% women, 18% men

Masculine—23% women, 26% men

Feminine—26% women, 25% men

In comparison, Allison Parelman's group of 201 female and 157 male married UCLA graduate students and their spouses had these results:

Androgynous—31% women, 32% men
Masculine—14% women, 34% men
Feminine—35% women, 8% men
Undifferentiated—20% women, 25% men

Adults tested in other studies are likely to score sex-typed, but among coparents only 23% of the women scored feminine and 28% of the men scored masculine. The group was fairly evenly divided among the four types. Men were most likely to score androgynous and least likely to score undifferentiated; the opposite was true with the women.

Looking at patterns among married couples, men scoring androgynous and feminine were most likely to pair with undifferentiated women, masculine men with masculine women, and undifferentiated men with feminine women.

Q: Did family types differ on the BSRI?

A: Differences among trends in scores in the six family types were:

	Men	*Women*
Intact marriages	Masculine and Androgynous	Masculine
Divorced	Masculine and Androgynous	Androgynous
Stepparents	Masculine	Feminine, Undifferentiated, Masculine
Lesbian and gay	Androgynous and Feminine	Undifferentiated
Fathers primary	Feminine and Androgynous	Feminine
Communal parents	Undifferentiated	Feminine

Q: Are egalitarian marriages happy?

A: I gave 84 role sharers (interviewed for this book and *The 50-50 Marriage*) a standard marital-satisfaction scale (Locke-Wallace), and then gave it to 22 couples identified by coordinators of women's studies around the United States as happily married for over twenty years. The results were very similar for both groups. Both male and female coparents have average scores of 115. In the happily married group, wives' scores are 119 and husbands' are 108. All the combined scores were divided into high, medium, and low categories to see if there were differences between the happily and less happily married couples. Forty percent of *The 50/50 Marriage* couples, 31% of the *50/50 Parenting* couples, and 33% of the happily married couples were in the high group. The Gough-Heilbrun personality inventory did not show any significant personality differences among the more or less happily married groups. (The inventory has 300 questions.) There were differences on the BSRI; the most happily married group was likely to score androgynous or masculine. This perhaps relates to the correlation between high self-esteem and high masculinity scores. However, there was no correlation between BSRI scores and the self-confidence scale of the Gough-Heilbrun Adjective Checklist (on that scale women scored slightly higher than men, 8.6 compared to 7.1).

Q: Describe other characteristics of the 84 role sharers.

A:

	Annual Income (%)
Less than $15,000	16
$15,000–24,999	24
$25,000–29,999	13
$30,000–39,999	14
Over $40,000	31

	Number of Children (%)
One	25
Two	54
Three	13
Four	6
Five	1

On child care, 40% of egalitarian individuals share child care evenly; 19% of the women do less than half, and 24% of the men do more than half. On housework, 36% reported even sharing; 29% of the women did less than half, and 21% of the men did more than half.

Of staying home with a sick child, 55% practiced even sharing, 24% of the women said they stay home more often, and 18% of the men said that they do. Eleven percent of the women and 20% of the men said that their spouse stays home more often.

Appendix 2
The Children

THE children surveyed in 1984 are raised by married parents, comparing egalitarian (E) and traditional (T) families. Truly egalitarian families are defined as those in which the parents spend within ten hours of each other on family work (child care and housework). These families were chosen from those surveyed for this book and for *The 50-50 Marriage*. Traditional families are defined as those in which the mother does more than half of the family work and does not have a full-time job. The traditional families were recommended by E parents in their areas, with the addition of 18 T children from Chico. Fathers of all the children have similarly high educational and occupational status, with the exception of 5 blue-collar T fathers compared to 1 blue-collar E father. The children were ages 8 to 18, with 12 the mean age, about equally divided between girls and boys.

Children's Characteristics

Some general findings are that T children commonly have more siblings. A higher percentage of E children scored masculine or androgynous on Sandra Bem's Sex-Role Inventory (BSRI), but the difference was not statistically significant. Undifferentiated scorers (those scoring low on both masculine and feminine) have significantly lower self-esteem scores than masculine and androgynous children. Some T boys were different from the other children in having lower self-esteem and less professional career aspirations.

Children of truly egalitarian married parents had significantly higher self-esteem scores on the Rosenberg measure than children of traditional parents. The difference between T and E boys—but not girls—approaches statistical significance. The breakdown of self-esteem and BSRI scores follows.

	Egalitarian Girls	*Egalitarian Boys*	*Traditional Girls*	*Traditional Boys*
	(N = 22)	*(N = 20)*	*(N = 18)*	*(N = 23)*
Rosenberg Self-Esteem Score	41.2	41.1	38.7	37.9
BSRI Masculinity Score	100.41	108.4	93.5	104.0
BSRI Femininity Score	97.8	96.4	102.2	85.4

Including children from various family styles interviewed for this book:

	Girls		*Boys*	
	Mean Score	*N*	*Mean Score*	*N*
Rosenberg Self-Esteem Scores	39.4	28	39.9	38
BSRI Masculinity Score	101.0		103.4	
BSRI Femininity Score	100.1		94.4	

Of the 66 children surveyed whose parents were interviewed for this book, the children in stepfamilies were most likely to have high self-esteem (46%), probably because they were older than the other groups of children (age correlation was found in Cieslikowski's surveys). When I divided the group into low, medium, and high scorers on self-esteem, I found that a third of the low-scoring children had divorced single parents, although they were only 14% (9) of the total number of children surveyed. This was the only noticeable difference between high and low self-esteem scorers; the low-scorer's fathers were not less involved in child care than other fathers.

Among the children of egalitarian and traditional parents surveyed by Margaret Ferrin Cieslikowski, most of the low self-esteem children were from traditional families (16 of 21). A few more were boys (12) than girls (9). The five E children with low self-esteem had clearly identifiable problems. A ten-year-old girl was on a kidney machine and a sixteen-year-old boy had experienced a divorce as a preschooler, after which his father and stepmother, with whom he lived, moved frequently, and his mother was unstable. The other three E children were two boys and a girl from the same family. They all complained more than other E children about not being able to talk with their parents, not having frequent family activities, and being "ordered around," especially by their father. Their parents divided family work evenly, but the children felt left out of making decisions.

Children's Survey Responses

A distillation of the children's survey responses follows, with "majority" votes underlined.

	Egalitarian Girls (%)			
	Both	*Mom*	*Dad*	*Neither*
Which parent (is):				
Strict	11.1	18.5	30	41
Demands mastery of school-related skills	33	17	33	17
Demands responsible behavior	<u>64.7</u>	17.6	11.8	5.9
Permissive	39	33	22	6
Warm	<u>68</u>	18	14	—
Easy to talk with	43	36	7	14
Someone you are proud of	<u>64</u>	26	10	—
Close to you	<u>80</u>	16	4	—
Interested and involved in your activities	<u>72</u>	11	11	6
Someone you play with	<u>70</u>	10	10	10
Makes decisions easily	47	23.5	11.8	17.7
The boss	<u>76</u>	12	12	—
Wins more arguments	<u>75</u>	25	—	—
Do you spend more time with	<u>54</u>	33	13	—

	Approve	*Disapprove*	*Neutral*
What is your attitude toward:			
Mothers working outside the home	<u>100</u>	—	—
The women's movement	<u>100</u>	—	—

	Egalitarian Boys (%)			
	Both	*Mom*	*Dad*	*Neither*
Which parent (is):				
Strict	11	19	35	35
Demands mastery of school-related skills	39	28	22	11

	Egalitarian Boys (%)			
	Both	*Mom*	*Dad*	*Neither*
Demands responsible behavior	77	16	17	—
Permissive	39	33	28	—
Warm	64	24	8	4
Easy to talk with	33	25	29	13
Someone you are proud of	80	8	8	4
Close to you	77	11	6	6
Interested and involved in your activities	76	16	4	4
Someone you play with	44	—	39	17
Makes decisions easily	50	28	11	11
The boss	72	6	22	—
Wins more arguments	70.6	—	29.4	—
Do you spend more time with	50	18.8	31.2	—

	Approve	*Disapprove*	*Neutral*
What is your attitude toward:			
Mothers working outside the home	83	—	17
The women's movement	89	—	11

	Traditional Girls (%)			
	Both	*Mom*	*Dad*	*Neither*
Which parent (is):				
Strict	19	24	24	33
Demands mastery of school-related skills	45	20	20	15
Demands responsible behavior	57	5	33	5
Permissive	29	48	24	—
Warm	60	25	10	5
Easy to talk with	26	53	16	5
Someone you are proud of	65	5	25	5
Close to you	45	35	15	5

	Traditional Girls (%)			
	Both	*Mom*	*Dad*	*Neither*
Interested and involved in your activities	60	25	10	5
Makes decisions easily	48	24	19	9
Someone you play with	55	11	6	28
The boss	41	18	41	—
Wins more arguments	23	18	41	18
Do you spend more time with	21	69	10	—
	Approve	*Disapprove*	*Neutral*	
What is your attitude toward:				
Mothers working outside the home	59	6	35	
The women's movement	56.3	12.5	31.2	

	Traditional Boys (%)			
	Both	*Mom*	*Dad*	*Neither*
Which parent (is):				
Strict	33.3	11.2	22.2	33.3
Demands mastery of school-related skills	43	13	13	31
Demands responsible behavior	63	5	27	5
Permissive	39	35	26	—
Warm	52	26	17	5
Easy to talk with	39	30	22	9
Someone you are proud of	83	4	13	—
Close to you	55	30	15	—
Interested and involved in your activities	27	9	59	5
Someone you play with	38	10	28	24
Makes decisions easily	41	23	27	9
The boss	28	9	58	5
Wins more arguments	38	14	43	5
Do you spend more time with	19	52	29	—

	Approve	*Disapprove*	*Neutral*
What is your attitude toward:			
Mothers working outside the home	37	21	42
The women's movement	55	9	36

E children's "both" responses on thirteen statements were significantly more frequent than T children's "both" responses (.002), as was their approval of women's rights (.001).

BSRI scores for the children whose parents were interviewed for this book follow (compiled by Vicki Moen).

Total Children = 65

Female	*Male*
8 feminine (12%)	6 feminine (9%)
3 masculine (5%)	14 masculine (22%)
10 androgynous (15%)	11 androgynous (17%)
5 undifferentiated (8%)	8 undifferentiated (12%)

Appendix 3
Other Research on Role Sharers

PERHAPS the first researcher on role sharers was John DeFrain, who began in 1974 to study shared, or what he called androgynous, parenting. His impetus was that he and his wife were both in college, working half time, and raising the first of their three children. DeFrain read a few pages about shared parenting in Jessie Bernard's *The Future of Marriage* and realized that nothing else on the subject had been written. For his dissertation, he compared coparent and traditional families, both middle class and blue collar, in Madison, Wisconsin, where he earned his Ph.D., and in Lincoln, Nebraska, where he teaches. He published an article on his findings about the Nebraska parents in 1979. DeFrain's unpublished study with Rebecca Braymen and mine with Margaret Ferrin Cieslikowski are the only such studies comparing the children of egalitarian and traditional parents that I have discovered. Cieslikowski wrote her M.A. thesis about this topic in 1985.

Norma Radin, at the University of Michigan, writes about nontraditional families in which fathers are the main child care providers. The middle-class families she studies are near Ann Arbor, Michigan. She has linked with Graeme Russell in Australia and Abraham Sagi (a former graduate student of hers) in Israel as they began their own studies of families in which the father did equal or more child care than the mother. Russell began his work independently of Radin around 1977, with seventy-one families described in his 1983 book *The Changing Roles of Fathers?* Radin's social work graduate student, Bonnie Carlson, wrote her dissertation comparing sixty Ann Arbor families in which one-third of the mothers worked full time and the fathers shared equally in child care. Another of Radin's former graduate students, Diane Ehrensaft, wrote in *Parenting Together* about forty San Francisco couples who share child care. In turn, her graduate student, Rick Sapp, wrote a dissertation on thirteen involved Bay Area fathers. Michael Lamb, a former University of Michigan faculty member who is now at the University of Utah, edits books about nontraditional families, including articles by Radin, Sagi, and Russell and his own investigations of fathers' and mothers' equal attachment and responsiveness to their infants.

In 1977 Linda Haas wrote her doctoral dissertation on thirty-one role-sharing couples in Madison, Wisconsin. Nearly half of these couples had children. Several articles were drawn from Haas's dissertation. Published in 1983, my book, *The 50-50 Marriage*, was the first using a national sample of egalitarian couples. William Beer reported on fifty-six husbands in New York who were involved in family work in *Househusbands: Men and Housework in American Families* (1983). Audrey Smith's and William Reid's *Role Sharing Marriages*, based on interviews with sixty-four couples in Wisconsin and New York, was published in 1985. Over half of Smith's and Reid's couples had children, described in one chapter.

Regarding BSRI scores, John DeFrain found that role-sharing wives had lower femininity scores than other married women and often had high masculinity scores. Russell found that fathers with high femininity and androgyny scores were more nurturant than those with high masculinity scores. These patterns did not hold up in his follow-up study of nine out of eighteen families who reverted to traditional family patterns. Radin found no differences in mothers' BSRI scores among the three groups of parents she studied: father as primary parent, mother as primary parent, and shared parenting. The third group of fathers did have higher femininity scores than the traditional fathers. Lamb found no correlations with BSRI scores among Swedish couples who choose to take parental leave. A dissertation study of sixty-nine Iowa couples also found no correlation of androgyny with role sharing.

Russell's study found only two couples in which a man scoring masculine was married to a woman scoring feminine. Only four out of eighty-nine couples surveyed for *The 50-50 Marriage* paired this way, compared to eighteen out of seventy-five traditional couples, in which 63 percent of the women scored feminine and 47 percent of the men scored masculine. Egalitarian couples were likely to score androgynous and masculine: The husband was slightly more likely to score androgynous and the wife masculine. Couples who were not able to put their beliefs about division of family work into practice often had an undifferentiated-scoring husband; although in another study the undifferentiated individuals were the least traditional in their views of marital roles. My conclusion is that a high masculinity component is necessary to put beliefs into action. Interestingly, there is a positive correlation between masculinity scores and self-esteem in the children surveyed for this book.

In Linda Haas's study of role sharers, two-thirds of the subjects had

had working mothers, compared to 50 percent of more conventional dual-career couples. In Norma Radin's sample, the mothers of both parents had worked in 25 percent of the families where the father was the main care giver. In contrast, none of the traditional spouses had employed mothers. Half of DeFrain's sample had working mothers during their school years, although Sapp's thirteen fathers mostly had homemaker mothers. Two-thirds of Smith and Reid's sample had mothers who worked outside the home, either full or part time, while the respondents were growing up. In Radin's study all of the wives in families where the father was the primary care giver worked or were full-time students. Two-thirds of Beer's sample had working wives: 36 percent of the men cited pragmatic reasons and 37 percent cited fairness as an explanation of why they shared family work.

Two-thirds of the husbands and one-third of the wives in Haas's Madison, Wisconsin, study had a lot of job flexibility. In DeFrain's sample, 67 percent of the parents stated that they had flexible working hours, but not flexible enough to mesh two work schedules and child care. In DeFrain's interviews with forty blue-collar families, who are less likely to role-share, 90 percent reported inflexible jobs. The men scored about as nurturant on Bem's personality scale as the middle-class men, but their jobs got in the way of child care. Nearly all of Beer's male respondents have flexible work situations. So did at least one spouse of each pair of Russell's couples. Thus egalitarian couples tend to score nontraditionally on the BSRI, grew up with employed mothers, have job flexibility as well as a middle-class status.

Role-Sharing References

William Beer, *Househusbands: Men & Housework in American Families* (New York: Praeger, 1983).

Bonnie Carlson, "Shared vs. Primarily Maternal Child Rearing: Effects of Dual-Career on Families with Young Children" (Unpublished dissertation, University of Michigan, 1980).

John DeFrain, "Androgynous Parents Tell Who They Are and What They Need," *Family Coordinator* 28, no. 2 (April 6, 1978): 237–243.

Diane Ehrensaft, *Parenting Together: Men and Women Sharing the Care of Their Children* (New York: Free Press, forthcoming).

Linda Haas, "Sexual Equality in the Family: A Study of Role-Sharing Couples" (Unpublished dissertation, University of Wisconsin, Madison, 1977).

Linda Haas, "Role-Sharing Couples: A Study of Egalitarian Marriages," *Family Relations* 29, no. 3 (July 1980): 289–296.

Linda Haas, "Determinants of Role-Sharing Behavior: A Study of Egalitarian Couples," *Sex Roles* 8, no. 7 (1982):747–760.

Linda Haas, "Parental Sharing of Childcare Tasks in Sweden," *Journal of Family Issues* 3, no. 3 (September 1982): 389–412.

Michael Lamb, ed., *The Role of the Father in Child Development* (New York: John Wiley & Sons, 1981).

Michael Lamb, ed., *Non-traditional Families: Parenting and Child Development* (Hillsdale, N.J.: Lawrence Erlbaum, 1982).

Michael Lamb and Abraham Sagi, eds., *Fatherhood and Family Policy* (Hillsdale, N.J.: Lawrence Erlbaum, 1983).

Michael Lamb, ed., *The Father's Role: Applied Perspectives* (New York: John Wiley & Sons, 1986).

Norma Radin, "Childrearing Fathers in Intact Families, I: Some Antecedents and Consequences," *Merrill-Palmer Quarterly* 27(1981): 491–514.

Norma Radin, "Primary Caregiving and Role-Sharing Fathers," in Michael Lamb, ed., *Non-traditional Families* (Hillsdale, N.J.: Lawrence Erlbaum, 1982).

Norma Radin and Rena Goldsmith, "Caregiving Fathers of Preschoolers: Four Years Later," *Merrill-Palmer Quarterly* (in press).

Norma Radin and A. Sagi, "Childrearing Fathers in Intact Families, II: Israel and the USA," *Merrill-Palmer Quarterly* 28(1982): 111–136.

Graeme Russell, *The Changing Role of Fathers?* (St. Lucia, Australia: University of Queensland Press, 1983).

Rick Sapp, "Shared Parent Fathers: Role Entry and Psychological Consequences of Participation in a Nontraditional Male Parent Role" (Ph.D. dissertation, The Wright Institute, 1984).

Audrey Smith and William Reid, *Role-Sharing Marriage* (New York: Columbia University Press, 1986).

Appendix 4
Resource Guide for Coparents

Books

Diane Ehrensaft. *Parenting Together: Men and Women Sharing the Care of Their Children*. Free Press, forthcoming. Based on interviews with Bay Area couples who share parenting.

Gayle Kimball. *The 50/50 Marriage*. Beacon, 1983. Interviews with 150 couples around the United States. Explains how to have an egalitarian marriage.

Gayle Kimball. *Life After College: Combining Career and Family*. Equality Press, 1986. Compares surveys of college students and dual-career couples. Includes bibliographies.

Debra Klinman and Rhiana Kohl. *Fatherhood U.S.A*. Garland, 1984. List of resources for fathers.

Sally Wendkos Olds. *The Working Parents' Survival Guide*. Bantam, 1983. Practical tips.

Letty Cottin Pogrebin. *Growing Up Free: Raising Your Child in the 80's*. McGraw-Hill, 1980. How to raise children in a sexist society.

Graeme Russell. *The Changing Role of Fathers?* University of Queensland Press (Australia), 1983. Describes a scholarly study of Australian families in which the father is highly involved in child rearing.

Marjorie and Morton Shaevitz. *Making It Together as a Two-Career Couple*. Houghton Mifflin, 1980. How to manage family work and child care and cope with "overload."

Audrey Smith and William Reid. *Role-Sharing Marriage*. Columbia University Press, 1986. A scholarly study of role-sharing couples (thirty-seven with children).

S. Adams Sullivan. *The Fathers' Almanac*. Doubleday, 1980. Practical suggestions for fathers' involvement with young children.

Videotapes

Barriers and Bridges: Male/Female Relationships, *Swedish Support Systems for Egalitarian Families*, *Parenting*, *Changing Families*, *Dual-Earner Families*, and *Men's Changing*

Roles. Thirty to fifty minutes. C/o Gayle Kimball, CSUC, Chico, CA, 95929. (Other tapes in the series are *Women and Careers*, *Women and Health*, and *Feminist Visions of the Future*.)

Research Centers

- Catalyst Career and Family Center
  250 Park Ave. So.
  New York, NY 10003

- Fatherhood Project
  Bank Street College of Education
  610 West 112 Street
  New York, NY 10025

Newsletters

- *Nurturing Today Quarterly*
  187 Caselli Ave.
  San Francisco, CA 94114

- Growing Child
  P.O. Box 620
  Lafayette, IN 47902

Notes

Chapter 1. Advantages of Equal Parenting

1. *U.S. Government Current Population Reports*, 1985 data, compiled by Marc Sexton.
2. Sarah Fenstermaker Berk, *The Gender Factory: The Apportionment of Work in American Households* (New York: Plenum Press, 1985), 66; Kate Keating, "How Is Work Affecting American Families? A Report from 32,500 Readers," *Better Homes and Gardens* 60, no. 2 (February 1982):22; Sar Levitan and Richard Belous, "Working Wives and Mothers: What Happens to Family Life?" *Monthly Labor Review* 104, no. 9 (September 1981):27.
3. Arlie Hochschild, interview with the author, San Francisco, January 21, 1987. See Hochschild, *The Second Shift* (New York: Random House, forthcoming).
4. Pamela Daniels and Kathy Weingarten, *Sooner or Later: The Timing of Parenthood in Adult Life* (New York: W. W. Norton, 1980), 38; Rosanna Hertz, *More Equal than Others: Women and Men in Dual-Career Marriages* (Berkeley: University of California Press, 1986), 141, 189.
5. *Corporations and Two-Career Families: Directions for the Future* (New York: Catalyst, 1981), 20, 21.
6. Joann Lublin, "Scenes from Two Marriages," *Wall Street Journal*, March 24, 1986, 26D.
7. Samuel Osherson, *Finding Our Fathers: The Unfinished Business of Manhood* (New York: Free Press, 1986), 4.
8. Anthony Astrachan, *How Men Feel and Their Response to Women's Demands for Equality and Power* (New York: Doubleday, 1986), 401, 402.
9. Elizabeth Mehren, "Life with Father and Other Tales of the Changing Family," *Los Angeles Times*, August 29, 1986, 6, 7. See also Ken Druck with James Simmons, *The Secrets Men Keep* (New York: Doubleday, 1985), 16, 18.
10. Douglas Besharov and Michelle Dally, "How Much Are Working Mothers Working?" *Public Opinion* 9, no. 4 (November/December 1986):48, 50.
11. Joseph Pleck, *Working Wives/Working Husbands* (Beverly Hills: Sage, 1985), 146, 150.

12. Gayle Kimball, *Life After College: Combining Career and Family* (Chico, Calif.: Equality Press, 1986).
13. Pleck, *Working Wives/Working Husbands*, 156; Pleck, "Husbands' and Wives' Family Work, Paid Work, and Adjustment," Working Paper No. 95 (Wellesley, Mass.: Center for Research on Women, 1982), 5-4, 5-5, 5-6; Sara Yogev, "Do Professional Women Have Egalitarian Marital Relationships?" *Journal of Marriage and the Family* 43, no. 4 (November 1981):868; Ross Thompson, "The Father's Case in Child Custody Disputes: The Contributions of Psychological Research," in Michael Lamb and Abraham Sagi, eds., *Fatherhood and Family Policy* (Hillsdale, N.J.: Lawrence Erlbaum, 1983), 69, 76.
14. Michael Lamb, telephone interview with the author, November 1984.
15. William Goode, "Why Men Resist," in Barrie Thorne and Marilyn Yalom, eds., *Rethinking the Family: Some Feminist Questions* (New York: Longman, 1982), 140. (Goode made the comment about men's loss of centrality.) See also "The American Male," *U.S. News and World Report* 98, no. 21 (June 3, 1985):44.
16. Janet Elder, "A Giant Step Forward for Parents and Child Care," *San Francisco Chronicle*, September 4, 1986, 26; Joseph Pleck, "Fathers & Infant Care Leave," in Edward Zigler and Meryl Frank, eds., *Infant Care Leave* (New Haven, Conn.: Yale University Press, forthcoming).
17. Forty-nine percent of working mothers agreed that children of working mothers almost always suffer: Jody Gaylin, "Do Kids Need a Stay-at-Home Mom?" *Redbook* 167, no. 4 (August 1986):78, 79. See also Yankelovich, Skelley, and White, Inc., *The General Mills Family Report, 1976–1977: Raising Children in a Changing Society* (Minneapolis: General Mills, 1977), 20; Nancy Chodorow and Susan Contratto, in Thorne and Yalom, eds., *Rethinking the Family*, 55. (They explain that Americans view the mother as "all powerful" in her ability to raise successful children.) See also Lydia O'Donnell, *The Unheralded Majority: Contemporary Women as Mothers* (Lexington, Mass.: Lexington Books, 1985), 80; Janice Mall, "Lack of Paid Maternity Leave Deplored," *Los Angeles Times*, September 30, 1983, 2.
18. Michael Lamb et al., "Effects of Paternal Involvement on Fathers & Mothers," in Robert Lewis and Marvin Sussman, eds., *Men's Changing Roles in the Family* (New York: Haworth Press, 1986), 7.
19. Berk, *The Gender Factory*, 207. (Most couples do not have equitable division of family work, but think it is fair anyway.) See also Robert Schafer and Patricia Keith, "Equity in Marital Roles Across the Family Life Cycle," *Journal of Marriage and the Family* 43, no. 2 (May 1981):363; "SuperDads," *The Futurist* 19, no. 3 (June 1985):48; Karen Barrett, "Two-Career Couples," *Ms.* 15, no. 9 (June 1984):39–40.
20. Hochschild, *The Second Shift;* Gayle Kimball, *The 50/50 Marriage* (Boston: Beacon, 1983), 246–252; Lucia Gilbert, *Men in Dual-Career Families* (Hillsdale, N.J.: Lawrence Erlbaum, 1985), 62. (About a third of the men were very involved.) See also Catalyst Career and Family Center, *Corporations and Two-Career Families*, 23. A poll of people age 19 to 37 showed that 76% supported family equality. A Roper poll found that 37% of women and 43% of men want a traditional marriage with the husband as sole earner. More preferred shared

responsibilities, yet few put their beliefs into practice. In a Gallop Poll of men, half felt they should share child care and housework with an employed wife. Almost as many husbands said they provided no help or only helped part of the time. Eighty-nine percent of the women reported that they do more than half or all the child care and housework, according to a *Redbook* survey of 46,000 readers. See the 1985 Virginia Slims American Women's Opinion Poll (conducted by the Roper Organization), as summarized in *Women and Work Research and Resource Letter*, University of Texas at Arlington, vol. 2, no. 1 (Fall 1986):2.

21. Edmund Morgan, *The Puritan Family* (New York: Harper and Row, 1966), 138–39.
22. Paul Olsen, *Sons and Mothers: Why Men Behave as They Do* (New York: Fawcett, 1982), 22.
23. Caryl Rivers, Rosalind Barnett, and Grace Baruch, *Beyond Sugar and Spice: How Women Grow, Learn and Thrive* (New York: Ballantine, 1979), 84–85.
24. Cheryl Hayes and Sheila Kamerman, eds., *Children of Working Parents: Experiences and Outcomes* (Washington, D.C.: National Academy Press, 1983), 164.
25. Leah Yarrow, "How to Get Your Husband to Help," *Parents* 57, no. 55 (May 1982):55.
26. "A Mother's Choice," *Newsweek* 107, no. 13 (March 31, 1986):46–51. See also Marjorie Hansen Shaevitz, *The Superwomen Syndrome* (New York: Warner Books, 1984); Matt Siden, "Like SuperMom, SuperDad Is Having Anything but a Super Time," *Los Angeles Times*, March 19, 1980.
27. Helen Rogan, "Executive Women Find It Hard to Balance Demands of Job, Home," *Wall Street Journal*, October 30, 1984, 33, 55.
28. Janice Mall, "About Women," *Los Angeles Times*, February 24, 1985, 14; "Executive Poll," *San Francisco Chronicle*, June 1, 1982; "U.S. Women Executives Report Sexual Bias," *San Francisco Chronicle*, November 19, 1982, 81; Karen Rubin, "Whose Job Is Child Care?" *Ms.* 15, no. 9 (March 1987):33.
29. Donna Alvarado, "The Castle Is Crumbling," *The Berkeley Gazette* 105, no. 114 (January 7, 1983).
30. A. Regula Herzog, Jerald Bachman, and Lloyd Johnston, "Paid Work, Child Care, and Housework: A National Survey of High School Seniors' Preferences for Sharing Responsibilities Between Husbands and Wives," *Sex Roles* 9, no. 1 (1983): 109–132; Mall, "About Women," 16; Kimball, *Life After College*; Cher Carrie Thomas, "The Work–Personal Life Relationship: A Study of Student Expectations" (Unpublished paper, California State University, Long Beach, 1986); Anne Mechung, "Talking Career, Thinking Job: Gender Differences in Career and Family Expectations of Berkeley Seniors" (University of California, Berkeley, Center for the Study, Education and Advancement of Women, November 1986); Catalyst, "New Roles for Men and Women: A Report on Educational Intervention with College Students" (1987).
31. See the Mall, Thomas, and Mechung reports above. One study found that youthful expectations were not an accurate predictor of women's adult roles: Karen Gerson, *Hard Choices* (Berkeley: University of California Press, 1985), 21.
32. Martha Zaslow et al., "The Early Resumption of Employment by Mothers:

Implications for Parent-Infant Interaction," *Journal of Applied Developmental Psychology* 6, no. 1 (January 16, 1986):11.

33. Molly Haskell, "Male Mommies in Anti-Women Movies," *San Francisco Chronicle*, June 26, 1983, 17–19.
34. Paula Selkow, "Effects of Maternal Employment on Kindergarten and First Grade Children's Vocational Aspirations," *Sex Roles* 11, no. 7/8 (October 1984):677–690; Cookie Stephan and Judy Carder, "The Effects of Dual-Career Families on Adolescents' Sex-Role Attitudes, Work and Family Plans, and Choices of Important Others," *Journal of Marriage and the Family* 47, no. 3 (August 1985):921.
35. See studies by Pruett, Radin, Russell, or Sagi, as cited in various notes in this chapter. See also Sanford Dornbush et al., "Single Parents, Extended Households, and the Control of Adolescents," *Child Development* 36, no. 2 (1985):332; John Santrock, Richard Warshak, and Gary Elliot, "Social Development and Parent Custody Interaction in Father Custody and Step-Mother Families," in Michael Lamb, ed., *Non-traditional Families: Parenting and Child Development* (Hillsdale, N.J.: Lawrence Erlbaum, 1983), 293; E. Mavis Hetherington, Martha Cox, and Roger Cox, "Effects of Divorce on Parents and Children," in Lamb, *Non-traditional Families*, 275.
36. Patricia Knaub, "Growing Up in a Dual-Career Family: The Children's Perspectives," *Family Relations* 35, no. 3 (July 1986):434, 435. A poll of 1,000 children discovered that 59% prefer a mother who works outside the home: "U.S. Children Fairly Content, Poll Indicates," *San Francisco Chronicle*, March 11, 1987. See also Nancy Sachs, "Latchkey to Success," *Parenting* 1, no. 2 (March 1987):17.
37. Anne Mechung, *Women, Work and Family* (Women's Resource Center, University of California, Berkeley).
38. Letty Cottin Pogrebin, *Family Politics: Love and Power on an Intimate Frontier* (New York: McGraw-Hill, 1983), 206, 207.
39. Norma Radin, "Primary Caregiving and Role-Sharing Fathers," in Michael Lamb, ed., *Non-traditional Families*, 191, 192; Margaret White, *Sharing Caring* (Englewood Cliffs, N.J.: Prentice-Hall, 1982), 101, 102; Kyle Pruett, *The Nurturing Father: Journey Toward the Complete Man* (New York: Warner Books, 1987), 75, 202, 208.
40. Norma Radin, "The Influence of Fathers on Their Sons and Daughters," *Social Work in Education* 8 (1986):80–81.
41. Warren Farrell, interview with the author, San Diego, September 1978; Pruett, *The Nurturing Father*, 49.
42. Ronald D'amico, Jean Havrin, and Frank Mott, "The Effects of Mothers' Employment on Adolescent and Early Adult Outcomes of Young Men and Women," in Hayes and Kamerman, eds., *Children of Working Parents*, 145. See also Phyllis Katz and Sally Boswell, *Flexibility and Traditionality in Children's Gender Roles* (Boulder, Colo.: Institute for Research on Social Problems), 44. See also N. Colangelo, D. Rosenthal, and D. Dettmann, "Maternal Employment and Job Satisfaction and Their Relationship to Children's Perceptions and Behaviors," *Sex Roles* 10, no. 9/10 (1984):693–702.

43. Sally Squires, "Whether Moms Work or Not Won't Hurt Kids, a Study Says," *San Francisco Chronicle*, September 2, 1985. (Report on a study by Adele Gottfried, Allen Gottfried, and Kay Bathurst, CSU, Northridge, and UCLA.)
44. Grace Baruch, Rosalind Barnett, and Caryl Rivers, *Lifeprints* (New York: McGraw-Hill, 1983), 31.
45. Nancy Fasciano, "When Mothers Work, Fathers Play," *Working Mother* (June 1983):44, 46; "Working Moms Have Well-Read Children," *San Francisco Chronicle*, June 26, 1986. (Report on a National Assessment of Education Progress survey.)
46. Michael Lamb, telephone interview with the author; Lamb, *Non-traditional Families*, 58; Susan Fogg, "The Working Mothers and Their Cheerful Babies," *Los Angeles Times*, April 16, 1981, 6; Liliane Floge, "The Dynamics of Child-Care Use and Some Implications for Women's Employment," *Journal of Marriage and the Family* 41, no. 1 (February 1985):152–53.
47. Dorothy Dinnerstein, *The Mermaid and the Minotaur* (New York: Harper and Row, 1976); Nancy Chodorow, *The Reproduction of Mothering* (Berkeley: University of California Press, 1978); Lillian Rubin, *Intimate Strangers: Men and Women Together* (New York: Harper and Row, 1983).
48. Michael McGill, *The McGill Report on Male Intimacy* (New York: Harper and Row, 1985), 118, 232.
49. Astrachan, *How Men Feel*, 401, 402.
50. Pruett, *The Nurturing Father*, 77; Martin Greenberg, *The Birth of a Father* (New York: Continuum Publishing, 1985), 19; Diane Ehrensaft, *Parenting Together: Men and Women Sharing the Care of their Children* (New York: Free Press, forthcoming); Gilbert, *Men in Dual-Career Families*, 82; Graeme Russell, *The Changing Role of Fathers?* (St. Lucia, Australia: University of Queensland Press, 1983), 127.
51. Herb Goldberg, telephone interview with the author, December 1983.
52. Daniels and Weingarten, *Sooner or Later*, 144.
53. Pleck, *Working Wives/Working Husbands*, 90, 154; Daniels and Weingarten, *Sooner or Later*, 71.
54. Russell, *The Changing Role of Fathers*, 107–8; Michael Lamb, "The Prenatal, Perinatal, and Infancy Periods," in Richard Lerner and Graham Spencer, eds. *Child Influences on Mental and Family Interaction* (New York: Academic Press, 1978), 145.
55. Baruch, Barnett, and Rivers, *Lifeprints*, 88; "Job, Family Stress Hit Women Harder, UCLA Study Finds," *San Francisco Chronicle*, December 9, 1984, 83.
56. Baruch, Barnett, and Rivers, *Lifeprints*, 82, 93, 141, 242; *Newsweek*, March 31, 1986, 47; Maureen Dowd, "Where Do Women Belong?" *San Francisco Chronicle*, December 12, 1983, 24.
57. "A Mother's Choice," *Newsweek* 107, no. 13 (March 31, 1986):46–51.
58. Phyllis Moen "The Two-Provider Family: Problems and Potentials," in Lamb, ed., *Non-traditional Families*, 24; Laurel Richardson, *The Dynamics of Sex and Gender* (Boston: Houghton Mifflin, 1981), 224; Baruch, Barnett, and Rivers, *Lifeprints*, 37, 104, 144; Myra Marx Ferree, "Class, Housework and Happiness and Women's Work and Life Satisfaction," *Sex Roles* 11, nos. 11, 12 (December 1984):

1058, 1060, 1063; Ronald Burke and Tamara Weir, "Relationship of Wives' Employment Status to Husband, Wife, Pair Satisfaction and Performance," *Journal of Marriage and the Family*, 38, no. 2, (May 1976):279–286; "Being Superwoman! Not All Bad," *California Women* 3 (1985):7.
59. Angus Campbell, Philip Converse, and Willard Rodgers, *The Quality of American Life* (New York: Russell Sage Foundation, 1976), 425, 426.
60. John DeFrain, "Androgynous Parents Tell Who They Are and What They Need," *Family Coordinator* 28, no. 2 (April 6, 1979):240; "Job, Motherhood an 'Unhealthy' Mix," *San Francisco Chronicle*, November 8, 1983. (Report on a survey by Barbarah Wolfe and Robert Haveman, University of Wisconsin.) See also Pleck, *Working Wives/Working Husbands*, 155.
61. Gail Schaper, "Married Working Mothers: An Analysis of Role Strain" (Unpublished dissertation, California School of Professional Psychology, 1983); Barbara Berg, "The Guilt That Drives Working Mothers Crazy," *Ms.* 15, no. 11 (May 1987):57. Berg states, "After two years of interviewing nearly 1,000 women . . . I learned that guilt was their greatest emotional problem."
62. "Female Managers' Drop-out Rate," *San Francisco Chronicle*, July 31, 1986. (Report on a *Fortune* magazine survey.) See also Paul Berg, "Women with MBAs Suffer More Stress," *San Francisco Chronicle*, October 22, 1985; Ruthe Stein, "Stanford MBA Women," *San Francisco Chronicle*, November 30, 1984, 31; Louise Bernikow, "We're Dancing as Fast as We Can," *Savvy* (April 1984):40–44; "Female Managers' Drop-out Rate," *San Francisco Chronicle*, July 3, 1986.
63. Davidson, *Staying Home Instead* (Lexington, Mass.: Lexington Books, 1986).
64. Elizabeth Nelson and Edward Nelson, "Is His Better than Hers? An Exploration of the Relationships Between Marital Roles and Well-Being" (Presented to the Western Social Science Association, April 1983); Bernadette Gray-Little and Nancy Burks, "Power and Satisfaction in Marriage: A Review and Critique," *Psychological Bulletin* 93, no. 3 (1983):513–538.
65. Campbell, Converse, and Rodgers, *The Quality of American Life*, 324; Richard Lerner and Graham Spanier, *Child Influences on Marital and Family Interaction* (New York: Academic Press, 1978), 174.
66. Ibid., 324.
67. DeFrain, "Androgynous Parents Tell Who They Are and What They Need," 240.
68. Arlene Skolnick, *The Intimate Environment* (Boston: Little Brown, 1978), 383.
69. Quoted in David Giveans and Michael Robinson, "Fathers and the Preschool-Age Child," in Shirley Hanson and Frederick Bozett, eds., *Dimensions of Fatherhood* (Beverly Hills: Sage, 1985), 127.

Chapter 2. How to Coparent

1. Rosalind Barnett and Grace Baruch, "Determinants of Fathers' Participation in Family Work," Working Paper No. 136 (Wellesley, Mass.: Wellesley College,

1986), 13. Also in *Journal of Marriage and the Family* 49, no. 1 (February 1987). Fathers spent 29.48 hours interacting with children and mothers 44.45 hours. Husbands of working wives spent 20% of the solo time with children. Fathers did less as children got older and spent more time with boys than girls.
2. Caryl Rivers, Rosalind Barnett, Grace Baruch, *Beyond Sugar and Spice* (New York: Ballantine, 1979), 198.
3. E. Mavis Hetherington, "Effects of Divorce On Parents and Children" in Michael Lamb, ed. *Non-traditional Families: Parenting and Child Development* (Hillsdale, N.J.: Lawrence Erlbaum, 1982), 276.
4. Lamb, ed., "Introduction," *Non-traditional Families.*
5. Janet Rausch, interview with the author, May 1985.
6. Kay Kuzma, *Prime-Time Parenting* (New York: Rawson, Wade, 1980), 265, 269; Sally Wendkos Olds, *The Working Parents Survival Guide* (New York: Bantam, 1983); Gloria Norris and Joann Miller, *The Working Mother's Complete Handbook* (New York: Plume Books, 1984); Marjorie Hansen Shaevitz and Morton Shaevitz, *Making it Together as a Two-Career Couple* (Boston: Houghton Mifflin, 1980); Kay Lowman, *Of Cradles and Careers: A Guide to Reshaping Your Job to Include a Baby in Your Life* (New York: New American Library, 1985); Renee Magid, *When Mothers and Fathers Work* (New York: AMACOM, American Management Association, 1987).
7. Jane Bryan-Jones, telephone interview with the author, February 1984.

Chapter 3. Democratic Discipline

1. Letty Cottin Pogrebin, *Family Politics: Love and Power on an Intimate Frontier* (New York: McGraw-Hill, 1983), 8.
2. Letty Cottin Pogrebin, *Growing Up Free: Raising Your Child in the 80's* (New York: McGraw-Hill, 1980), 161–167.
3. Norma Radin and Grame Russell, "Increased Father Participation and Child Development Outcome," in Michael Lamb, ed., *The Role of the Father in Child Development* (New York: John Wiley, 1981), 200–201.
4. Caryl Rivers, Rosalind Barnett, and Grace Baruch, *Beyond Sugar and Spice: How Women Grow, Learn and Thrive* (New York: Ballantine, 1979), 9.
5. Jane Bryan-Jones, telephone interview with the author, February 1984.
6. Janet Rausch, interview with author, May 1985.
7. Ellen Galinsky, *Between Generations: The Stages of Parenthood* (New York: Berkeley Books, 1982), 3.
8. Louise Bates Ames and Frances Ilg, *Five Year Old: Sunny and Serene* (New York: Dell, 1979).
9. Ronnie Friedland and Carol Kort, *The Mothers' Book: Shared Experiences* (Boston: Houghton Mifflin, 1981), 91.
10. James Dobson, *The Strong-Willed Child* (Weaton, Ill.: Tyndale, 1978), 15.

11. Adele Faber and Elaine Mazlish, *Liberated Parents, Liberated Children* (New York: Avon, 1974), 13; *How To Talk So Your Children Will Listen and Listen So Your Children Will Talk* (New York: Avon, 1982).
12. Jane Nelson, *Positive Discipline* (Fair Oaks, Calif.: Adlerian Counseling Center, 1981).
13. Diana Baumrind, "Rejoinder to Lewis's Reinterpretation of Parental Firm Control Effects: Are Authoritative Families Really Harmonious?" *Psychological Bulletin* 94, no. 1 (July 1983):132–142.
14. Rita Dunn and Kenneth Dunn, *How To Raise Independent and Professionally Successful Daughters* (Englewood Cliffs, N.J.: Prentice-Hall, 1977), 84.
15. George Gallup, Jr., "Where Parents Go Wrong," *San Francisco Chronicle*, December 13, 1984. (Those surveyed observed that parents are too permissive.)
16. Rudolph D. Dreikurs, with Vicki Soltz, *Children: The Challenge* (New York: Hawthorne Books, 1964).
17. Jean Illsley Clark, *Self-Esteem: A Family Affair* (Minneapolis: Winston Press, 1978).
18. Thomas Gordon, *P.E.T. in Action* (New York: Bantam, 1978).
19. Farber and Mazlish, *Liberated Parents, Liberated Children*, chapter 5.
20. Paul Wood and Bernard Schwartz, *How To Get Your Children To Do What You Want Them To Do* (New York: Prentice-Hall, 1977), 29–41.
21. William Duffy, *Sugar Blues* (New York: Warner Books, 1976).
22. Deborah Rozman, *Meditating With Children: The Art of Concentrating and Centering* (Boulder Creek, Calif.: University of the Trees, 1975); Martha Belknap, "Taming Your Dragons: A Collection of Creative Relaxation Activities for Home and School" (East Aurora, N.Y.: D.O.K. Publishers [P.O. Box 605, East Aurora, N.Y. 14052], 1986).
23. Diana Baumrind, telephone interview with the author, December 4, 1984.
24. "How American Teens Feel," *San Francisco Chronicle*, April 1, 1984, A18.
25. William Masters and Virginia Johnson, *The Pleasure Bond* (Boston: Little, Brown, 1974).

Chapter 4. Raising Girls and Boys with Options

1. Benjamin Spock, quote on jacket cover of Letty Cottin Pogrebin, *Growing Up Free: Raising Your Children in the 80's* (New York: McGraw-Hill, 1980).
2. Letty Cottin Pogrebin, telephone interview with the author, November 19, 1983.
3. Herb Goldberg, *The New Male* (New York: Signet, 1979), 6.
4. Barbara Powell, *How To Raise a Successful Daughter* (Chicago: Nelson-Hall, 1979), 50.
5. Rodney Cate and Alan Sugawara, "Sex Role Orientation and Dimensions of Self-esteem among Middle Adolescents," *Sex Roles* 15, no. 3/4 (1986):145; P. P. Wong, G. Kettlewell, and C. F. Sproule, "On the Importance of Being Masculine: Sex Role Attribution and Women's Career Achievement," *Sex Roles* 12,

no. 7/8 (April 1985):757; Ellen Piel Cook, *Psychological Androgyny* (New York: Pergamon, 1985), 94.

6. Jerome Kagan and Howard Moss, *Birth to Maturity: A Study in Psychological Development* (New York: John Wiley & Sons, 1962), 275.
7. Norma Radin and Grame Russell, "Increased Father Participation and Child Development Outcomes," in Michael Lamb and Abraham Sagi, eds., *Fatherhood and Family Policy* (Hillsdale, N.J.: Lawrence Erlbaum, 1983), 198, 199; J. Brooks-Gunn, "The Relationship of Maternal Beliefs about Sex Typing to Maternal and Young Children's Behavior," *Sex Roles* 14, no. 1/2 (January 1986):22.
8. Lamb and Sagi, *Fatherhood and Family Policy*, 198, 199; David Lynn, *Daughters and Parents: Past, Present and Future* (Monterey, Calif.: Brooks/Cole, 1979), 89.
9. David Lynn, *The Father: His Role in Child Development* (Monterey, Calif.: Brooks/Cole, 1974), 128.
10. Powell, *How To Raise a Successful Daughter*, 51–65; Graeme Russell, *The Changing Role of Fathers?* (St. Lucia, Australia: University of Queensland Press, 1983), 179.
11. Lala Steelman and Brian Powell, "The Social and Academic Consequences of Birth Order: Real, Artifactual, or Both?" *Journal of Marriage and the Family* 47, no. 1 (February 1985):118.
12. Abraham Sagi, "Antecedents and Consequences of Various Degrees of Paternal Involvement in Child Rearing: The Israeli Project," in Michael Lamb, ed., *Nontraditional Families: Parenting and Child Development* (Hillsdale, N.J.: Lawrence Erlbaum, 1982), 222.
13. Phyllis Katz and Sally Boswell, *Flexibility and Traditionality in Children's Gender Roles* (Boulder, Colo.: Institute for Research on Social Problems), 40.
14. Lynn, *Daughters and Parents*, 89.
15. Eleanor Maccoby and Carol Jacklin, *The Psychology of Sex Differences* (Stanford, Calif.: Stanford University Press, 1974), 302.
16. Carol Gilligan, *In a Different Voice* (Cambridge, Mass.: Harvard University Press, 1982).
17. Carol Tavris and Carole Wade, *The Longest War: Sex Differences in Perspective* (San Diego, Calif.: Harcourt Brace Jovanovich, 1984), 246; Lillian Rubin, *Woman of a Certain Age: The Mid Life Search For Self* (New York: Harper and Row, 1979), 55.
18. Janice Mall, "About Women," *Los Angeles Times*, February 12, 1984, 14.
19. Beverly Fagot and Richard Hagan, "Aggression in Toddlers: Response to Assertive Acts of Boys & Girls," *Sex Roles* 12, no. 3/4 (1985):341, 349.
20. June Statham, *Daughters and Sons: Experiences of Non-sexist Childraising* (New York: Basil Blackwell, 1986), 28.
21. Caryl Rivers, Rosalind Barnett, and Grace Baruch, *Beyond Sugar and Spice: How Women Grow, Learn and Thrive* (New York: Ballantine, 1979), 58.
22. Mildred Hamilton, "Are Girls Smarter than Boys?" *San Francisco Chronicle*, February 12, 1984. See also Bette Whitelock Tyron, "Beliefs About Male & Female Competence Held by Kindergartners," *Sex Roles* 6, no. 1 (February 1980):85, 86.
23. E. Yuchtman-Yaar and R. Shapira, "Sex as a Status Characteristic: An Exam-

ination of Sex Differences in Locus of Control," *Sex Roles* 7, no. 2 (February 1981):158.

24. Carol Tavris with Alice Baumgartner, "How Would You Like To Be Different?" *Redbook* 160, no. 4 (February 1983):92–95.
25. Barbara Kerr, *Smart Girls, Gifted Women* (Columbus: Ohio Psychology Publishing, 1985), 83; Lori Schwartz and William Markham, "Sex Stereotyping in Children's Toy Advertisement," *Sex Roles* 12, no. 1/2 (January 1985):158, 159.
26. Katz and Boswell, *Flexibility and Traditionality in Children's Gender Roles*, 35.
27. Myra Sadker and David Sadker, "Sexism in the Schoolroom of the 80's," *Psychology Today* 19, no. 3 (March 1985):54, 56, 57.
28. Gloria Contreras, "A Gender-Balancing Resource List," *Social Education* 51, no. 3 (March 1987): 200–205. (This is a very useful article for secondary school and college levels. Other articles in the issue include material for elementary schools.) See also Resources for Sex Equity in Education, Women's Action Alliance, 370 Lexington Ave., New York, N.Y. 10017; Nancy Schniedewind and Ellen Davidson, *Open Minds to Equality: A Sourcebook* (Englewood Cliffs, N.J.: Prentice-Hall, 1983); TABS newsletter (Aids for Ending Sexism in School), 744 Carroll St., Brooklyn, N.Y. 11215; June Shapiro, Slyvia Kramer, and Catherine Hunerberg, *Equal Their Chances: Children's Activities for Non-sexist Learning* (Englewood Cliffs, N.J.: Prentice-Hall, 1981); "Celebrating a Decade of Equity 1977–87," Women's Educational Equity Act Publishing Center, 55 Chapel St., Newton, Mass. 02160 (contains guides for curricula for all grade levels, career guidance, etc.); "Non-Sexist Teacher: Overcoming Bias in Teacher-Student Interation," The Mid-Atlantic Center for Sex Equity, The American University, U.S. Department of Education, 3301 New Mexico Ave., Washington, D.C. 20016; "Audiovisual Resources, Project Sex Equity in Education," California State Department of Education, Sacramento, CA 94244-2720, 1987.
29. Marie Richmond-Abbott, *Masculine and Feminine: Sex Roles over the Life Cycle* (Reading, Mass.: Addison-Wesley, 1983), 187.
30. Judy Pearson, *Gender and Communication* (Dubuque, Iowa: William C. Brown, 1985); Nancy Henley, *Body Politics* (Englewood Cliffs, N.J.: Prentice-Hall, 1977).
31. Letty Cottin Pogrebin, telephone interview with the author, November 19, 1983.
32. Richmond-Abbott, *Masculine and Feminine*, 78.
33. Ibid., 283; Melvin Kohn, "The Effects of Social Class on Parental Values and Practices," in Patricia Voydanoff, ed., *Work and Family: The Changing Roles of Men and Women* (Palo Alto, Calif.: Mayfield, 1984), 125.
34. Catherine Emihovich, Eugene Gaier, and Nareen Cronin, "Sex-Role Expectation Changes by Fathers for Their Sons," *Sex Roles* 11, no. 9/10 (November 1984):862, 866, 867.
35. Peter Dworkin, "SRI Turns a Profit from Psychology," *San Francisco Chronicle*, November 7, 1984, 31. Americans were categorized by marketing researchers as the "Outer Directeds" (68%) who "live their lives driven by signals from others," and the "Inner Directeds" (19%) who value inner growth and experiences. Only 11% of Americans are "societally conscious," and only 2% are "In-

tegrated"—psychologically mature and understanding. The coparents in my studies are like the "Inner Directeds," who, although a minority, are the fastest growing group. This is another indication that role sharers are unusual but are harbingers of a future trend.

36. Letty Cottin Pogrebin, telephone interview with the author, November 19, 1983.
37. Statham, *Daughters and Sons,* 178.
38. "Thinking About the Unthinkable, Resource List," *Ms.* 13, no. 11 (May 1985):131–32.
39. "Action Agenda for Equalizing Girls' Options," *Voice for Girls* 29, no. 2 (Spring 1985):11.
40. Russell, *The Changing Role of Fathers?* 179; see appendix 3 for studies by Braymen, Carlson, DeFrain, Radin, and Sagi.

Chapter 5. Children's Views

1. Margaret Ferrin (now Cieslikowski), "Sex Role Identity and Self-Esteem of Children Reared by Egalitarian Parents" (Master's thesis, California State University, Chico, 1985).
2. Graeme Russell and Norma Radin, "Increased Paternal Participation: The Father's Perspective," in Michael Lamb and Abraham Sagi, eds., *Fatherhood and Family Policy* (Hillsdale, N.J.: Lawrence Erlbaum, 1983), 152; Victor Gecas and Michael Schawalbe, "Parental Behavior and Adolescent Self-Esteem," *Journal of Marriage and the Family* 48, no. 1 (February 1986):38, 44; Rebecca Braymen and John DeFrain, "Sex-Roles and Behaviors of Children Reared by Androgynous Parents" (Unpublished paper presented at Groves Conference on Marriage and Family, Washington, D.C., April 26-29, 1979). See also Braymen and DeFrain, "Equalitarian Marriages: Sex-Role Attitudes and Behaviors of Children" (Unpublished paper, University of Nebraska).
3. David Lynn, *Daughters and Parents: Past, Present, and Future* (Monterey, Calif.: Brooks/Cole, 1979), 138.
4. Norma Radin, "Primary Caregiving and Role-Sharing Fathers," in Michael Lamb, ed., *Non-traditional Families: Parenting and Child Development* (Hillsdale, N.J.: Lawrence Erlbaum, 1982), 191; Norma Radin and Graeme Russell, "Increased Father Participation and Child Development Outcomes," in Lamb and Sagi, *Fatherhood and Family Policy;* Abraham Sagi, "Antecedents and Consequences of Various Degrees of Paternal Involvement in Child-Rearing: The Israeli Project," in Lamb, *Non-traditional Families,* 205–222.
5. David Lynn, *The Father's Role in Child Development* (Monterey, Calif.: Brooks/Cole, 1974), 127.
6. Gloria Nemerowicz, *Children's Perceptions of Gender and Work Roles* (New York: Praeger, 1979), 162, 163.
7. Corrie Anders, "Study Of U.S. Teens Finds Generation Gap Has Closed," *San Francisco Chronicle,* April 1, 1984, A18.

8. Morris Rosenberg, *Society and Adolescent Self-Image* (Princeton, N.J.: Princeton University Press, 1965), 17–18.
9. We gave the children the Bem Sex-Role Inventory (with definitions added for children) designed to measure degrees of masculinity, femininity, androgyny, or undifferentiation. The E children had a higher percentage of masculine and androgynous scores than T children, but the difference was not statistically significant. T girls gave themselves higher femininity scores than E girls. High self-esteem was related to a high masculinity score on the Bem Sex-Role Inventory and a low self-esteem score was associated with scoring undifferentiated, meaning low on both masculinity and femininity. Bonnie Carlson reported that egalitarian mothers were least likely to be androgynous and their daughters were most feminine. The mothers who were the primary care givers had the least feminine daughters. (See Carlson, "Shared vs. Primarily Maternal Child Rearing: Effects of Dual-Career on Families with Young Children," *Dissertation Abstracts* 4, no. 9 (March 1981):3599-B.) See also Stanley Coppersmith, *The Antecedents of Self-Esteem* (San Francisco: W.H. Freeman, 1967), 109–10.
10. Carol Tavris and Carole Wade, *The Longest War: Sex Differences in Perspective* (San Diego: Harcourt Brace Jovanovich, 1984), 67; Deborah Stipetz, "Sex Differences in Children's Attributions for Success and Failure on Math and Spelling Tests," *Sex Roles* 11, no. 1/2 (December 1984):969, 972; Florence Rosenberg and Roberta Simmons, "Sex Differences in the Self Concept in Adolescence," *Sex Roles* 1, no. 2 (1975):155; Norma Radin, "Primary Caregiving and Role-Sharing Fathers," in Michael Lamb, *Non-traditional Families*, 192, 201.
11. Norma Radin, "Effects of Equal Parenting on Children" (Paper presented at the Conference on Equal Parenting: Families of the Future, California State University, Chico, February 9, 1985); Sagi, "The Israeli Project," 205–222; Robert Bradley, "Fathers and the School-aged Child," in Shirley Hanson and Frederick Bozett, eds., *Dimensions of Fatherhood* (Beverly Hills, Calif.: Sage, 1985), 160–1; Ross Parke, *Fathers* (Cambridge, Mass.: Harvard University Press, 1981), 43, 45.
12. Marie Richmond-Abbott, *Masculine and Feminine: Sex Roles over the Life Cycle* (Reading, Mass.: Addison-Wesley, 1983), 199; Lynda Madaras, "Talking to Boys About Sex," in Ollie Pocs, ed., *Human Sexuality 86/87*, Annual Editions (Guilford, Conn.: Dushkin Publishers, 1986), 41; Shirley Zussman, "Talking Sex," *Children; For Today's Parent*, Rodale Press 1, no. 5, (March 1987):106. (A list of useful books about sex is included.) John Santrock, Richard Warshak, and Gary Elliot, "Social Development and Parent-Custody Interaction in Father-Custody and Step-mother Families," in Lamb, *Non-traditional Families*, 293; John Hildebrand, "Inspire Your Children: Don't Nag Them," reprinted from *Newsday* in *San Francisco Chronicle*, March 4, 1986, 19; Earl Schaefer, University of North Carolina, Chapel Hill, "Prediction of Child Academic Competence from Maternal Modernity During Infancy" (a copy of a paper presented to the American Education Research Association, New Orleans, April 26, 1984).
13. Lynn, *Daughters and Parents*, 89.

14. Barbara Powell, *How to Raise a Successful Daughter* (Chicago: Nelson-Hall, 1979), 48.
15. Stanrock, Warshak, and Elliot, "Social Development and Parent-Custody Interaction," 293; Hildebrand, "Inspire Your Children," 19; Schaefer, "Prediction of Child Academic Competence"; David Perlman, "Kids with One Sibling Tops on Test, Study Says," *San Francisco Chronicle*, May 28, 1985.

Chapter 6. Coparents' Perspectives

1. Joseph Veroff, Elizabeth Douvan, and Richard Kulka, *The Inner American: A Self-Portrait, from 1957–1976* (New York: Basic Books, 1981), 177, 178. In their national survey, 85% of the husbands and 87% of the wives reported that their marriages were about equal. Wives, however, were more likely to express resentment, perhaps because over 80% of the couples reported that women do most of the housework. Among dual-earner couples in the same survey, about a third indicated that husbands share child care equally. See also Philip Blumstein and Pepper Schwartz, *American Couples* (New York: William Morrow, 1983), 145, 146, 326. Less than 2% share equally, according to a Texas study: L. Nyquist et al., "Household Responsibilities for Middle-class Couples," *Sex Roles* 12, nos. 1 and 2 (January 1985): 26. See also Sarah Fenstermaker Berk, *The Gender Factory: The Apportionment of Work in American Households* (New York: Plenum Press, 1985), 207; Lucia Albino Gilbert, *Men in Dual-Career Families* (Hillsdale, N.J.: Lawrence Erlbaum, 1985), 63.
2. Mark Kotkin, "Roles Among Married and Unmarried Couples," *Sex Roles* 9, no. 9 (1983):975–985.
3. C. Cowan et al., "Transitions to Parenthood: His, Hers, Theirs," *Journal of Family Issues* 6, no. 4 (December 1985):464; Lynn White, Alan Booth, and John Edwards, "Children and Marital Happiness: Why the Negative Correlation?" *Journal of Family Issues* 7, no. 2 (June 1986):139.
4. Lance Laurence, *Couple Constancy: Conversations with Today's Happily Married People* (Ann Arbor, Mich.: VMI Research, 1982), 35.
5. The 1985 Virginia Slims American Women's Opinion Poll (conducted by the Roper Organization) as summarized in *Women and Work Research and Resource Letter*, University of Texas at Arlington, 2, no. 1 (Fall 1986):2. A poll of people age 19 to 37 showed that 76% supported family equality. A Roper poll found that 37% of women and 43% of men want a traditional marriage with the husband as sole earner. More preferred shared responsibilities, yet few put their beliefs into practice. In a Gallop Poll of men, half felt they should share child care and housework with an employed wife. Almost as many husbands said they provided no help or only helped part of the time. Eighty-nine percent of the women reported that they do more than half or all the child care and housework, according to a *Redbook* survey of 46,000 readers.
6. Blumstein and Schwartz, *American Couples* 145, 146, 326. See also Laura Lein

and Lydia O'Donnell, "Talk, Talk, Talk: Negotiating Housework Can Take More Time Than Doing It," *Working Mothers* 6, no. 9 (September 1983):76–77.

7. Interview with Lucia Gilbert, March 9, 1987. "Entitlement" is her term for men's common expectation that women are responsible for family work. See also Jessie Bernard, *The Female World* (New York: The Free Press, 1980), 502; Sandra Stanley, Janet Hunt, and Larry Hunt, "The Relative Deprivation of Husbands in Dual-Earner Households," *Journal of Family Issues* 7, no. 1 (March 1986):11.
8. L. Locke and K. Wallace, "Short Marital Adjustment and Prediction Tests: Their Reliability and Validity," *Marriage and Family Living* 21, no. 3 (1959):251–55. In another study the mean was 115.6: See Allison Parelman, *Emotional Intimacy in Marriage: A Sex-Role Perspective* (Ann Arbor, Mich.: VMI Research Press), 88. In an Ohio study of families with school-age children, the mean for women was 95 and 104 for men: See Graham Spanier, Robert Lewis, and Charles Cole, "Marital Adjustment over the Family Life Cycle," *Journal of Marriage and the Family* (May 1975):270. One study found mean scores of dual-worker couples with preschool children of 115 for androgynous scorers, 100 for masculine, 100 for feminine, and 93 for undifferentiated: Kristina Cooper, Laurie Chassin, and Antoinette Zeiss, "The Relation of Sex-Role Self-Concept and Sex-Role Attitudes to the Marital Satisfaction and Personal Adjustment of Dual-Worker Couples with Pre-School Children," *Sex Roles* 12, no. 1/2 (1985):326. Another study found that marital satisfaction predicted "paternal satisfaction": Shirley Feldman, Sharon Nash, and Barbara Aschenbrenner, "Antecedents of Fathering," *Child Development* 54, no. 30 (December 1983): 1632.
9. The same 84 couples also filled out a 300-question personality inventory called the Adjective Checklist (designed by Gough and Heilbrun). Twenty-five subscales include traits such as self-confidence, nurturance, and dominance. My thesis was that the most happily married couples would be most confident and nurturant, but the thesis was not proved valid by the Adjective Checklist as there were no significant differences between groups. The couples also completed the Bem Sex-Role Inventory. The most happily married group was likely to score androgynous or masculine. Several other studies have also found a correlation with androgyny and marital happiness (see, for example, Allison Parelman, *Emotional Intimacy in Marriage*, 11), although others have found no correlation. High masculinity scores correlate with high self-esteem (as was true for children surveyed for this book), which is required for the self-disclosure on which intimacy is based.
10. Graeme Russell, "The Father Role and Its Relation to Masculinity, Femininity and Androgyny," *Child Development* 49, no. 4 (December 1978):1179; Cooper, Chassin, and Zeiss, "Relation of Sex-Role Self-Concept and Sex-Role Attitudes," 326; Christina Cooper, Laurie Chassin, Sanford Braver, Antoinette Zeiss, and Katherine Khavari, "Correlates of Mood and Marital Satisfaction among Dual-Worker and Single-Worker Couples," *Social Psychology Quarterly* 49, no. 4 (1986):322, 325.
11. John Antill and John Cunningham, "Self-Esteem as a Function of Masculinity

in Both Sexes," *Journal of Consulting and Clinical Psychology* 47, no. 4:784; J. Rendely, R. Holmstrom, and S. Karp, "The Relationship of Sex-Role Identity, Lifestyle and Mental Health in Suburban Homemakers," *Sex Roles* 11, no. 9/10 (1984):839–848. A Boston study of middle-class families found that men's peer groups often ridicule men for doing family work, seen as "effeminate or weak behavior." "You're getting us in trouble" with our wives was a common reaction to a man doing housework; self-esteem is required to resist this pressure: Laura Lein, "Male Participation in Home Life," in Patricia Voydanoff, ed., *Work and Family: Changing Roles of Men and Women* (Palo Alto, Calif.: Mayfield, 1984), 246.

12. William Coysh, "Predictive and Concurrent Factors Relate to Fathers' Involvement in Childbearing" (Paper presented to the American Psychological Association, California, 1983), 1, 3; Linda Haas, "Role-Sharing Couples: A Study of Egalitarian Marriages," *Family Relations* 29, no. 3 (July 1980):289–296; Linda Haas, "Determinants of Role-Sharing Behavior: A Study of Egalitarian Couples," *Sex Roles* 8, no. 7 (1982):747–760; Mark deTurck and Gerald Miller, "Effects of Husbands' and Wives' Social Cognition on Their Marital Adjustment, Conjugal Power, and Self-Esteem," *Journal of Marriage and The Family* 48 (November 1986), 722.
13. In a Boston study, women's but not men's marital happiness gained with increases in the father's child care activities; men who were not as involved in child care felt positive about their marriage, but had low self-esteem: Rosalind Barnett and Grace Baruch, "Determinants of Fathers' Participation in Family Work," Working Paper No. 136 (Wellesley, Mass.: Wellesley College Center for Research on Women, revised 1986), 5.
14. Lizanne Leach, "Egalitarian Marriage: Some Differences Between Those Who Share and Those Who Don't," (Master's thesis, California State University, Chico, 1983), 49.
15. Norma Radin, "Childrearing Fathers in Intact Families I: Some Antecedents and Consequences," *Merrill-Palmer Quarterly* 27 (1981):491–514. Many of the fathers interveiwed by Rick Sapp also identified with their mothers and were critical of their fathers' lack of contact with the family: Rick Sapp, "Shared Parent Fathers: Role Entry and Psychological Consequences of Participation in a Nontraditional Male Parent Role (Ph.D. dissertation, The Wright Institute, 1984).
16. Audrey Smith and William Reid, *Role-Sharing Marriage* (New York: Columbia University Press, 1986), 135; John DeFrain, "Androgynous Parents Tell Who They Are and What They Need," *Family Coordinator* 28, no. 2:237–243; Rick Sapp, "Shared Parent Fathers."
17. Graeme Russell and Norma Radin, "Increased Paternal Participation: The Fathers' Perspective," in Michael Lamb and Abraham Sagi, eds., *Fatherhood and Family Policy* (Hillsdale, N.J.: Lawrence Erlbaum, 1983), 160.
18. Norma Radin, "Effects of Equal Parenting on Children" (Paper presented to California State University, Chico, Conference on Equal Parenting, February 6, 1985); Smith and Reid, *Role-Sharing Marriage*, 89; Haas, "Role-Sharing Couples," 291.

19. William Coysh, "Predictive and Concurrent Factors," 3.
20. Graeme Russell and Norma Radin, "Increased Paternal Participation, 160; Lois Hoffman, "Increased Fathering: Effects on the Mother," in Lamb and Sagi, eds., *Fatherhood and Family Policy,* 182; Janice Hood, *Becoming A Two-Job Family* (New York: Praeger, 1983), 190; Linda Haas, "Fathers and Childcare in the 80's" (copy of plenary speech given to the annual meeting of the Indiana Council on Family Relations, February 23, 1982).
21. Linda Haas, "Determinants of Role-Sharing Behavior," 756. Only six of the thirty-one Madison couples studied by Linda Haas reported a history of the husband earning a great deal more than his wife. (See appendix 3 for bibliographical references to studies on role sharing.) Lucia Gilbert, *Men in Dual-Career Families* (Hillsdale, N.J.: Lawrence Erlbaum, 1985), 69, 71.
22. Arlie Hochschild, interview with the author, San Francisco, January 21, 1987, about her book *The Second Shift* (New York: Random House, forthcoming). Hochschild did not find any differences between black families and white families in role sharing, although John Scanzoni and others have suggested that black spouses are more egalitarian.
23. Diane Ehrensaft, *Parenting Together: Men and Women Sharing the Care of Their Children* (New York: Free Press, forthcoming). Many of the role-sharing parents interviewed by Diane Ehrensaft, Linda Haas, and John DeFrain, but not by Norma Radin, were influenced by feminism. Graeme Russell's involved parents in Australia were likely not to believe in innate differences between men's and women's ability to raise children. A linked attitude is liberal political beliefs.
24. Norma Radin, "Primary Caregiving and Role-Sharing Fathers," in Michael Lamb, ed., *Non-traditional Families: Parenting and Child Development* (Hillsdale, N.J.: Lawrence Erlbaum, 1982), 192. Radin found that involved fathers did more direct teaching of their sons than of their daughters, although the daughters did benefit from the educational enrichment.
25. Richard Lerner and Graham Spanier, eds., *Child Influences on Marital and Family Interaction* (New York: Academic Press, 1978), 170, 171; Linda Nyquist et al., "Household Responsibilities for Middle Class Couples," *Sex Roles* 12, no. 1/2 (January 1985):26.
26. Lance Laurence, *Couple Constancy,* 33; E. Denmark, J. Shaw, and S. Ciali, "The Relationship Among Sex Roles, Living Arrangements and the Division of Household Responsibilities," *Sex Roles* 12, no. 5/6 (1985):617–625; Jeanette Lauer and Robert Lauer, "Marriages Made to Last," *Psychology Today* 19, no. 6 (June 1985):26.
27. Doug Smith, "Long-Married Pairs Share Unhappiness," *Los Angeles Times,* June 22, 1981, 17; Karen Barnett, "Two-Career Couples: How They Do It," *Ms.* (June 1984); Elaine Walster and G. William Walster, *Equity Theory and Research* (Boston: Allyn and Bacon, 1978), 178; Coysh, "Predictive and Concurrent Factors Related to Fathers' Involvement," 1, 3; John Antill, Sandra Cotton, and Susan Tindale, "Egalitarian or Traditional: Correlates of the Perception of an Ideal Marriage," *Australian Journal of Psychology* 35, no. 110 (1983):245; Sara Yogev and Jeanne Brett, "Perceptions of the Division of Housework and Childcare and Marital Satisfaction," *Journal of Marriage and the Family* 47, no. 3 (Au-

gust 1985):609; Lucia Gilbert, *Men in Dual-Career Families*, 50, 61; DeFrain, "Androgynous Parents Tell Who They Are and What They Need," 240–241; Bebe Moore Campbell, *Successful Women, Angry Men* (New York: Random House, 1986), 219; Allison Parelman, *Emotional Intimacy in Marriage*, 11; Bernadette Gray-Little and Nancy Burks, "Power and Satisfaction in Marriage: A Review and Critique," *Psychological Bulletin* 93, no. 3 (1983):513, 534, 535.

Marital studies range from couples with a new baby—which found that marital satisfaction at six months after the birth of the child correlates with the extent to which the parents share child care and housework—to studies of couples married over fifty years. This ties in with findings by Elaine Walster and William Walster that even the more benefited partner feels dissatisfied when there is inequity in the relationship.

28. Elisabeth Nettle and Jane Loevinger, "Sex Role Expectations and Ego Levels in Relation to Problem Marriages," *Journal of Personality and Social Psychology* 45, no. 3 (1983):685; Boas Shamir, "Unemployment and Household Labor," *Journal of Marriage and the Family* 48, no. 1 (February 1986):205; Laurie Chassin, Antoinette Zeiss, Kristina Cooper, and Judith Reaven, "Role Perceptions, Self-Role Congruence and Marital Satisfaction in Dual-Worker Couple with Pre-School Children" *Social Psychology Quarterly* 48, no. 4 (1985):310.
29. Joan Huber and Glenna Spitze, "Considering Divorce: An Expansion of Becker's Theory of Marital Instability," *American Journal of Sociology* 86, no. 1 (1980):85.
30. Robert Levenson and John Gottman, "Martial Interaction: Physiological Linkage and Affective Exchange," *Journal of Personality and Social Psychology* 3, no. 3 (1983):595; deTurck and Miller, "The Effects of Husbands' and Wives' Social Cognition," 722.
31. Blumstein and Schwartz, *American Couples*, 139.
32. Mary Benin and Barbara Wienstedt, "Happiness in Single- and Dual-Earner Families," *Journal of Marriage and the Family* 47, no. 4 (November 1985):975–983.
33. "The Perils of Dual-Careers," *Time*, May 13, 1985, 67.
34. C. Pietrowski and R. Repetti, "Dual-Earner Families," in Beth B. Hess and Marvin Sussman, eds., *Women and the Family: Two Decades of Change* (Binghamton, N.Y.: Haworth Press, 1984), 117; Faye Crosby, *Relative Deprivation and Working Women* (New York: Oxford University Press, 1982), 159. However, a recent study comparing single-worker and dual-worker families found that women who did not work had higher marital satisfaction scores: Chassin, Braver, Zeiss, and Khavari, "Correlates of Mood and Marital Satisfaction Among Dual-Worker and Single-Worker Couples," 326.
35. Grace Baruch, Rosalind Barnett, and Caryl Rivers, *Lifeprints* (New York: McGraw-Hill, 1983), 38.
36. S. Yogev, "Do Professional Women Have Egalitarian Marital Relationships?" *Journal of Marriage and the Family* 43, no. 4 (1981):865–871.
37. Elizabeth Mehren, "Working Wives: Negative Effect on Husbands?" *Los Angeles Times*, March 31, 1986, 1. Mehren cites a study by Kathleen Pottick et al. See also R. Burke and T. Weir, "Relationship of Wives' Employment Status to

Husband, Wife and Pair Satisfaction and Performance," *Journal of Marriage and the Family* 38, no. 2 (1976):279–287; Dana Hiller and William Philliber, "Predicting Marital and Career Success among Dual-Worker Couples," *Journal of Marriage and the Family* 44, no. 1 (February 1982):53–62.

38. S. Hardesty and N. E. Betz, "The Relationships of Career Salience Attitudes toward Women to Marital Adjustment in Dual-Career Couples," *Journal of Vocational Behavior* 17, no. 2 (1980):242–252.
39. Thomas Harrell and Jane Baack, "Dual Career Couples: Anxiety of MBA Couples Compared with Traditional Couples." (Research Report No. 889, Graduate School of Business, Stanford University, July 1986); Fern Schumer Chapman, "Executive Guilt: Who's Taking Care of the Children?" *Fortune* 115, no. 4 (February 16, 1987):30, 31, 35.
40. Beth B. Hess and Marvin Sussman, eds., *Women and the Family: Two Decades of Change* (Binghamton, N.Y.: Haworth Press, 1984), 106.
41. Francine Klagsbrun, "Secret and Pleasures of Long-Lasting Marriage," *Ms.* 13, no. 12 (June 1985):41–93.
42. See also Judith Wallerstein, *Surviving the Break-Up: How Children and Parents Cope with Divorce* (New York: Basic Books, 1980), 14. Beckstein and I surveyed 300 individuals of various ages, 184 women and 116 men, 127 in California and 73 in Ontario (tabluated by Vicki Pesetti).
43. Shirley Gilbert, "Self-Disclosure, Intimacy and Communication in Families," *Family Coordinator* 25, no. 3 (July 1976):225, 226.
44. Douglas Abbott and Géne Brody, "The Relation of Child Age, Gender, and Number of Children to the Marital Adjustment of Wives," *Journal of Marriage and the Family* 47, no. 11 (February 1985):78, 81–83. Yet other studies show that parents of boys are less likely to divorce.
45. Abner Boles, "Martial Satisfaction during the Transition to Parenthood" (Paper delivered at American Psychological Association meeting, California, 1983), 1.
46. Nick Stinnett and John DeFrain, *Secrets of Strong Families* (New York: Berkeley Books, 1985), 67.
47. David Rice, *Dual-Career Marriage* (New York: Free Press, 1979), 3; Uma Sekaran, *Dual-Career Families* (San Francisco: Jossey-Bass, 1986), 176, 180, 198.
48. Bruce Chadwick, Stan Albrecht, and Philip Kunz, "Marital and Family Role Satisfaction," *Journal of Marriage and the Family* 38, no. 3 (August 1976):432, 439; Michael Sporakowski and George Hughston, "Prescriptions for Happy Marriage: Adjustments and Satisfactions of Couples Married for 50 or More Years," *Family Coordinator* 27, no. 4 (October 1978):326.
49. Dolores Curran, *Traits of a Healthy Family* (Minneapolis, Minn.: Winston Press, 1983), 5.
50. Catalyst Career and Family Center, *Corporations and Two-Career Families: Directions for the Future* (New York: Catalyst, 1981).
51. Cher Carrie Thomas, "Keeping It All in Balance: Strategies from Southern California Women," Unpublished paper, Psychology Department, California State University, Long Beach, 1986. See also Aasta Lubin, *Managing Success: High-Echelon Careers and Motherhood* (New York: Columbia University Press, 1987), 47–53.

Chapter 7. Involving Fathers

1. Joseph Pleck, personal correspondence to the author, December 31, 1986; Michael Lamb, Joseph Pleck, and James Levine, "Effects of Increased Paternal Involvement on Children," in Robert Lewis and Robert Salt, eds., *Men In Families* (Beverly Hills: Sage, 1986), 141.
2. Barbara Kantrowitz, "The Real 'Mr. Moms,'" *Newsweek* 107, no. 18 (March 31, 1986):54; referred to as "The New Fathering" in Anthony Astrachan, *How Men Feel and Their Response to Women's Demands for Equality and Power* (New York: Doubleday, 1986), 231; Stephen Grubman-Black, "Some Images and Reflections of Fathers in the Popular Media: Fallacy, Fiction, Fantasy, Fact," *University of Dayton Review* (Special Issue on Men) 18, no. 2 (Winter-Spring 1986–1987):83–92.
3. Perry Garfinkel, *In A Man's World* (New York: New American Library, 1985). (He states, "For most men life is a long search for reunion with their lost fathers.") See also Samuel Osherson, *Finding Our Fathers: The Unfinished Business of Manhood* (New York: Free Press, 1986); Mark Gerzon, *A Choice of Heroes: The Changing Faces of American Manhood* (Boston: Houghton Mifflin, 1982), 58. (Fathers "were important but distant. We didn't count on them"); Gloria Emerson, "Some American Men," *Psychology Today* 20, no. 4 (April 1986):80. She reported that most of the men she interviewed expressed "a wounded tenderness for their fathers . . . the sadness of lost connection. The father-son relationship emerges as perhaps the pivotal force in a man's life."
4. Rick Sapp, personal correspondence to the author, May 17, 1985, based on his dissertation "Shared Parent Fathers," The Wright Institute, 1984; Shirley Feldman, Sharon Nash, and Barbara Aschenbrenner, "Antecedents of Fathering," *Child Development* 54 (December 1983):1632; Lucia Gilbert, interview, March 9, 1987. See her *Men In Dual-Career Families* (Hillsdale, N.J.: Lawrence Erlbaum, 1985).
5. White House Press Release, "Father's Day, 1982: A Proclamation," April 27, 1982.
6. Page Smith, *Daughters of the Promised Land* (Boston: Little, Brown, 1970), 64.
7. Michael Lamb, telephone interview with the author, May 17, 1984.
8. Robert Sayers, *Fathering: It's Not The Same* (Larkspur, Calif.: Nurturing Family School, 1983). The Sayers material in this chapter was obtained by a telephone interview with the author, September 9, 1984.
9. David Keirsey and Marilyn Bates, *Please Understand Me: Character and Temperament Types* (Del Mar, Calif.: Gnosology Books, 1984).
10. Keith Thompson, "What Men Really Want," Interview with Robert Bly, *New Age* 7, no. 10 (May 1982):31–51.
11. John Nicholson, *Men and Women: How Different Are They?* (Oxford: Oxford University Press, 1984), 131; Kyle Pruett, *The Nurturing Father* (New York: Warner Books, 1987):34–35.
12. Colette Jones, "Father-Infant Relationships in the First Year of Life," in Shirley Hanson and Frederick Bozett, eds., *Dimensions of Fatherhood* (Beverly Hills: Sage, 1985), 103.

13. Ross Thompson, "The Father's Case in Child Custody Disputes," in Michael Lamb and Abraham Sagi, eds., *Fatherhood and Family Policy* (Hillsdale, N.J.: Lawrence Erlbaum, 1983), 75, 91.
14. Graeme Russell and Norma Radin, "Increased Paternal Participation: The Father's Perspective," in Michael Lamb and Abraham Sagi, eds., *Fatherhood and Family Policy* (Hillsdale, N.J.: Lawrence Erlbaum, 1983), 197, 202; Ross Parke, *Fathers* (Cambridge, Mass.: Harvard University Press, 1981), 69, 71, 72.
15. Warren Farrell, telephone interview with the author, September 12, 1982; Susan Basow, *Gender Stereotypes: Traditions and Alternatives* (Monterey, Calif.: Brooks/Cole, 1986), 232.
16. Joseph Pleck, personal correspondence to the author, December 31, 1986.
17. Pierre Mornell, *Passive Men, Wild Women* (New York: Simon and Schuster, 1979).
18. Warren Farrell, *Why Men Are The Way They Are* (New York: McGraw-Hill, 1986).
19. Lucia Gilbert, *Men in Dual-Career Families*, 46, 66. See also chapter 6 in this book.
20. Pamela Daniels and Kathy Weingarten, *Sooner or Later: The Timing of Parenthood in Adult Life* (New York: W. W. Norton, 1980), 71.
21. Letty Cottin Pogrebin, *Growing Up Free: Raising Your Child in the 80s* (New York: McGraw-Hill, 1980), 155; Jane Adams, "I Liked It Better When It Was Him Tarzan, Me Jane," *Working Mother* 4, no. 7 (November 1981):71; Nijole Benokraitis, "Fathers in the Dual-Earner Family," in Hanson and Bozett, eds., *Dimensions of Fatherhood*, 256.
22. Debra Klinman, telephone interview with the author, December 1983.
23. William Goode, "Why Men Resist," in Barrie Thorne, ed., *Rethinking the Family: Some Feminist Questions* (New York: Longman, 1982), 144; Rosalind Barnett and Grace Baruch, "Determinants of Fathers' Participation in Family Work," Working Paper No. 136 (Wellesley, Mass.: Wellesley College Center for Research on Women), 20; Shirley Feldman, Sharon Nash, and Barbara Aschenbrenner, "Antecedents of Fathering," *Child Development* 54, no. 30 (December 1983):1628–1636.
24. Norma Radin, "Primary Caregiving and Role-Sharing Fathers," in Michael Lamb, ed., *Non-traditional Families: Parenting and Child Development* (Hillsdale, N.J.: Lawrence Erlbaum, 1982), 185.
25. "Letters to Father Earth," *Father Earth News* (Fathering Support Services, 44 Washington Blvd., Oak Park, IL 60302) 1, nos. 4, 5 (April 1985):7.
26. Dianne Hales, "Turning Tough Guys into Tender Fathers," *Family Circle* 98, no. 10:30. A study of fathers who participated in a parent education program found that both children and fathers reported positive changes: Robert Levant and Gregory Doyle, "An Evaluation of a Parent Education Program for Fathers of School-Aged Children," *Family Relations* 32, no. 1 (January 1983):33, 44; Michael Lamb, ed., *The Father's Role: Applied Perspectives* (New York: John Wiley, 1986), 21.
27. Hal Yoergler, telephone interview with the author, July 1983.
28. Debra Klinman, telephone interview with the author, December 1983.

29. S. Adams Sullivan, *The Father's Almanac* (New York: Doubleday, 1980).
30. Stanley Cath, Alan Gurwitt, and John Ross, *Father and Child* (Boston: Little, Brown, 1982), 108.
31. Alice Rossi, "American Sociological Association, 1983 Presidential Address," *American Sociological Review* 49, no. 1 (February 1984):13, 15.
32. W. Lambert, W. Hamers, and N. Frasure-Smith, *Child-Rearing Values: A Cross National Study* (New York: Praeger, 1979).

Chapter 8. Coparenting after Divorce

1. Jamie Talan, "What Divorce Does to Kids," *San Francisco Chronicle*, October 1, 1986, 22, 24; Sandra Hoffert, "Updating Children's Life Course," *Journal of Marriage and the Family* 41, no. 1:93.
2. Children raised by single mothers tend to have lower educational and occupational achievement and more divorces of their own. See Daniel Mueller and Philip Cooper, "Children of Single Parent Families: How They Fare as Young Adults," *Family Relations* 35 (January 1986):169, 174. See also E. Milling Kinard and Helen Reinherz, "Effects of Marital Disruption on Children's School Aptitudes and Achievement," *Journal of Marriage and the Family* 48, no. 2 (May 1986):285. However, Eiduson concluded that family type has "no systematic effect on the child's development." See Bernice Eiduson, "Comparative Socialization Practices in Traditional and Alternative Families," in Michael Lamb, ed., *Non-traditional Families: Parenting and Child Development* (Hillsdale, N.J.: Lawrence Erlbaum, 1982), 344.
3. Judith Wallerstein and Joan Kelly, *Surviving the Breakup: How Children and Parents Cope with Divorce* (New York: Basic Books, 1980), 14.
4. Margaret Madden and Ronnie Janoff-Bulman, "Blame, Control and Marital Satisfaction: Wives' Attributions for Conflict in Marriage," *Journal of Marriage and the Family* 43, no. 3 (1981):663.
5. G. P. Spanier and P. C. Glick, "Marital Instability in the U.S.: Some Correlates and Recent Changes," *Family Relations* 31, no. 3 (1981):329.
6. Paul Glick, "How American Families Are Changing," *American Demographics* 6, no. 1 (January 1984):23.
7. E. Mavis Hetherington and Margaret Hagan, "Divorced Fathers: Stress, Coping and Adjustment," in Michael Lamb, ed., *The Father's Role: Applied Perspectives* (New York: John Wiley, 1986), 106.
8. Linda Bird Francke, *Growing Up Divorced* (New York: Linden Press, 1983), 11.
9. Judith Wallerstein, "Children of Divorce: Preliminary Report of a Ten-Year Follow-Up of Young Children," *American Journal of Orthopsychiatry* 54, no. 3 (July 1984):451.
10. Francke, *Growing Up Divorced*, 11.
11. E. Mavis Hetherington, Martha Cox, and Roger Cox, "Effects of Divorce on Parents and Children," in Michael Lamb, ed., *Non-traditional Families*, 234.
12. Deborah Luepnitz, *Child Custody: A Study of Families after Divorce* (Lexington,

Mass.: Lexington Books, 1982), 7–8; James Peterson and Nicholas Zill, "Marital Disruption, Parent-Child Relationships and Behavior Problems in Children," *Journal of Marriage and the Family* 48, no. 2 (May 1986):300.

13. Francke, *Growing Up Divorced* (Francke describes the stages in chapters 5, 6, and 7); Wallerstein and Kelly, *Surviving the Breakup*, 165.
14. Linda Bird Francke, "Why Divorce Is a Bigger Trauma for Sons," *San Francisco Chronicle*, July 12, 1983.
15. Ibid.
16. John Santrock, Richard Warshak, and Gary Elliot, "Social Development and Parent-Custody Interaction in Father-Custody and Step-mother Families," in Michael Lamb, ed., *Non-traditional Families*, 293, 294, 296. John Guidubaldi of Kent State University also found that boys did better in the sole custody of fathers than of mothers, although boys in single-mother families did as well if they were in contact with their fathers: see Talan, "What Divorce Does to Kids," 22.
17. Dorothy Huntington, interview with the author, September 14, 1984.
18. Wallerstein, "Children of Divorce," 448; Warner Troyer, *Divorced Kids* (New York: Harcourt Brace Jovanovich, 1979), 144.
19. Marie Richmond-Abbott, "Sex-Role Attitudes of Mothers and Children in Divorced, Single-Parent Families," *Journal of Divorce* 8, no. 1 (Fall 1984):64.
20. Persia Wooley, *The Custody Handbook* (New York: Summit Books, 1979), 124, 307; Miriam Galper, *Co-Parenting* (Philadelphia: Running Press, 1978), 88; Morris Shepard and Gerald Goldman, *Divorced Dads* (New York: Berkeley Books, 1980), 116.
21. Erica Goode, "The Trauma of Divorced Fathers," *San Francisco Chronicle*, May 18, 1984, 25; Bernard Goldberg, "All Dads Aren't Deadbeats," *San Francisco Examiner*, "This World," December 7, 1986, 20.
22. Wallerstein, "Children of Divorce," 230–243.
23. Wallerstein and Kelly, *Surviving the Breakup*, 309.
24. Lenore Weitzman, *The Divorce Revolution: The Unexpected Social and Economic Consequences for Women and Children in America* (New York: Free Press, 1985); "Fathers Who Skip Out," *San Francisco Chronicle*, June 19, 1983, A1; "Dad No Help for Half of Single Moms," *Sacramento Bee*, November 24, 1986, A12.
25. Luepnitz, *Child Custody*, 67.
26. Ibid., 150.
27. Madonna Bowman and Constance Ahrons, "Impact of Legal Custody Status on Fathers' Parenting Post Divorce," *Journal of Marriage and the Family* 47, no. 2 (May 1, 1985):482.
28. Galper, *Co-Parenting*, 16.
29. Isolina Ricci, *Mom's House, Dad's House* (New York: Macmillan, 1980), 169.
30. Ciji Ware, *Sharing Parenting after Divorce* (New York: Viking, 1982), 228.
31. E. Mavis Hetherington, "Effects of Divorce on Parents and Children," in Michael Lamb, ed., *Non-traditional Families*, 276. See also Cheryl Hayes and Sheila Kamerman, eds., *Children of Working Parents* (Washington, D.C.: National Academy Press, 1983), 88.

32. Melanie Rohn, *The Written Connection* (P.O. Box 572, Chandler, AZ 85244-9980); George Neumann, *101 Ways to Be a Long-Distance Super-Dad* (Mountain View, Calif.: Blossom Valley Press, 1984).
33. Nancy Weston, personal correspondence with the author, March 5, 1984.
34. George Bach, *Pairing* (New York: Avon Books, 1970), 202–4.
35. Issue on Divorce Mediation, *Journal of Divorce* 8, no. 3/4 (Spring/Summer 1985); Nancy Fasciano, "A More Peaceful Parting," *Working Mother* 7, no. 10 (October 1984):150.

Chapter 9. Stepparenting

1. Mark Fine, "Perceptions of Stepparents," *Journal of Marriage and the Family* 48, no. 3 (August 1986):537; Andrew Cherlin and James McCarthy, "Remarried Couple Households: Data from the June, 1980 Current Population Survey," *Journal of Marriage and the Family* 47, no. 1 (February 1985):23; Mark Rosin, "Stepfathers and Stepkids—Can They Get Along?" *Parents* 62, no. 4 (April 1987):22.
2. Elizabeth Dolan and Jean Lown, "The Remarried Family: Challenges and Opportunities," *Journal of Home Economics* 77, no. 3 (Fall 1985):36; Sarah Ramsey, "Stepparent Support of Children," *Family Relations* 35, no. 3 (July 1986):362; Lawrence Ganong and Marilyn Coleman, "A Comparison of Clinical Empirical Literature on Children in Stepfamilies," *Journal of Marriage and the Family* 48, no. 2 (May 1986):314; Lawrence Ganong and Marilyn Coleman, "The Effects of Remarriage on Children: A Review of the Empirical Literature," *Family Relations* 33, no. 3 (July 1984):389–406; Clifford Sager et al., *Treating the Remarried Family* (New York: Brunner/Mazel, 1983), 227.
3. In 1985, 755 California State University, Chico, students were surveyed; 198 students reported that their parents were divorced. Of those students that lived in a stepfamily, only 17% picked "painful" as the most accurate adjective to describe their experience with a stepparent. More frequent first choices were: "added a new person to learn from" (31%), "added complexity to my life" (26%), "added a new person to love" (25%). Female students were more likely to respond, "added a new person to love."
4. Emily Visher and John Visher, "Children in Stepfamilies," *Psychiatric Annals* 12, no. 9 (September 1982):834.
5. Sager et al., *Treating the Remarried Family*, 232.
6. Bryan Robinson and Robert Barret, *The Developing Father: Emerging Roles in Contemporary Society* (New York: Guilford Press, 1986), 127, 131, 132.
7. Sanford Dornbush et al., "Single Parents, Extended Households, and the Control of Adolescents," *Child Development* 56 (1985):332, 333, 338.
8. Natalie Hall, "Stepfamily Complexity," *Stepfamily Bulletin* (Fall 1985):4.
9. Barbara Finley, Charles Starnes, and Fausto Alvarez, "Recent Changes in Sex-

Role Ideology among Divorced Men and Women: Some Possible Causes and Implications," *Sex Roles* 12, no. 5/6 (March 1985):640, 642, 650, 656, 657.

10. Emily Visher, telephone interview with the author, February 1, 1984.
11. Tommie Hamner and Pauline Turner, *Parenting in Contemporary Society* (Englewood Cliffs, N.J.: Prentice-Hall, 1985), 188.
12. Sager et al., *Treating the Remarried Family*, 228; Emily Visher and John Visher, *How To Win as a Stepfamily* (New York: Dembner 1982), 82; Kay Pasley, "Characteristics Studied," *Stepfamily Bulletin* (Fall 1984):7. In a recent study, however, college students were more positive in their evaluation of stepmothers than stepfathers. (See Fine, "Perceptions of Stepparents," 538.)
13. Robinson and Barret, *The Developing Father*, 133.
14. Joy Schulenburg, *Gay Parenting* (New York: Anchor/Doubleday, 1985), 34; Brenda Maddox, "Homosexual Parents," *Psychology Today* 15, no. 2 (February 1982):68; Richard Green, "Sexual Identity of 37 Children Raised by Homosexual or Transsexual Parents," *American Journal of Psychiatry* 35, no. 6 (June 1978):692; Joe Gantz, *Whose Child Cries: Children of Gay Parents Talk About Their Lives* (Rolling Hills Estates, Calif.: Jalmar Press, 1983), xix. The children of lesbian parents in this study had self-esteem scores similar to other children surveyed. Additional material about lesbian parents may be published in a periodical: write to the author for that information.
15. Elizabeth Einstein, *The Stepfamily: Living, Loving and Learning* (New York: Macmillan, 1982), 12.
16. John Florentine and John Visher, "Stepfathering," in Robert Sayers, ed., *Fathering: It's Not the Same* (Larkspur, Calif.: Nurturing Family School, 1983), 59.
17. Ibid., 60.
18. Robinson and Barret, *The Developing Father*, 127.
19. Ibid., 133.
20. Ed Winter-Tamkin and Marilyn Winter-Tamkin, "Children and the Stepfamily Puzzle," *Nurturing News* 7, no. 3 (September 1985):10, 15. See also Peter Jolin, *How to Succeed as a Stepparent* (New York: New American Library, 1981); Larry Jensen and Janet Jensen, *Stepping into Stepparenting: A Practical Guide* (Palo Alto, Calif.: R & E Publishers, 1981).
21. Einstein, *The Stepfamily*, 23–24.
22. Ibid., 53.
23. Vicki Jarmulowsti, "The Blended Family: Who Are They?" *Ms.* 13, no. 8 (February 1985):34.
24. Stan Albrecht, "Correlates of Marital Happiness among the Remarried," *Journal of Marriage and the Family* 34, no. 45 (November 1979):862.
25. Einstein, *The Stepfamily*, 55. See also Jeannette Lofas, "Discipline and Structuring," *The Stepfamily Foundation Newsletter* (Fall 1983):3.
26. Jeannette Lofas with Dawn Sova, *Stepparenting: A Complete Guide to the Joys, Frustrations and Fears of Stepparenting* (New York: Zebra Books, 1985), 132, 133.
27. Emily Visher and John Visher, *Stepfamilies: A Guide to Working with Stepparents and Stepchildren* (New York: Brunner/Mazel, 1979); Emily Visher and John Visher, *Stepfamily Workshop Manual* (Towson, Md.: Stepfamily Association, 1983).

Chapter 10. Communal Parenting

1. Michael Weiss, *Living Together; A Year in the Life of a City Commune* (New York: McGraw-Hill, 1974).
2. *Utopian Classroom* (543 Frederick St., San Francisco, CA 94117). See also Kerista, *Lifestyle Package Design and Experience: Art and Writing of the Kerista Commune* (San Francisco: Performing Arts Society, 1984).
3. Pierrepont Noyes, *My Father's House: An Oneida Boyhood* (New York: Farrar and Rinehart, 1937), 23. Richard De Maria, *Communal Love at Oneida* (New York: Edwin Mellen Press, 1978); Louis Kern, *An Ordered Love: Sex Roles and Sexuality in Victorian Utopias—The Shakers, The Mormons and the Oneida Community* (Chapel Hill: University of North Carolina Press, 1981).
4. *Communities: Journal of Cooperation* (Twin Oaks, Rt. 4, Louisa, VA 23093); Corinne McLaughlin and Gordin Davidson, *Builders of the Dawn: The Network of New Age Communities* (Walpole, N.H.: Stillpoint, 1985); Ron Roberts, *The New Communes* (Englewood Cliffs, N.J.: Prentice-Hall, 1971); Oliver Popenoe and Cris Popenoe, *Seeds of Tomorrow: New Age Communities That Work* (San Francisco: Harper and Row, 1984).
5. Kathleen Kinkade, *A Walden Two Experiment* (New York: William Morrow, 1973).
6. A more recent account is provided by Ingrid Komar, *Living the Dream: A Documentary Study of the Twin Oaks Community* (Norwood, Penn.: Harvard Univ. Center for Jewish Studies, Communal Societies and Utopian Studies Book Series, 1983), 232.
7. Bernice Eiduson, "Children of the 60's," *American Journal of Orthopsychiatry* 53, no. 3 (July 1983):405, 412; Rosabeth Moss Kanter, Dennis Jaffe, and D. Kelly Weisberg, "Coupling, Parenting, and the Presence of Others: Intimate Relationships in Communal Households," *Family Coordinator* 24 (October 1975): 433; Charley Johnston and Robert Deisher, "Contemporary Communal Childrearing," *Communities: A Journal of Cooperative Living: Children in Community*, no. 9 (July-August 1974):27; Rosabeth Moss Kanter, *Communes: Creating and Managing the Collective Life* (New York: Harper and Row, 1973), 351–352.
8. Eiduson, "Children of the 60's," 353, 430, 432.

Chapter 11. Help for Employed Parents

1. "A National Policy for Infant Care," *San Francisco Chronicle*, January 25, 1985.
2. General Mills, *Families at Work: Strengths and Strains, 1980–81* (9200 Wayzata Blvd., Minneapolis, MN 55440), 19.
3. Candace Trunzo, "Mixing Children and Jobs," *Money* 9, no. 11 (November 1980):81; Dana Friedman, "Are Work-Family Concerns Really Women's Issues?" *BusinessLink: The Report on Management Initiatives for Working Parents* 2, no. 2 (Summer 1986):3; see also in the same issue, "Work/Family Research in Progress," *BusinessLink*, 7. (This is a useful newsletter; write to P.O. Box 669,

Summit, NJ 07901). See also Fern Schumer Chapman, "Executive Guilt: Who's Taking Care of the Children?" *Fortune* 115, no. 4 (February 16, 1987):35.

4. Gail Schaper, telephone interveiw with the author about her dissertation "Married Working Women: An Analysis of Role Strain as a Function of Coping Strategy," July 1984.
5. Gayle Kimball, *Life after College: Combining Career and Family* (Chico, Calif.: Equality Press, 1986).
6. Ellen Galinsky, telephone interview with the author, January 3, 1984; see her coauthored chapter (with Diane Hughes), "Women in the Workforce," in Adele Gottfried and Allen Gottfried, eds., *Maternal Employment and Children's Development* (forthcoming).
7. Mary Morse, "Childcare in Sickness and in Health," *New Age Journal* (February 1986):14–15.
8. Dana Friedman, *Working Parents Project* (New York: Carnegie Corp., 1982), 6. A study of dual-earner couples found that they bought services such as child care rather than receiving help from employees or other couples: Rosanna Hertz, *More Equal Than Others: Women and Men in Dual-Career Marriages* (Berkeley: University of California Press, 1986), 14.
9. Katy Butler, "How Bay Area Firms View Ruling on Leaves," *San Francisco Chronicle*, March 31, 1984, 98.
10. Michael Lamb, telephone interview with the author, May 17, 1984.
11. Norma Radin, "Primary Caregiving Fathers of Long Duration," in Phyllis Bronstein and Carolyn Pape Cowan, eds., *Fatherhood Today: Men's Changing Roles in the Family* (New York: John Wiley, forthcoming).
12. Rosabeth Moss Kanter, *The Change Masters* (New York: Simon and Schuster, 1984).
13. Catalyst, "Why Should Companies Think about Women?" (February 1983):3; Janet Elder, "A Giant Step Forward for Parents and Child Care," *San Francisco Chronicle*, September 4, 1986 (reprinted from *The New York Times*).
14. Catalyst, "Career and Family: Maternity and Parental Leaves of Absence" (March 1983):6.
15. Meg Franklin, lecture at a conference on The Working Family: Perspectives and Prospects in the U.S. and Sweden, San Francisco, May 10, 1984; and interview with the author, February 21, 1987.
16. Birgitta Silén, "The Truth About Sexual Equality," *Inside Sweden* (April 1987):13 (available free of charge: S-105 53, Stockholm, Sweden); Staffan Herrstrom, "Swedish Family Policy," *Current Sweden* (Swedish Institute, Stockholm) (September 1986):5.
17. Janice Mall, "Lack of Paid Maternity Leave Deplored," *Los Angeles Times*, September 30, 1983, 2.
18. Barbara Kantrowitz, "Changes in the Workplace," *Newsweek* (March 31, 1986): 57: fewer than 10% of children are in licensed day-care centers.
19. Joseph Pleck, "Fathers and Infant Care Leave," in Edward Zigler and Meryl Frank, eds., *Infant Care Leave* (New Haven, Conn.: Yale University Press, forthcoming.)

20. Economic Policy Council of UNA-USA, "Work and Family in the United States: A Policy Initiative" (New York: United Nations Assoc., December 1985), 2.
21. Olivia Schieffelin Nordberg, "The Cost of Child Care," *Working Mother* 8, no. 2 (February 1985):85.
22. Sheila Kamerman, "The Child-Care Debate," *Working Woman* (November 1983):132; Chapman, "Executive Guilt," 31.
23. Kantrowitz, "Changes in the Workplace," 57; Chapman, "Executive Guilt," 33; Uma Sekaran, *Dual-Career Families* (San Francisco: Jossey-Bass, 1986), 139–144.
24. John Fernandez, *Child Care and Corporate Productivity: Resolving Family/Work Conflicts* (Lexington, Mass.: Lexington Books, 1986), 14; Economic Policy Council of UNA-USA, "Work and Family in the United States," 12, 34.
25. Donna Fenn, "The Kids Are All Right," *Inc.* 7, no. 1 (January 1985):48, 50; See also Candy Cooper, "State-of-the-Art Child Care Hits Town," *San Francisco Examiner,* March 29, 1987, B-1, B-2. There are around a dozen on-site child care centers for state employees. A director observed that the center is having "a great impact on attendance, morale and productivity."
26. General Mills, *Families at Work,* poll by Louis Harris and Associates (General Mills, 1981), 48; Chapman, "Executive Guilt," 35.
27. Fernandez, *Child Care and Corporate Productivity,* 41.
28. Catalyst, "National Resources on Parenting and Child Care" (1982) (250 Park Ave. So., New York, NY 10003). Such organizations include the Texas Institute for Families, the Center for Parenting Studies at Wheelock College in Boston, The Bank Street College of Education in New York, Columbia University's School of Social Work, the Conference Board (the research arm of the Fortune 500 companies), and Catalyst Career and Family Center of New York. Also in New York, Children at Work: Employer-Supported Child Care provides companies with feasibility studies, develops and manages workshops for employees on site, provides training and resources for existing child care providers, and developed a workbook for employers. Work/Family Directions provides similar services in Boston.
29. Jeanne Lesem, "Finding Jobs for the 'Trailing Spouses,'" *Los Angeles Times,* February 10, 1984, 28.
30. Catalyst, "Corporate Relocation Practices: A Report on a Nationwide Survey" (June 1983):5.
31. Joseph Pleck, "Employment and Fatherhood: Issues and Innovative Policies," in Michael Lamb, ed., *The Father's Role: Applied Perspectives* (New York: John Wiley, 1986), 391; Joyce Sullivan, "Family Support Systems Paychecks Can't Buy," in Patricia Voydanoff, ed., *Work and Family: Changing Roles of Men and Women* (Palo Alto, Calif.: Mayfield Publishing, 1984), 315.
32. John DeFrain, "Androgynous Parents Tell Who They Are and What They Need," *Family Coordinator* 28, no. 2 (April 6, 1979):237–243.
33. Audrey Smith and William Reid, *Role-Sharing Marriage* (New York: Columbia University Press, 1986), 136.

34. Halcyone Bohen and Ana Maria Viceros-Long, *Balancing Jobs and Family Life* (Philadelphia: Temple University Press, 1981), 127, 135; "Spouses That Pass in the Night," *San Francisco Chronicle*, August 7, 1983.
35. "Finding Time for Work and Family," *Work Times* (New Ways to Work, 149 Ninth St., San Francisco, Calif. 94103) 1, no. 1 (Summer 1982):7.
36. General Mills, *Families at Work*, 48.
37. Jane Bryan-Jones, telephone interview with the author, February 1984; Fernandez, *Child Care and Corporate Productivity*, 165.
38. Technical assistance about how to design and implement a school-age care program is provided by the School-Age Child Care Project, Wellesley College Center for Research on Women. The project provides a newsletter and other publications and works with demonstration sites.
39. Joseph Pleck, "Employment and Fatherhood," 388.
40. "A Mother's Choice," *Newsweek* 107, no. 13 (March 31, 1986):46–51.
41. Ibid.
42. Other federal supports for low-income children include: Head Start, AFDC (Aid to Families with Dependent Children), WIN (Work Incentive Program) to train AFDC recipients, and the child care food program.
43. Children's Defense Fund, *CDF Reports* (122 C St. NW, Washington, DC 20001).
44. "Study Says Child Care Still Hurting From Cuts," *San Francisco Chronicle*, September 25, 1984.
45. Maria Eden, "Parenting in Paris," *Working Mother* (March 1984):65–69.
46. Earl Grollman and Gerri Sweden, *The Working Parent Dilemma* (Boston: Beacon Press, 1986), 26; ABC, "After the Sexual Revolution," July 30, 1986. See the *SACC Newsletter*, a publication of the School-Age Child Care Project, Wellesley College Center for Research on Women, Wellesley, Mass. 02181.
47. Chapman, "Executive Guilt," 30, 35, note 39 in chapter 7.

Chapter 12. The Future of Parenting

1. John Naisbitt, *Megatrends: Ten New Directions Transforming Our Lives* (New York: Warner Books, 1982), 249.
2. Marvin Cetron, "Getting Ready for the Jobs of the Future," *Futurist* 17, no. 3 (June 1983):15.
3. Alvin Toffler, *The Third Wave* (New York: Bantam, 1981), 109, 215.
4. Andrew Cherlin and Frank Furstenberg, Jr., "The Shape of the American Family in the Year 2000" (American Council of Life Insurance, Social Research Services, Fall 1982), 3.
5. "Nation: Snapshot of a Changing America," *Time* 126, no. 9 (September 2, 1985):16.
6. Cherlin and Furstenberg, "The Shape of the American Family in the Year 2000," 14; Naisbitt, *Megatrends*, 232.
7. Naisbitt, *Megatrends*, 251. Current employees are not eager to work at home "telecommuting." In a poll, 7% reported wanting to work at home, 36% would

like to split their time between home and office, and 56% would continue going to the office everyday: Alex Kotlowitz, "Working at Home While Caring for a Child Sounds Fine—In Theory," *Wall Street Journal*, March 30, 1987, 25.

8. Naisbitt, *Megatrends*, 251.
9. Joseph Pleck, personal correspondence with the author, December 31, 1986.
10. Carol Pearson, "Coming Home: Four Feminist Utopias and Patriarchal Experiences," in Marlene Barr, ed., *Future Females: A Critical Anthology* (Bowling Green, Ohio: Bowling Green State University Press, 1981); Susan Lees, "Motherhood in Feminist Utopias," in Ruby Rohlich and Elaine Baruch, eds., *Women in Search of Utopia* (New York: Schockan, 1984).
11. L. Colette Jones, "Father-Infant Relationships in the First Year of Life," in Shirley Hanson and Frederick Bozett, eds., *Dimensions of Fatherhood* (Beverly Hills: Sage, 1985), 105.
12. Keith Schneider, "Repro Madness," *New Age Journal* (January 1986):36, 37.
13. Pamela Sargent, ed., *Bio-Futures* (New York: Vintage Books, 1976).
14. Dolores Hayden, "Making Housing Work for People," *Ms.* 12, no. 1 (January 1984):69.
15. Gerda Werkerle, "Women in the Urban Environment," in Catharine Stimpson et al., eds., *Women and the American City* (Chicago: University of Chicago Press, 1981), 202.
16. Matrix, *Making-Space: Women and the Man-made Environment* (London: Pluto Press, 1984), 4.
17. Susan Saegert, "Masculine Cities and Feminine Suburbs," in Stimpson et al., *Women and the American City*, 95–96.
18. "A New Housing Ideal for the Modern Woman," *San Francisco Chronicle*, December 4, 1979, 22 (study by Donald Rothblatt, Jo Sprague, and Daniel Garr). See also Sylvia Fava, "Women's Place in the New Suburbia," in Gerda Werkerle, Rebecca Peterson, and David Marley, eds., *New Space for Women* (Boulder, Colo.: Westview Press, 1981), 135.
19. Margaret Mead, "New Towns To Set New Lifestyles," *The Town Forum: A Journal of Creative Community*, series 2, no. 3 (Spring 1976):25.
20. Ibid.
21. Eklal Kueshana, *The Ultimate Frontier* (Stelle, Ill.: Stelle Group, 1982).
22. Oliver Popenoe and Cris Popenoe, *Seeds of Tomorrow: New Age Communities That Work* (San Francisco: Harper and Row, 1984), 46.
23. Linda Guinn, telephone interview with the author, August 29, 1983.
24. Dolores Hayden, "Speculations on the Future of Housing, Work and Family Life" (Paper presented at conference on women's culture, California State University, Long Beach, November 6, 1983).
25. Dolores Hayden, *Redesigning the American Dream: The Future of Housing, Work and Family Life* (New York: W.W. Norton, 1984), 180-189, 197, 229.
26. In addition to *Yentl*, *Tootsie*, and *Victor/Victoria*, previous gender-bending films had the following characters, as described by film professor Tom Reck: 1) Katharine Hepburn masqueraded as a man in *Sylvia Scarlet*, a 1935 costume drama, fooling Cary Grant. 2) Greta Garbo did exactly the same in *Queen Cristina* (1933), also a costume drama, fooling John Gilbert. 3) Cary Grant in *I Was a*

Male War Bride (1949) played an Englishman who married a WAC (Ann Sheridan). In order to qualify for entry into the United States, under the "war bride" program, he had to masquerade as a woman. 4) Anthony Perkins in *Psycho* (1960) assumed the identity of his dead mother to commit his famous shower murder. 5) Debbie Reynolds in *Goodbye Charlie* (1964) played a male friend of Tony Curtis who dies and comes back to life as (yes) Debbie Reynolds. Curtis is faced with the dilemma of finding himself falling in love with a good male friend. 6) I would not discount *Some Like It Hot* just because it is essentially comic. The "statement" is there; it is just not delivered in sermon form. Certainly, Daphne (the Curtis character) learns what it is like to be a best friend to another female and (as he hears Marilyn Monroe's recitation of agony) what it feels like to be a victim of men. The Lemmon character (Josephine) at first finds being a woman is a pain the neck (being constantly pinched, etc.), but then discovers advantages (being chased, sought after, seduced). See Joan Mellon, *Big Bad Wolves: Masculinity in the American Film* (New York: Pantheon, 1977).

27. Sandra Bem, "Androgyny vs. the Tight Little Lives of Fluffy Women and Chesty Men," *Psychology Today* 5, no. 4 (September 1975):60. Some psychologists caution that what is really significant in the BSRI is the high masculinity score, not the high femininity score. They believe that good adjustment is associated with instrumental traits and adjustment is more true of androgynous women than androgynous men. Studies indicate that girls and women who score low on femininity and high on masculinity have higher achievement motivation, higher grades, and more prestigious professional careers than sex-typed females. Some studies do not find much difference between androgynous and masculine scoring women, or feminine and undifferentiated women, which concurs with the thesis that a high masculinity score is most significant in self-esteem and achievement. See also John Antill and John Cunninghamm, "Self-Esteem as a Function of Masculinity in Both Sexes," *Journal of Consulting and Clinical Psychology* 47, no. 4:784; J. Rendely, R. Holmstrom, and S. Karp, "The Relationship of Sex-Role Identity, Lifestyle and Mental Health in Suburban Homemakers," *Sex Roles* 11, no. 9/10 (1984):839–848. A Boston study of middle-class families found that men's peer groups often ridicule men for doing family work, seen as "effeminate or weak behavior." "You're getting us in trouble" with our wives was a common reaction to a man doing housework; self-esteem is required to resist this pressure: Laura Lein, "Male Participation in Home Life," in Patricia Voydanoff, ed., *Work and Family: Changing Roles of Men and Women* (Palo Alto, Calif.: Mayfield, 1984), 246. See also P.P. Wong, G. Kettlewell, and C.F. Sproule, "On the Importance of Being Masculine: Sex Role Attribution and Women's Career Achievement," *Sex Roles* 12, no. 7/8 (April 1985):757; Ellen Piel Cook, *Psychological Androgyny* (New York: Pergamon, 1985), 94.
28. Janet Spence and Robert Helmreich, *Masculinity and Femininity: Their Psychological Dimensions, Correlates and Antecedents* (Austin, Tex.: University of Texas Press, 1978).
29. Sandra Bem, "On the Utility of Alternative Procedures for Assessing Psychological Androgyny," *Journal of Consulting and Clinical Psychology* 45, no. 2 (1977):196; Bem, "Androgyny vs. The Tight Little Lives," 60.

30. Rendely, Holmstrom, and Kays, "The Relationship of Sex-Role, Lifestyle, and Mental Health in Suburban American Homemakers," 839.
31. Spence and Helmreich, *Masculinity and Femininity*, 163, 218; Ellen Lenny, "Androgyny: Some Audacious Assertions toward Its Coming of Age," *Sex Roles* 5, no. 6 (1979):739, 742, 760.
32. Diana Baumrind, "Are Androgynous Individuals More Effective Persons and Parents?" *Child Development* 53, no. 1 (February 1982):64, 68; Donnie Hoffman and Linda Fidell, "Characteristics of Androgynous, Undifferentiated, Masculine and Feminine Middle-class Women," *Sex Roles* 5, no. 6 (1979):777–78.
33. Graeme Russell, "The Father Role and Its Relation to Masculinity, Femininity and Androgyny," *Child Development* 49, no. 4 (December 1978):1179.
34. Lenny, "Androgyny: Some Audacious Assertions toward Its Coming of Age," 739, 742, 760.
35. B. Abrahams, S. Feldman, and S. Nash, "Sex-Role Self-Concept and Sex-Role Attitudes: Enduring Personality Characteristics or Adaptations to Changing Life Situation?" *Developmental Psychology* 14 (1978):393–400.
36. Warren Farrell, telephone interview with the author, September 12, 1982.
37. Jo Freeman, *The Politics of Women's Liberation* (New York: David McKay, 1975), 48–49.
38. Margaret Leahy, *Development Strategies and the Status of Women* (Boulder, Colo.: Lynne Rienner, 1986).
39. Keith Thompson, "What Men Really Want," Interview with Robert Bly, *New Age* 7, no. 10 (May 1982):31–51; Steve Chappel, "The New Men's Movement: In Search of the Beast Within," *Image* Magazine, *San Francisco Examiner*, January 11, 1987, 12–19, 30–37.
40. Herb Goldberg, "Why Is the Men's Movement Not 'Happening'?" *Transitions* (Coalition of Free Men) 3, no. 2 (Spring/Summer 1983):1.
41. Robert Brannon, "Are the 'Free Men' a Faction of Our Movement?" *M.: Gentle Men for Gender Justice*, cycle 2, no. 7 (Winter 1981–82):30.
42. Press conference statement in *Brother* (News Quarterly of the National Organization for Changing Men) 1, no. 2 (Summer 1983):5.
43. Herb Goldberg, interview with the author, Chico, California, 1979.
44. Jack Kammer, personal correspondence with the author, January 6, 1987.
45. Sylvia Ann Hewlett, *A Lesser Life: The Myth of Women's Liberation in America* (New York: William Morrow, 1986).
46. Gloria Steinem, *Outrageous Acts and Everyday Rebellions* (New York: Holt, Rinehart, and Winston, 1983), 361; Interview with the author, Chico, March 1984.
47. Betty Friedan, *The Second Stage* (New York: Summit Books, 1981), 160, 203.
48. Letty Cottin Pogrebin, *Family Politics: Love and Power on an Intimate Frontier* (New York: McGraw-Hill, 1983), 2.
49. Steinem, *Outrageous Acts*, 149.
50. Toffler, *The Third Wave*, 44–45.
51. David Giveans, ed., *Nurturing Today: For Self and Family Growth* (formerly *Nurturing News*) (187 Caselli Ave., San Francisco, CA 94114).
52. Contact the Swedish Information Society, 825 Third Ave., New York, NY 10022, for bibliography.

Index

Acknowledgments

THE book required the efforts of many people. Paul Gunther and Susan Suntree went through the entire manuscript, leaving a trail of useful red-inked comments behind them. Brad Glanville, Carol Burr, and Jill Nachreiner provided their editorial skills in various chapters. Emily and John Visher commented on the step-parenting chapter, Robert Sayers and Joseph Pleck reacted to the chapter on fathers, Bill Rector commented on the children's chapter, and Ellen Galinsky critiqued the chapter on work place supports. Phoenix Wheeler reacted to the group chapter. Robin Wilson and Joseph Pleck commented on the final chapter.

Thanks to Patrice Graham and Paul Lau who typed the manuscript through multiple revisions. Ms. Graham and Paula Hamman also typed interview transcriptions. Thanks also to Nancy Herndon, the copyeditor at Lexington Books, who contributed a great deal.

My son Jed's father, Les Hait, and his wife, Donna Hait, made it possible for me to write this book by faithfully taking care of Jed for twenty-four hours on the weekend so I could jog, then sit glued to the typewriter.

Jed provided a reality check for theories I read about and is teaching me about what it means to be a parent, to know unconditional love, and to learn patience and that the positive works better than the negative.

Programming data on the computer was done by Jeanette Alosi, data entered by Charles Abbleby, Paul Lau, Molly Campbell, Shirley Goodgame, and Milo Wilde. Thanks also to Babette Lightner and Pamela and Erin Grams. Students in my "Sex Roles of the Future" course helped me to develop ideas about changing families.

The lifeblood of the book is the parents and children who were willing to frankly tell me their experiences. My deepest thanks go to them. Interviewees who gave me written permission to acknowledge their contribution to the book are, in no particular order:

Raleigh Foss
Mark Cornetta
Denise R. Wheeler
Garret D. Bonnema
Antonia Woods Ellis
Linda Boynton
Michael Robinson
Carol Christensen
Kendall Link
Jason Cromwell
Dave McAllister
Carol J. Levin
Dan McDougall-Treacy
Roger Lininger
Cheryl Orr
Linda Stevens
Leah Stanton Harvey
Bertrand B. Pogrebin
Rita Askew
Deborah Cohen
Linda Shopes
S. Diane Nofs
Gail Goldstein
Jane Bryan-Jones
Maureen Powers
Leroy McDermott
Jerry Block
Partha L. Buell
Arza E. Ralph
Greenville B. Whitman
Sheldon Praiser
Kathleen A. Moneymaker
Neal Eddy
G. Nicholas Golden
Mary Greer
Susan Suntree
Monica Foss
Elizabeth Wise
Cat Carney
Melody D. Bonnema
Dan Butler
Gayle A. Butler
Maureen Pierce
Karen Zweig
Jody Link
Bonnie Cromwell
Pamela Smith
Steve Deutsch
David McDonald
Nareta Lininger
Mary Gordon
Judith Massimi
Robert C. Fox
Gale R. McCullough
John Cornetta
Ron Angle
Laurel Leone
Vicki Runquist
Donovan C. Snyder
Wayne Runquist
Hardy Jones
Brad Powers
Kay Sohl
Patty Hoagland
Karl H. Schwerin
Joaneen Hodnett

Neil J. Whitman
Kenneth R. Lake
June Myrwang
Carol Knudtson Eddy
Sharon E. Budd
Bob Speer
Annette Van Dyke
Deb Stranges
Jock Young
Gree Decker
Peter Woods Ellis
Mike Boynton
Kathy Robinson
Steve Christensen
Bob Zweig
Cheryl Howard
Linda M. Powers
Jo Durand
Gayle McDougall-Treacy
Lou McDonald
Mary Anne Mize
Earl Stevens
Frances Maher
Letty Cottin Pogrebin
Jim Kraemer
Steffen Saifer
Jeanne Angle
Steve Wegener
Kathleen O'Connor
Joanne Montegomery
Paul Runquist
Bill Cassady
Diane McDermott
Brunie Block
Jane Kirchman
Curtis Davis
Ken Hodnett
Chris Nelson
Bruce Goldstein
Steve Myrwang
Hilary Emmer
Beckie Harvey
Ed Buryn

About the Author

GAYLE KIMBALL, Ph.D., is professor of women's studies at California State University, Chico. She is the author of *The 50-50 Marriage* and the editor of *Women's Culture: The Women's Renaissance of the 70's*. She has also written a booklet entitled *Life After College: Combining Career and Family* and produced nine instructional videotapes about women, men, and families. Kimball is the mother of a seven-year-old son, Jed. She is looking forward to writing a book about how employed parents cope and a ten-year follow-up of role-sharing couples and their children. She welcomes letters from readers about their experiences. Please write to Dr. Gayle Kimball, EWS-420, California State University, Chico, CA 95929.

Survey for Parents

I would like to include your views in my next book, which is about model social supports for employed parents and their children. Please respond to these questions and add additional comments describing your experiences. Please ask your children to give their views on the survey for children, which follows. Please send to: Gayle Kimball, EWS–420, California State University, Chico, CA 95929.

1. Based on your own experience and observation, what do you think is the effect on children of having employed parents? You might want to discuss different age groups in your reply.
2. Overall, would you say the impact on your children of having employed parents is: excellent ____ good ____ does not make a difference ____ poor ____ .
3. What is the ideal way to care for children with employed parents? Include what employers, schools, legislators, and others can do to recognize the needs of families.
4. Please include the following information as well.

   Gender __________

   Marital status __________

   Age __________

   Occupation ____________________

Number of children ____________

Ages of children ____

State in which you live ____________

Highest educational degree ____________

Survey for Children

1. Your age is __________ .
2. Your year in school is __________ .
3. Are you female __________ or male __________ ?
4. You live in what state? ____________________
5. Your career goal is ____________________________________ .
6. What is the highest educational degree you plan to obtain?
   ____
7. If you plan to have children, how long do you plan to stay home with the first child? ____________________
8. Do you plan to have 0 ______ , 1 ______ , 2 ______ , 3______ , 4______ , or more ______ children?
9. Based on observation of your friends, do you think the impact on preschool children of having an employed mother is excellent __________ , good __________ , doesn't make a difference __________ , depends on the parent __________ , or is poor __________ ?

   Comment ____

   ____

   ____

   _______________________________________ .

10. Please answer question #9 again for school-age youngsters: The impact is excellent ________ , good ________ , doesn't make a difference ________ , depends on the parent ________ , or is poor ________ .

    Comment ____________________

    ____

    ____

    ____________________ .

11. Was your mother employed before you were five years old?
    yes ______ no ______
    Was the impact on your development excellent ________ , good ________ , didn't make a difference ________ , or poor ________ ?

    Explain ____________________

    ____

    ____

    ____________________ .

12. My mother is a fulltime homemaker ________ , works part time ________ , or works full time ________ .
    She has a job as a ________ .
    Is the current impact of your mother's employment on your development excellent ________ , good ________ , doesn't make a difference ________ , or poor ________ ?

    Comment ____________________

    ____

    ____

    ____________________ .

13. Looking at the amount of time you spend with your father, is it about equal to the amount of time you spend with your mother ________, much less than the amount of time you spend with your mother ________, or much more than the amount of time you spend with your mother ________?

    Comment ____

    ____

    ____

    ____.

14. What do you think is the ideal way to care for young children when both parents need to work outside the home?

    ____

    ____

    ____

    ____.